Dictionary of A

The Wordsworth
Dictionary of Anagrams

–

Michael Curl

Wordsworth Reference

First published as *The Anagram Dictionary* by Robert Hale,
London, 1982.

This edition published 1995 by Wordsworth Editions Ltd,
Cumberland House, Crib Street, Ware, Hertfordshire SG12 9ET.

ISBN 1-85326-350-8

Printed and bound in Denmark by Nørhaven.

The paper in this book is produced from pure wood
pulp, without the use of chlorine or any other substance
harmful to the environment. The energy used in its
production consists almost entirely of hydroelectricity
and heat generated from waste materials, thereby
conserving fossil fuels and contributing little to the
greenhouse effect.

Thy genius calls thee not to purchase fame
In keen iambics, but mild anagram:
Leave writing plays, and choose for thy command
Some peaceful province in Acrostic Land.
Where thou mayest wings display and altars raise
And torture one poor word ten thousand ways.

Dryden

Contents

Ars Magna—The Great Art

A Brief History of Anagrams

According to some historians, anagrams originated in the fourth century B.C. with the Greek poet Lycophron, who found favour with the rich and mighty by devising flattering anagrams of their names. Other sources claim that anagrams date further back to the sixth century B.C. when they were used by Pythagoras and his disciples, who found philosophical meanings therein.

It was believed at this time that anagrams had a mystical significance, and they were at times used in prophecy. Alexander the Great, during the siege of Tyre, dreamed one night of a satyr dancing in the woods. His soothsayers, when they were called on to interpret the dream, revealed that the letters of the word 'satyr' could be transposed to spell 'Tyre is thine'. On the following day the city of Tyre fell to Alexander, thus justifying the soothsayers' faith in anagrams.

Anagrams were also known to the Romans, though most surviving example of Roman anagrams are imperfect. An anagrammatic significance has been attached to the most famous example of Roman word play, the so-called SATOR word square. This word square was first discovered during excavation of the site of the Roman city at Cirencester. It was found inscribed on a wall, and reads as follows:

```
R O T A S
O P E R A
T E N E T
A R E P O
S A T O R
```

This can be translated as 'Arepo the sower guides the wheels at work' or more freely as 'God controls the universe'. The word square was for many years believed to be of early Christian origin, and it was pointed out by one scholar that the letters could be arranged like this:

```
              A
              P
              A
              T
              E
              R
A P A T E R N O S T E R O
              O
              S
              T
              E
              R
              O
```

The A and the O were said to stand for Alpha and Omega—the beginning and the end. This theory lent weight to the view that the SATOR word square was used—as was the pictorial symbol of a fish—in early Christian communities, fearful of persecution, as a cryptic affirmation of the faith.

Various other anagrams were proposed, such as RETRO SATANA TOTO OPERE ASPER (Begone, Satan, cruel in all thy works). Such speculations, however, were ended when another example of the word square was found at Pompeii, the dating of which proved that the square was definitely of pre-Christian origin. So the AREPO word square remains a mystery. Is it merely a piece of clever popular wordplay—the Roman equivalent of our crossword puzzles—or does it have some deeper significance?

After the Greeks and Romans, anagrams did not appear again to any extent until the thirteenth century. They were then used by the Jewish Cabbalists, who again found mystical significance in them.

The popularity of anagrams spread rapidly among the learned of Europe in the Middle Ages. They were especially popular in France, where one Thomas Billon was appointed Royal Anagrammatist to King Louis XIII. King Charles IX of France was also fond of anagrams and delighted in the fact that the name of his mistress Marie Touchet could be transposed to JE CHARME TOUT (the letters I and J at that time being interchangable, as were U and V).

Also in France, a certain André Pujon, discovering that his name could be transposed to PENDU A RION, and having great faith in the mystical nature of anagrams, committed a murder in the town of Rion so that he could be hanged there, thus fulfilling the anagrammatic prophecy.

The principal activity of anagrammatists in the Middle Ages, however, was in forming anagrams on religious texts. One of the most popular texts for this exercise was the Angel's Salutation in Mark's gospel: AVE MARIA, GRATIA PLENA, DOMINUS TECUM (Hail Mary, full of grace, the Lord is with thee). Devoted anagrammatists found literally thousands of different anagrams of this phrase, as, for example: VIRGO SERENA, PIA, MUNDA ET IMMACULATA (Virgin serene, holy, pure and immaculate). It is said that one man alone produced over 3,000 different anagrams from this phrase.

One of the most famous mediaeval anagrams was that based on Pilate's question at the trial of Jesus—QUID EST VERITAS? (What is truth?)—to form the reply VIR EST QUI ADEST (It is the man before thee).

Many authors used pseudonyms based on anagrams. François Rabelais used the name Alcofribas Nasier and Calvinus was the pen-name of Alcuinus. Voltaire was the pseudonym of Arouet 1.j. (Arouet le jeune or Arouet the younger). Honoré de Balzac used the pseudonym Lord Rhoone for some of his earlier works.

In the seventeenth century it was also common practice for scientists to record the results of their research in anagram form if further verification was needed before the discoveries could be published openly. Galileo, Huygens and Robert Hooke, among others, used this system, the purpose being to stake their claim to the discovery and to prevent anyone else from claiming the credit.

In the nineteenth century there was a vogue for forming anagrams from the names of prominent people. Usually these were rather unsophisticated by today's standards—for example, TEAR IT, MEN, I ATONE from MARIE ANTOI-NETTE. Occasionally, however, there were examples which have never been bettered, as, for example, FLIT ON, CHEERING ANGEL for FLORENCE NIGHTINGALE or I LEAD, SIR for DISRAELI. These two anagrams, incidentally, are both the creations of Lewis Carroll, who also challenged his readers to form one word from the letters in NEW DOOR— the answer being, of course, ONE WORD.

The Victorian era was the heyday of the cognate anagram— transposing the letters of a common word or phrase to form another word or phrase with some relevance to the original— turning ASTRONOMER into MOON STARER, for example. Many of the cognate anagrams listed in the appendix origin-ated in this period.

Today the anagram lives on mainly within the confines of the crossword puzzle, where one may discover such little gems as these:

Tree producing fir cone (7)	CONIFER
New Orleans in Italy (7)	SALERNO
Supersonic instruments (10)	PERCUSSION
Soldiers armed with guns? (9)	GUARDSMEN
Noiseless wild animals (9)	LIONESSES
The raffia-weaving business (6)	AFFAIR
They are used for duplicating clients' letters (8)	
	STENCILS

And finally:

INDICATORY ANAGRAM BOOK (10)	DICTIONARY

A

Aaronic ocarina
aba baa
abaca Caaba
abactor acrobat
abactors acrobats
abas baas; Saab; Saba
abash Sabah
abates sea-bat
abba baba
abbas babas
abbé babe
abbés babes
ABC cab
Abdera abrade
abed bade; bead
Abel able; albe; bael; bale; blae;
    Elba; Labe
abele Albee
abet bate; beat; beta
abetment batement
abets baste; bates; beast; beats;
    besat; Sebat; tabes
abhorrent earthborn
abides biased
ablaut tabula
able Abel; albe; bael; bale; blae;
    Elba; Labe
abled baled; blade
abler baler; blare; blear
ables bales; Basel; Basle; blaes;
    blasé; sable
ablest ablets; bleats; stable; tables
ablet blate; bleat; table
ablets ablest; bleats; stable; tables
abling baling
ablution Abutilon
ably blay
Abo boa
aboard abroad; Baroda
abode adobe
abord board; broad
aborded boarded
abording boarding
abords adsorb; boards; broads
abort boart; Rabot; tabor
aborted borated; tabored
aborting borating; taboring
aborts boarts; Strabo; tabors
Abos boas
about U-boat

abrade Abdera
abridge brigade
abridged brigaded
abridges brigades
abridging brigading
abrin bairn; brain; Brian
abroad aboard; Baroda
absit baits
absorber reabsorb
absorbers reabsorbs
abstain Tsabian
abstains Tsabians
abuser bursae
abusers surbase
abut buat; tabu; tuba
Abutilon ablution
abuts buats; tabus; tubas
aby bay
abysmal balsamy
acarian Acarina
acaridan Arcadian
Acarina acarian
acates sea-cat
accidents desiccant
accoil calico
accompt compact
accompts compacts
accoutred accoutred
accourting accoutring
accoustrement accoutrements
accoutred accourted
accoutrements accoustrement
accoutres coruscate; court case
accoutring accourting
accoyld cacodyl
accretions Cestracion
accrued cardecu
accrues accurse; accuser
accurate carucate
accurse accrues; accuser
accursed cardecus
accurses accusers
accused succade
accuser accrues; accurse
accusers accurses
acer acre; care; race
acerb brace; caber; cabré
acerous carouse
acers acres; cares; carse; races;
    scare; scrae; sérac

13

aces   aesc; case
ache   each
achenes   enchase
aches   chase
acid   cadi
acids   asdic; cadis
acid test   dictates
aciform   Formica
acme   came; mace
acmes   maces
acmite   micate
acne   ance; Caen; cane
acnode   canoed; deacon
acnodes   deacons
acol   coal; cola
aconites   canoeist
acre   acer; care; race
acred   arced; cadre; cared; cedar;
    raced
acres   acers; cares; carse; races;
    scare; scrae; sérac
acrid   caird; daric; Dirac
acrobat   abactor
acrobats   abactors
acrolein   Caroline; Cornelia;
    creolian
across   Oscars
acrostic   Socratic
acroter   creator; reactor
acroters   creators; reactors
act   cat
acted   cadet
actinal   alicant
actinide   indicate
actinides   indicates
action   atonic; cation
actioning   incognita
actions   cations; Scotian
active   Cavite
acton   canto; cotan; octan
actons   cantos; Octans
actor   Crato; Croat; taroc
actors   castor; Castro; Croats; scrota;
    tarocs
actress   casters; Castres; recasts
acts   cast; cats; scat
acture   curate
acute   Ceuta
acutes   cuesta
ad   da
Adamites   diastema
Adar   Arad
add   dad

adder   aredd; dared; dread
adders   dreads; sadder
addle   dedal; laded
addles   saddle
addresser   readdress
adds   dads
adeem   Medea
adeems   seamed
Adeline   aliened; delaine
Aden   Dane; dean; Edna
Adeni   Andie; Denia; Diane; Edina
Adenis   Sendai
adept   pated; taped
adepts   pasted
adermin   Amerind; inarmed
ad finem   infamed
adhere   header; hedera
adhered   redhead
adherent   neatherd
adherents   neatherds
adherer   reheard
adheres   headers; sheared
adios   aidos
adit   dita
adits   ditas; staid
adjuster   readjust
adjusters   readjusts
Adler   alder
Adlestrop   Portslade
ad lib   Blida
adminicle   medicinal
administer   mistrained
admire   Mérida
admirer   married
admires   misread
admonition   domination
admonitive   dominative
admonitor   dominator
admonitors   dominators
adobe   abode
adore   oared; oread
adored   deodar
adorer   roared
adorers   Drosera
adores   oreads; soared
adoring   Gordian; gradino; roading
adorn   Donar
adorned   road-end
adown   downa
adpress   spreads
ad rem   armed; derma; dream
adret   dater; rated; tared; trade;
    tread

adrets daters; stared; trades; treads
Adrian Andria; radian
adroitly dilatory; idolatry
adroitness intradoses
adry dray; yard
ads das; sad
adsorb abords; boards; broads
adsum Dumas; mauds
adult dault
adults daults
adverb braved
adverts starved
advise Davies; visaed
adze daze
adzes dazes
ae ea
aerometer areometer
aerometers areometers
aerometric areometric
aerometry areometry
aery Ayer; eyra; yare; year
aesc aces; case
aesir Aries; arise; raise; Riesa; serai;
  Seria
aestival salivate
aether heater; hereat; reheat
afar Afra
affair raffia
affirmer reaffirm
affirmers reaffirms
afield failed
afire feria
Afra afar
afreets feaster; sea-fret
afro faro
aft fat
afters faster; strafe
agar Agra; raga
age gae
aged egad; gade; gaed
ageless sea-legs
agelong Legnago
Agen gane; gean; gena
age-old gaoled; old age
ages gaes; sage
agger eggar
aggers eggars; sagger; seggar
aggress saggers; seggars
agin Agni; gain; Gina
agist gaits
agister gaiters; sea-girt; stagier;
  strigae; triages
agnail Anglia; Ilagan

agname manage
agnamed managed
agnames manages; Mesagna
Agnes geans; genas; Senga
Agni agin; gain; Gina
agnise easing
agnostic coasting; coatings
ago Goa
agone Genoa; Onega
agonised diagnose; San Diego
Agra agar; raga
agree eager; eagre
agreed dragée; geared
agrees eagres; grease
agrin garni; grain
ah ha
ahem hame; Mahé
aid Dai; Ida
Aidan Diana; naiad
aide idea
aided idea'd
aider aired, irade; redia
aiders irades; raised
aides aside; ideas; Sadie
Aidin India
aidos adios
aids dais; Dias; Sadi; said; Sida
aiglet ligate; taigle
aiglets ligates; taigles
ail Ali
ailed Delia; ideal
aileron alerion; alienor
ailerons alerions; alienors; Rosaline
ailing nilgai
ailment aliment
ailments aliments; manliest;
  salt-mine
ails Isla; Lias; Lisa; sail; sial
aim Mia
aimed amide; media
aimless Melissa; mesails; samiels;
  seismal
aims Amis; Mais; Siam; sima
ain't Tain; Tina
Aintree retinae; trainee
air Ira; ria
air-beds braised; darbies; sea-bird
aired aider; irade; redia
airers raiser; Sérrai; sierra
airless sailers; serails; serials
airman Marian; marina
airmen marine; Marnie; remain
airn Iran; Nair; rain; rani

15

airs Asir; Isar; rias; sair;
sari
airt rait
airted raited; tirade
airts astir; raits; sitar; Sitrâ; stair;
stria; tarsi; Trias
airy Iyar
aisle Elias
aisled deasil; ideals; ladies;
sailed
aisles eassil; laisse; lassie
Aisne anise; Siena
ait ita; tai
aits Asti; itas; sati; sita
ajar raja
Akron Koran; krona
Ala Dagh Galahad
Alan anal; lana; nala
Alaric racial
alarm malar; ramal
alarming marginal
alarmingly marginally
alarmist alastrim
alas Sala
Alastrim alarmist
alb lab
Alba Baal; Bala
Alban banal; Laban
albe Abel; able; bael; bale; blae;
Elba; Labe
Albee abele
albeit albite
albert labret; tabler
Alberta ratable
Alberti librate; triable
alberts blaster; labrets; stabler;
tablers
Albi bail; Bali
albino Albion; Alboin
Albion albino; Alboin
albite albeit
Alboin albino; Albion
albs labs; slab
alburnum laburnum
alchemic chemical
alchemist St. Michael
Alcinoüs unsocial
alcove coeval; Levoca
alcoves coevals
Alcuin Lucian; Lucina; uncial
alder Adler
aldern darnel; enlard; lander
alders sardel

Aldine alined; Daniel; Delian;
denial; lead-in; nailed
Aldis dalis; dials; slaid
Aldred ladder; larded; raddle
Aldus lauds; udals
ale e-la; lea
Alec Clea; lace
alecost lactose; locates; scatole;
talcose
Alecto locate
aleft fetal
alegar laager
alerce cereal
alerion aileron; alienor
alerions ailerons; alienors; Rosaline
alert alter; artel; later; ratel; taler
alerted altered; related; treadle
alerting altering; integral; relating;
triangle
alerts alters; artels; laster; ratels;
salter; slater; staler; stelar; tarsel
ales Elsa; leas; sale; seal; slae
alevin alvine; venial
alexin xenial
alfa fa-la
al fine finale
Alfred fardel; flared
alga gala
algae galea
Algenib Belgian; Bengali
Algeria regalia
Algerian regalian
Algerines releasing
Algernon non-glare
Algiers lea-rigs
algin align
algor argol; goral; largo
algum almug; glaum; mulga
Ali ail
alibility liability
alible Belial; Biella; labile; liable
alicant actinal
Alice Celia; ileac
alien aline; anile; Elian; liane
alienation alineation
alienator rationale
alienators senatorial
aliened Adeline; delaine
alienism Milesian
alienist Latinise; litanies
alienists Latinises
alienor aileron; alerion
alienors ailerons; alerions; Rosaline

aliens alines; lianes; saline; Selina; silane
align algin
aligned dealing; leading
aligner engrail; learing; nargile; realign; reglial
aligners engrails; realigns; Salinger; sanglier; seal-ring
alignment lamenting
aligns signal
aliment ailment
aliments ailments; manliest; salt-mine
aline alien; anile; Elian; liane
alineation alienation
alined Aldine; Daniel; Delian; denial; lead-in; nailed
alines aliens; lianes; saline; Selina; silane
alining nailing
aliped elapid; paidle; Pleiad
alipeds elapids; lapides; paidles; palsied; Pleiads
Alister realist; retails; saltier; saltire; slatier
alit Atli; Lita; tail; tali
Allan nalla
allées sallee
allegorist legislator
allegorists legislators
allergies galleries
allergy gallery; largely; regally
alliance canaille
all in Lalin
allonge galleon
allonges galleons
allot atoll
allots atolls
allows sallow
alloy loyal
allude aludel
alludes aludels
allure laurel
allured udaller
allures laurels
ally y'all
alma lama
almah halma; hamal
almas lamas
alme Elam; Elma; lame; leam; Lema; male; meal
Almeric Carmiel; claimer; miracle; reclaim

almes lames; leams; males; meals; Salem; samel; Selma
almond dolman; old man
almonds dolmans
almoner nemoral
alms lams; slam
alms-fee females
almug algum; glaum; mulga
alnage Angela; anlage; galena; lagena
alod load; odal
alods loads; odals
aloetics societal
aloft float; flota
alone Olean
along Golan; Logan; longa; NALGO
alp lap; pal
alpine Epinal; penial; pineal
alpines spaniel
alpinist pintails
alps laps; pals; salp; slap
als sal
Alsager laagers
Al Sirat lariats
also Laos; sola
Altair atrial; lariat; latria
altar ratal; talar
altars astral; talars; tarsal
alter alert; artel; later; ratel; taler
alterant alternat
altered alerted; related; treadle
altering alerting; integral; relating; triangle
altern antler; learnt; rental; ternal
alternat alterant
alters alerts; artels; laster; ratels; salter; slater; staler; stelar; tarsel
Althing halting; lathing
altitude latitude
altitudes latitudes
altitudinal latitudinal
altitudinarian latitudinarian
altitudinarians latitudinarians
altitudinous latitudinous
alto lota; tola
altos Salto; Talos; tolas
altruism ultraism
altruist ultraist
altruistic ultraistic
atruists ultraists
aludel allude
aludels alludes

alum   maul; Mula
alumna   manual
Alva   aval; lava; Vaal
Alvin   anvil; nival; Vilna
alvine   alevin; venial
Alvis   salvi; silva; vails; valis; vials
alyssum   asylums
am   ma
amain   amnia; anima; mania
amarant   Maranta
amass   Assam; massa
amassing   siamangs
amateurs   Satu-Mare
amber   bream; embar
ambers   breams; embars; Sambre
amble   blame; Mabel; Melba
ambled   balmed; bedlam; beldam;
   blamed; lambed
ambler   blamer; marble; ramble
amblers   blamers; marbles; rambles
ambles   blames
ambling   balming; blaming;
   lambing
ambo   boma; M'Bao; Moab
ambones   bemoans
ambos   bomas; Sambo
Ambridge   game-bird
ameers   Mersea; seamer
amelcorn   cornmeal
amen   mane; mean; Mena; name
amenable   nameable
amend   maned; Medan; menad;
   named
amende   amened; demean
amender   enarmed; meander;
   renamed
amenders   meanders
amendes   demeans
amends   desman; menads
amened   amende; demean
amening   meaning
amenity   any time
amens   manes; manse; means;
   Mensa; names; samen
ament   Manet; meant
amentia   animate
aments   mantes; stamen
amerce   raceme
amerced   creamed; racemed
amerces   racemes
amercing   creaming; Germanic;
   Mérignac
American   Cinerama; in camera

Americas   mesaraic
Amerind   adermin; inarmed
amherst   hamster
amhersts   hamsters
amic   mica
amices   camise
amid   maid
amide   aimed; media
amides   mid-sea
Amiens   amines; inseam; mesian
Amin   main; mina
amine   animé, en ami; Maine;
   Menai; minae
amines   Amiens; inseam; mesian
amir   Mari; Mira; rami; rima
Amis   aims; Mais; Siam; sima
amiss   missa
ammeter   metamer
ammeters   metamers
amnesties   meatiness; seminates
amnia   amain; anima; mania
Amon   moan; mona; Oman
among   mango
amorets   maestro
amortise   atomiser; Timor Sea
amortises   atomisers
Amos   moas; soma
amount   moutan
amounts   moutans
amoves   vamose
Amoy   Mayo
amp   map; pam
ample   maple; pelma
ampler   Marple; palmer
amply   palmy
amps   maps; pams; samp; spam
amused   Medusa
amuser   Maseru; mauser
amusers   Erasmus; masseur;
   mausers
amuses   assume; Seamus
Amy   may; Mya; yam
an   na
anacreontic   canceration
anadem   maenad
anadems   maenads
anal   Alan; lana; nala
analog   Angola
analogist   nostalgia
anan   anna; nana
anapest   peasant
anapests   peasants
ance   acne; Caen; cane

ancestor enactors; Escatrón
ancestral Lancaster
Anchises inchases
anchor archon; Charon; rancho
anchored rondache
anchorites chain-store
anchors archons; ranchos
anchovies schiavone
ancients canniest; instance
ancile Celina; inlace
ancon Conan
ancones sonance
and dan
andante at an end; Dantean
Andersen ehsnared
Andes Danes; deans; Desna; sedan; snead
Andie Adeni; Denia; Diane; Edina
Andrew Darwen; dawner; wander; warden; warned
Andria Adrian; radian
Androcles colanders
ane ean; Ena; nae
anear arena
aneath Athena
aneled leaden; leaned; nealed
aneling eanling; leaning; nealing
anemic cinema; iceman
anemograph phanerogam
anerly nearly
Aneto atone; oaten; Onate
anew Ewan; wane; wean
angel angle; Galen; genal; glean
Angela alnage; anlage; galena; lagena
angelic anglice; Galenic
angelical Galenical
angels angles; gleans
Angelus lagunes
anger range; Regan; renga
angered derange; en garde; enraged; grandee; grenade
angering enraging
angers ranges; Sanger; serang
angina Nagina
angle angel; Galen; genal; glean
angled dangle; Glenda
angler regnal
angles angels; gleans
Anglet tangle
Anglia agnail; Ilagan
Anglic lacing
anglice angelic; Galenic

anglist lasting; salting; slating; staling
Angola analog
angora Aragon
angostura Argonauts
angrier earring; grainer; rearing
angriest astringe; ganister; gantries; granites; ingrates; inert gas; reasting
angriness ranginess
angry rangy
angst gants; gnats; stang; tangs
ani Ian
anil lain; nail
anile alien; aline; Elian; liane
anima amain; amnia; mania
animal lamina; manila
animals laminas
animas Maasin; manias; Manisa; Samian
animate amentia
animated diamante
animé amine; en ami; Maine; Menai; minae
anis Isna; Nias; Nisa; sain; Sian
anise Aisne; Siena
anker Karen; naker; nerka
ankers Karens; nakers
ankh hank; Kahn; khan
ankhs hanks; khans; shank
ankled Kendal
anklets asklent
anlage alnage; Angela; galena; lagena
Ann Nan
anna anan; nana
annalist santalin
Annam manna
annas nanas
Anne Enna
Annie inane
annoyed anodyne
annuities insinuate
anodyne annoyed
anoint nation
anointed antinode
anoints nations; onanist
Anselm lemans; mensal
answer awners
answers rawness
ant Nat; tan
antagonist stagnation
ant-bears ratsbane

ante   Aten; etna; neat; Tean
anted   Dante
antedate   edentata
anteing   antigen
antes   etnas; nates; Nesta; Senta;
  stane; stean; Teans
anthem   hetman
anthems   hetmans
anther   Tehran; thenar
anthers   thenars
anthesis   shanties
anthropophagus   phonautographs
anticor   carotin; Cortina
antigen   anteing
Antigone   negation
Antilope   antipole
antimonial   antinomial; lamination
antimonic   antinomic
antimony   antinomy
antinode   anointed
antinomial   antimonial; lamination
antinomic   antimonic
antinomy   antimony
antipole   Antilope
antipyretic   pertinacity
antique   quinate
antiques   quantise
antiseptic   psittacine
antitrade   attainder
antler   altern; learnt; rental; ternal
antlers   rentals; saltern; sternal
antra   ratan
antres   astern; sterna
Antirm   martin
antrum   Truman
ants   Stan; tans
anvil   Alvin; nival; Vilna
anvils   silvan
any   nay
any time   amenity
aorist   satori
ape   pea
apert   pater; peart; Petra; prate;
  taper; trape
apertly   pteryla
apertures   repasture
apery   payer; Peary; repay
apes   apse; peas; spae
apheresis   Pharisees
aphetic   hepatic
aphis   apish; spahi
apices   spicae
Apis   pais; Pias; Pisa

apish   aphis; spahi
aplite   Pilate
apodes   soaped
appal   papal
apparent   trappean
appealing   lagniappe
appel   apple; pepla
appels   apples
append   napped
appends   snapped
appertains   satin-paper
apple   appel; pepla
apples   appels
applies   lappies
appraised   disappear
appress   sappers
apricots   piscator
April   Pilar; prial
aprons   parson; Prosna
apse   apes; peas; spae
apses   passé; spaes
apso   soap
apsos   psoas; soaps
apt   pat; tap
aptly   patly
aptness   patness
aptote   teapot
aptotes   teapots
ar   Ra
Arab   arba; Raab
arable   Arbela
Arabs   arbas; Basra; sabra
Arad   Adar
Aragon   angora
Aram   mara; Rama
Aramaic   cariama
Aran   Nara; rana
Aras   Saar; Sara
Arawaks   Sarawak
arba   Arab; Raab
arbas   Arabs; Basra; sabra
Arbela   arable
arbiter   rarebit
arbiters   rarebits
arbute   Tauber
arc   car
Arcadian   acaridan
arcading   cardigan
arcadings   cardigans
arced   acred; cadre; cared; cedar;
  raced
arch   char; rach
archaism   charisma; machairs

arched chared
archeress searchers
arches chares; chaser; eschar;
  raches; search
Archie cahier
arching chagrin; charing
archon anchor; Charon; rancho
archons anchors; ranchos
Archy chary
arcing caring; racing
arcked carked; dacker; racked
arcking carking; racking
arco Cora; Orca; Roca
arcs cars; scar
Ardea aread
ardeb Bader; bared; beard; bread;
  Breda; debar
ardebs beards; breads; debars;
  sabred; serdab
Ardèche reached
Arden dearn; Derna
ardent endart; ranted; red ant
are ear; era
aread Ardea
areca Ceará
ared dare; dear; eard; rade; read
aredd adder; dared; dread
arede deare; eared; Reade
aredes deares; erased; Red Sea;
  reseda; seared
areding dearing; deraign; gradine;
  grained; reading
arefies faeries; freesia; sea-fire
arefy faery; Freya
arena anear
areometer aerometer
areometers aerometers
areometric aerometric
areometry aerometry
ares arse; ears; eras; rase; sear;
  sera
aret rate; tare; tear
arête eater; reate; Taree
arêtes easter; eaters; reates; reseat;
  saeter; teaser; Teresa
arets aster; astre; earst; rates; reast;
  resat; stare; strae; tares; tears; teras
arett tater; tetra; treat
aretted treated
aretting treating
aretts stater; taster; taters; tetras;
  treats
argent garnet

argentic catering; citrange;
  creating; reacting
Argentine tangerine
arghan hangar
argil grail; Lairg
Argive garvie; rivage
Argives garvies; rivages
argol algor; goral; largo
argon groan; Ongar; orang; organ
Argonauts angostura
Argonne Garonne
Argos sargo
argot groat
argots groats
argue auger
argues augers; sauger; Segura;
  usager
Argus gaurs; sugar
Arician Icarian
arid dari; raid
aridness sardines
Aries aesir; arise; raise; Riesa; serai;
  Seria
ariette iterate
ariettes iterates; treaties; treatise
aright graith
aril lair; liar; lira; rail; rial
ariot ratio
arise aesir; Aries; raise; Riesa; serai;
  Seria
arisen arsine; Resina
arises raises; serais
arish hairs; Shari
arising raising
arista tarsia; tiaras
aristae Astaire; asteria; atresia
arked daker; drake; raked
arking raking
arkose soaker
arks Kars; sark
Arlberg garbler
arles earls; lares; laser; lears; reals;
  seral
Arlon loran; Lorna
arm mar; ram
Armagh Graham
armaments men-at-arms
armed ad rem; derma; dream
Armenian Marianne
armet mater; tamer; trema
armets master; maters; stream;
  tamers
armful fulmar

armfuls fulmars
armies maires
arming ingram; margin
armlet martel
armlets martels
armpit impart
armpits imparts
armrest smarter
arms mars; rams
Armstrong strongarm
army Mary; Myra
Arne earn; nare; near; Rena
Arnhem Herman
arnica carina; crania
Arno Nora; Oran; roan; Rona
Arnold Landor; lardon; Roland;
  Ronald
aroid radio
aroids radios
aroint ration
aroints rations
arose soare
aroynt notary
Arp par; rap
arpent enrapt; entrap; panter;
  parent; trepan
arpents entraps; panters; parents;
  trepans
arrect carter; crater; tracer
arrest arrêts; raster; raters; Sartre;
  starer; terras
arrester rearrest
arresters rearrests
arresting astringer
arrests rasters; starers
arrêt rater; terra
arrêts arrest; raster; raters; Sartre;
  starer; terras
arride raider
arrides raiders
arrish Harris; shirra; sirrah
arrive Rivera; varier
arrives variers
arrowy yarrow
arse ares; ears; eras; rase; sear; sera
arsenate serenata
arsenide nearside
arsenite stearine
arses rases; rasse; sears
arsine arisen; Resina
arsis saris
arson roans; sonar
art rat; tar

artel alert; alter; later; ratel; taler
artels alerts; alters; laster; ratels;
  salter; slater; staler; stelar; tarsel
Artemis imarets; maestri; maister;
  misrate; semitar; St. Marie
artesian Erastian; resinata
Arteveld traveled
article recital
articles recitals; sterical
artisan tsarina
artisans tsarinas
artist sittar; strait; strati;
  traits
artiste attires; striate; tastier
artists sittars; straits; tsarist
artless lasters; salters; slaters;
  tarsels
Artois ratios
arts rats; star; tars; tsar
artsman Mansart; mantras
artsmen martens; sarment;
  smarten
arty tray
arums ramus; rusma; Sarum
Arun raun
Arundel launder; lurdane; rundale
arval larva; lavra
Arve aver; rave; vare; Vera
ary Ayr; ray
aryl Lyra; ryal
aryls ryals
Asben banes; beans
ascend dances
ascender reascend
ascenders reascends
ascension canonises
ascent enacts; secant; stance
ascents secants; stances
ascertain Cartesian; sectarian
ascertains Cartesians; sectarians
Ascot coast; coats; costa; Tosca
ascribe Brescia
ascription crispation
asdic acids; cadis
ash has
ash-bin banish
ashen Hanse; Shane
ashet haste; hates; heats
ashets hastes; tashes
ashler lasher
ashlers lashers
ashore hoarse
ashy hays; shay

Asians Niassa
aside aides; ideas; Sadie
asides dassie
Asir airs; Isar; rias; sair; sari
Aske kaes; keas; sake
asked kades
asker kesar; rakes; reaks; saker;
  skear
askers kesars; sakers; skears
askew wakes; wekas
asklent anklets
asleep elapse; please; sapele
asp pas; sap; spa
aspen napes; neaps; panes; peans;
  sneap; spane; spean
aspens sneaps; spanes; speans
asper pares; parse; pears; prase;
  presa; rapes; reaps; spaer; spare;
  spear
asperge presage
asperged presaged
asperger presager
aspergers presagers
asperges presages
aspergill pillagers
asperging presaging
aspers parses; passer; repass;
  spaers; spares; sparse; spears
asperse Parsees
aspersed repassed
asperses Passeres; repasses
aspersing repassing
asphalt taplash
asphodel pholades
aspic Capis; picas; spica
aspirant partisan
aspirants partisans
aspirate parasite; septaria
aspirates parasites; satrapies
aspire paries; Persia; praise
aspired despair; diapers; praised
aspires paresis; praises; Serapis
aspiring praising
asport pastor; portas; sap-rot
asports pastors
aspread parades
asps pass; saps; spas
Assam amass; massa
assaying gainsays
assemble beamless
assent sanest; snaste; stanes;
  steans
assenter earnests; sarsenet

assentor senators; star-nose;
  treasons
assentors star-noses
assents snastes
assert asters; astres; reasts; stares;
  Stresa
asserter reassert; serrates
asserters reasserts
assertion Señoritas
assertor oratress; roasters
asses sasse
asset sates; seats; tasse; Tessa
assets tasses
assignor Signoras
assist stasis
assistant Satanists
assort roasts
assot oasts; stoas; Tasso
assuage sausage
assuages sausages
assume amuses; Seamus
Astaire aristae; asteria; atresia
asteism Matisse; samites; tamises
astelic Castile; elastic; laciest;
  latices
aster arets; astre; earst; rates; reast;
  resat; stare; strae; tares; tears; teras
asteria aristae; Astaire; atresia
asterid astride; diaster; disrate;
  staired; tirades
asterids diasters; disaster; disrates
asterism maisters; misrates;
  semitars
astern antres; sterna
asters assert; astres; reasts; stares;
  Stresa
asthenics Caithness
Asti aits; itas; sati; sita
astilbe bestial; stabile
astir airts; raits; sitar; Sitra; stair;
  stria; tarsi; Trias
Astor roast; rotas; Sarto; taros;
  Troas
astral altars; talars; tarsa;
astray satyra; tayras
astre arets; aster; earst; rates; reast;
  resat; stare; strae; tares; tears; teras
astres assert; asters; reasts; stares;
  Stresa
astrex extras; taxers
Astrid triads
astride asterid; diaster; disrate;
  staired; tirades

astringe angriest; ganister;
　gantries; granites; inert gas;
　ingrates; reasting
astringer arresting
astute statue
aswim swami
aswing sawing
asylums alyssum
asyndetic syndicate
at ta
atabal balata
atabeg tea-bag
atabegs tea-bags
at an end andante; Dantean
ate eat; eta; tae; tea
ateliers earliest
Aten ante; etna; neat; Tean
atheism Hamites
atheist staithe
atheists staithes
Athena aneath
Athens hasten; snathe; sneath;
　thanes
a'thing hating
athirst tartish
Athlone ethanol
Athos hoast; hosta; oaths; shoat
atingle elating; gelatin; genital
atlas Salta
Atli alit; Lita; tail; tali
atoc Cato; coat
atoll allot
attolls allotts
atom moat
atomies atomise; osmiate
atomise atomies; osmiate
atomiser amortise; Timor Sea
atomisers amortises
atomises osmiates
atomists somatist
atoms moats; stoma
atonal Latona
at once octane
atone Aneto; oaten; Onate
atoned donate; nodate
atoner ornate
atones Easton; Seaton
atonic action; cation
atresia aristae; Astaire; asteria
Atreus Auster; Seurat
atrial Altair; lariat; latria
atrip parti; tapir
atrocity citatory

Ats sat
attainder antitrade
attar Tatar
attempered temperated
attempering temperating
attended dentated
attentive tentative
attic tacit
attics static
attire ratite; Tiaret
attires artiste; striate; tastier
attrite tattier; titrate
attrition titration
attune Tetuán
attuned taunted
attunes tetanus
attuning taunting
auction caution
auctionary cautionary
auctioned cautioned; education
auctioning cautioning
auctions cautions
auger argue
augers argues; sauger; Segura;
　usager
auks skua
auld dual; laud; udal
aumbry bay rum
aunt tuan; tuna
aunter nature; Neutra; tea-urn
aunters natures; saunter; tea-urns
auntie uniate
aunties sinuate
aunts tunas
aural Laura
auric curia
auricled radicule
Auster Atreus; Seurat
Australian saturnalia
authoress share-outs
avails saliva; salvia; Valais
aval Alva; lava; Vaal
Avalon Avlona; Valona
avarice caviare
ave Eva; vae
avenge geneva
avenger engrave
avengers engraves
avens Evans; naves; Sevan; vanes
aver Arve; rave; vare; Vera
Averno Verona
avers raves; saver; vares
averse reaves; Varese

avert   taver; trave
averted   tavered
avertible   veritable
averting   tavering; vintager
averts   starve; tavers; traves; vaster
Aves   save; vaes; vase
avid   diva, Vida
Aviles   Leavis; valise
avine   Neiva
Avis   siva; visa
avital   Latvia
Avlona   Avalon; Valona
avocations   Nova Scotia
avocet   octave
avocets   octaves
Avon   nova
avoset   ovates
avulse   values
awe   wae
a-weather   wheatear
awed   wade
aweless   weasels
awes   wase

awesome   waesome
awing   Wigan
awl   law
awls   laws; slaw
awn   wan
awned   dewan; waned
awner   Narew
awners   answer
awning   waning
awns   sawn; swan
awry   wary
Axel   axle
axes   Saxe
axle   Axel
axle-pin   explain
axle-pins   explains
axons   Naxos; Saxon
aye   yea
Ayer   aery; eyra; yare; year
Ayr   ary; ray
azin   Nazi
azym   mazy

B

baa   aba
Baal   Alba; Bala
Baalite   labiate
Baalites   labiates; satiable
baas   abas; Saab; Saba
baba   abba
babas   abbas
babbled   blabbed
babbler   blabber; brabble
babblers   blabbers; brabbles
babbling   blabbing
babe   abbé
babes   abbés
backer   reback
backers   rebacks
backets   backset; setback
backfire   fire-back
backfires   fire-backs
back-rest   brackets
backset   backets; setback
backsets   setbacks
backside   dies back
backward   drawback
backwards   drawbacks
bacco   caboc
bacon   banco; Coban

bacterial   calibrate
baculites   bisulcate
bad   dab
bade   abed; bead
Bader   ardeb; bared; beard; bread;
   Breda; debar
badge   begad
badger   barged; garbed
badly   baldy
bael   Abel; able; albe; bale; blae;
   Elba; Labe
bag   gab
bagarre   barrage
bagarres   barrages
bagel   belga; gable
bagels   belgas; gables
bagnio   gabion
bagnios   gabions
bags   gabs
Bahai   Bahia
Bahia   Bahai
baht   bath
bahts   baths
bail   Albi; Bali
bailer   librae
bails   basil; labis

Baird braid; rabid
bairn abrin; brain; Brian
bairns brains
baiter barite; terbia
baits absit
bake beak
baker brake; break
bakers basker; brakes; breaks
bakes beaks
baking ink-bag
Bala Alba; Baal
balancer barnacle
balancers barnacles
balas balsa; basal; Sabal
balata atabal
bald blad
balder bedral; blared
baldies disable
baldy badly
bale Abel; able; albe; bael; blae;
  Elba; Labe
baled abled; blade
baleen enable
baler abler; blare; blear
balers blares; blears
bales ables; Basel; Basle; blaes;
  blasé; sable
Bali Albi; bail
baling abling
ballast ballats
ballats ballast
balm lamb
balmed ambled; bedlam; beldam;
  blamed; lambed
balmier Mirabel; mirable; remblai
balmiest timbales
balming ambling; blaming;
  lambing
balms lambs
balsa balas; basal; Sabal
balsamic cabalism
balsamy abysmal
Balt blat
Balts blast; blats
baluster rustable
bam Mab
ban nab
banal Alban; Laban
banalities insatiable
banco bacon; Coban
bander Brenda
banderol Oberland
banderole bandoleer

banderoles bandoleers; endorsable
bandoleer banderole
bandoleers banderoles; endorsable
bandore broaden
bandores broadens
bane bean
banes Asben; beans
banger graben
bangers grabens
bangle Bengal
Bangor barong; brogan
banish ash-bin
banishes banshies
bank nabk
banker barken
bankers barkens
banks nabks
bans nabs; snab
banshies banishes
bantam batman
bantams batsman
banter Barnet
banterings string-bean
banzai Zabian
bar bra; Rab
barbed dabber
barbel rabble
barbels rabbles; slabber
barbet rabbet
barbets rabbets; stabber
bard brad; drab
bards brads; drabs
bardy Darby
bare bear; brae
bared ardeb; Bader; beard; bread;
  Breda; debar
barege bargee
Bareilly reliably
barely barley; bleary
bares baser; bears; braes; saber;
  sabre
barest baster; bestar; breast; Tarbes
bargained gabardine
barge begar; Berga; garbe
barged badger; garbed
bargee barege
barge in bearing
barges garbes
barges in bearings
barging garbing
Bari rabi
baric Carib; rabic
barite baiter; terbia**

baritone obtainer
baritones obtainers
barium Umbria
barked braked; debark
barken banker
barkens bankers
barking braking
Barkis Biskra
barley barely; bleary
barn bran
barnacle balancer
barnacles balancers
Barnet banter
barney Bayern; Bernay
Barnsley blarneys
Baroda aboard; abroad
barong Bangor; brogan
barongs brogans
barony baryon
barque Braque
barracan barranca
barrage bagarre
barrages bagarres
barranca barracan
barret barter
barrets barters
Barrie Ribera
bars bras
Barsac scarab; Scarba
Barsacs scarabs
Bart brat
barter barret
barters barrets
Barts brast; brats
baryon barony
barytes betrays
basal balas; balsa; Sabal
basaltic cabalist
based beads
Basel ables; bales; Basle; blaes;
  blasé; sable
basely belays
baser bares; bears; braes; saber;
  sabre
bases basse
basest basset; bastes; beasts
bashed bedash
basil bails; labis
basin sabin
basinet Antibes; besaint; bestain
basinets bassinet; besaints;
  bestains
basins sabins

basis bassi
basker bakers; brakes; breaks
basketwork work-basket
backing ink-bags
Basle ables; bales; Basel; blaes;
  blasé; sable
Basra Arabs; arbas; sabra
basse bases
Bassein sabines
basset basest; bastes; beasts
bassi basis
bassinet basinets; besaints;
  bestains
bast bats; stab; tabs
bastard tabards
baste abets; bates; beast; beats;
  besat; Sebat; tabes
baster barest; bestar; breast; Tarbes
basters bestars; breasts
bastes basest; basset; beasts
bastion obtains
basto boast; boats; sabot; Sobat
Basuto U-boats
bat tab
bate abet; beat; beta
batement abetment
bates abets; baste; beast; beats;
  besat; Sebat; tabes
bath baht
bather bertha; breath
bathers berthas; breaths
bathes Shebat
bathos boshta
baths bahts
batman bantam
bats bast; stab; tabs
batsman bantams
battels battles; tablets
battens test-ban
batter tabret
batters tabrets
battier biretta; ratbite
battle tablet
battler blatter; brattle
battlers blatters; brattles
battles battels; tablets
baud daub
baulk Kabul
bawble wabble
bawbles wabbles
bawler warble
bawlers warbles
bay aby

27

bayed   beady
Bayern   barney; Bernay
bayou   boyau
bay rum   aumbry
bazar   zabra
bazars   zabras
bead   abed; bade
beadiest   diabetes
beads   based
beadsmen   beam-ends; bedesman
beady   bayed
beak   bake
beaks   bakes
be-all   Bella; label
beam   bema; Emba
beam-ends   beadsmen; bedesman
beamers   besmear
beamless   assemble
beamy   embay; maybe
bean   bane
beans   Asben; banes
bean soup   subpoena
bean tree   Tenebrae
bear   bare; brae
bear-cat   cabaret
bear-cats   cabarets
beard   ardeb; Bader; bared; bread;
   Breda; debar
bearded   breaded
bearding   breading
beards   ardebs; breads; debars;
   sabred; serdab
bearing   barge in
bearings   barges in
bears   bares; baser; braes; saber;
   sabre
bearskin   breaks in; inbreaks
beast   abets; baste; bates; beats;
   besat; Sebat; tabes
beasts   basest; basset; bastes
beat   abet; bate; beta
beater   berate; rebate
beaters   berates; rebates
Beatles   belates
beats   abets; baste; bates; beast;
   besat; Sebat; tabes
beaut   Butea; taube; tubea
beauts   taubes
beavered   bereaved
becalms   scamble
Béchar   breach; Rechab
becharm   brecham; chamber;
   chambré

becharmed   chambered
becharming   chambering
becharms   brechams; chambers
becked   bedeck
bed   deb
bedash   bashed
bedaub   daubed
bedeck   becked
bedel   bleed
bedell   belled
bedels   bleeds
bedesman   beadsmen; beam-ends
bedim   imbed
bedims   imbeds
bedlam   ambled; balmed; beldam;
   blamed; lambed
bedlams   beldams
bedless   blessed
bedrail   ridable
bedral   balder; blared
bedrid   bidder; birded; brided
bedroom   boredom; broomed
bedrop   probed
beds   debs
bed-sit   bidets; debits
bedsore   sobered
beduck   bucked
bedung   bunged
bedust   bestud; busted; debuts
bedusts   bestuds
beeches   beseech
beech-fern   free-bench
beefier   freebie
bee-fly   feebly
been   bene
beer   bere; bree
beers   beres; brees
beet   bete
beetroot   boot-tree
beets   beset; betes
beflum   fumble
beflums   fumbles
begad   badge
begar   barge; Berga; garbe
begild   bilged
begin   being; binge
begins   beings; besing; binges
begird   bridge
begirds   bridges
begrudge   buggered; debugger
begrudges   debuggers
behest   Thebes
bein   Beni; bien; bine

being   begin; binge
beings   begins; besing; binges
Beira   Beria; Eibar
belated   bleated
belates   Boatles
belating   bleating; tangible
belays   basely
beldam   ambled; balmed;
   bedlam; blamed; lambed
beldame   bemedal
beldames   bemedals
beldams   bedlams
belga   bagel; gable
belgas   bagels; gables
Belgian   Algenib; Bengali
Belgians   Bengalis; singable
Belial   alible; Biella; labile; liable
belied   debile; edible
Bella   be-all; label
belled   bedell
bellied   delible
bellows   Boswell
belonged   englobed
belonging   englobing
below   bowel; elbow
belt   blet
Beltane   tenable
belts   blest; blets
beluga   blague
bema   beam; Emba
bemean   bename
bemeans   benames
bemete   beteem
bemetes   beteems
bemire   bireme
bemires   biremes
bemoans   ambones
bemoil   emboil; emboli; mobile
bemoiled   emboiled
bemoiling   emboiling
bemoils   emboils; mobiles
ben   neb
bename   bemean
benames   bemeans
bendier   inbreed
bends   S-bend
bendy   by-end
bene   been
Bengal   bangle
Bengali   Algenib; Belgian
Bengalis   Belgians; singable
Beni   bein; bien; bine
Benoni   bonnie

bens   nebs; sneb
berate   beater; rebate
berated   betread; debater; rebated
berates   beaters; rebates
berating   rebating
bere   beer; bree
bereaved   beavered
beres   beers; brees
Berga   barge; begar; garbe
Beria   Beira; Eibar
Bernard   brander
Bernay   barney; Bayern
berried   briered
bertha   bather; breath
berthas   bathers; breaths
berthing   brighten
besaint   Antibes; basinet; bestain
besainted   bestained
besainting   bestaining
besaints   basinets; bassinet;
   bestains
besat   abets; baste; bates; beast;
   beats; Sebat; tabes
beseech   beeches
beset   beets; betes
besing   begins; beings; binges
besings   bigness
besit   bites
besmear   beamers
besom   mebos
besotted   obtested
besotting   obtesting
best   bets
bestain   Antibes; basinet; besaint
bestained   besainted
bestaining   besainting
bestains   basinets; bassinet;
   besaints
bestar   barest; baster; breast; Tarbes
bestarred   redbreast
bestars   basters; breasts
bestead   debates
bestial   astilbe; stabile
bestiary   sybarite
bestill   billets
bestir   bister; bistre; biters; tribes
bestrew   webster
bestrews   websters
bestuck   buckets
bestud   bedust; busted; debuts
bestuds   bedusts
beta   abet; bate; beat
bete   beet

beteem bemete
beteems bemetes
betes beets; beset
betid bidet; debit
betided debited
betiding debiting
betrays barytes
betread berated; debater; rebated
betreads breasted; debaters
betrim timber; timbre
betrims timbers; timbres
betrod debtor
bets best
Betsy bytes
Bette Tebet
Betti Tibet
bever breve
bevers breves
Bevis vibes
bey bye
beys byes
bheesti bhistee
bhistee bheesti
biased abides
bicorn bicron
bicron bicorn
bid dib
bidder bedrid; birded; brided
bide dieb
bidet betid; debit
bidets bed-sit; debits
bids dibs
Biel bile
Biella alible; Belial; labile; liable
bien bein; Beni; bine
bier Brie; Ribe
biers birse; Ribes
big gib
Big Ben ebbing
big end binged
biggin gibing
bigness besings
bigoted dog-bite
Bikaner break in; inbreak
bike kibe
bikes kibes
bilboes lobbies
bile Biel
bilged begild
billets bestill
bilobed lobbied
biltong bolting
bin nib

binary brainy
binder brined; inbred; rebind
binders rebinds
bind over ovenbird
binds over ovenbirds
bine bein; Beni; bien
binge begin; being
binged big end
binges begins; beings; besing
bins nibs; snib
biogeny obeying
bionic niobic
bird drib
bird-call call-bird
bird-calls call-birds
birded bedrid; bidder; brided
birdie Bridie
birding briding
bird-like Kilbride
birds dribs
bireme bemire
biremes bemires
biretta battier; ratbite
birettas ratbites
birled bridle
birles birsle
biros Boris
birse biers; Ribes
birsle birles
birsled bridles
birsles ribless
bis sib
Biskra Barkis
bister bestir; bistre; biters; tribes
bistre bestir; bister; biters; tribes
bistro orbits
bisulcate baculites
bit Tib
biter rebit; Tiber; tribe
biters bestir; bister; bistre;
      tribes
bites besit
bito obit
bittern Britten
bizarre brazier
blabbed babbled
blabber babbler; brabble
blabbers babblers; brabbles
blabbing babbling
black earth blackheart
blackheart black earth
blad bald
blade abled; baled

blae Abel; able; albe; bael; bale; Elba; Labe

blaes ables; bales; Basel; Basle; blasé; sable

blague beluga

Blake bleak

blame amble; Mabel; Melba

blamed ambled; balmed; bedlam; beldam; lambed

blamer ambler; marble; ramble

blamers amblers; marbles; rambles

blames ambles

blaming ambling; balming; lambing

blare abler; baler; blear

blared balder; bedral

blares balers; blears

blarneys Barnsley

blasé ables; bales; Basel; Basle; blaes; sable

blast Balts; blats

blasted stabled

blastema lambaste

blaster alberts; labrets; stabler; tablers

blasters stablers

blasting stabling

blat Balt

blate ablet; bleat; table

blats Balts; blast

blatter battler; brattle

blatters battlers; brattles

blay ably

bleak Blake

blear abler; baler; blare

blears balers; blares

bleary barely; barley

bleat ablet; blate; table

bleated belated

bleating belating; tangible

bleats ablest; ablets; stable; tables

bleed bedel

bleeds bedels

blessed bedless

blessing glibness

blest belts; blets

blet belt

blets belts; blest

Blida ad lib

blinder brindle

blinders brindles

blister bristle

blisters bristles

blithe thible

bloated lobated

bloater Latrobe

bloaters sortable; storable

bloating bog-Latin; obligant

bloats oblast

Blois boils

blonde bolden; Döbeln

blondes boldens

bloods 'sblood

bloomer rebloom

bloomers reblooms

blore borel

blot bolt

blots bolts

blotted bottled

blotter bottler

blotters bottlers

blotting bottling

blouse boules; obelus

bloused doubles

blow bowl

blowed bowled

blower bowler

blowers bowlers

blowing bowling

blows bowls

blude blued

bludge bugled; bulged

bludger burgled

blue Lebu

blued blude

bluenose nebulose

bluenotes bluestone

bluer ruble

blue-rot boulter; trouble

blues bulse

bluest bustle; sublet; subtle

bluestone bluenotes

blunge bungle

blunged bungled

blunger bungler

blungers bunglers

blunges bungles

blunging bungling

blur burl

blurs burls; slurb

blushes bushels

bluster bustler; butlers; subtler

blusters bustlers

bo ob

boa Abo

boar bora

board   abord; broad
boarded   aborded
boarder   broader
boarding   abording
boardings   signboard
boardroom   Broadmoor
boards   abords; adsorb; broads
boars   boras
boart   abort; Rabot; tabor
boarts   aborts; Strabo; tabors
boas   Abos
boast   basto; boats; sabot; Sobat
boaster   boaters; borates
boasters   Botsares
boasting   bostangi
boasts   sabots
boater   borate
boaters   boaster; borates
boat-hook   book-oath
boat-hooks   book-oaths
boathouse   houseboat
boathouses   houseboats
boats   basto; boast; sabot; Sobat
bobac   cabob
bobak   kabob
boches   bosche
bode   Obed
Boden   boned
Boer   bore; Ebro; robe
Boers   bores; brose; robes; sober
bog   gob
bogeys   goes by
bog-Latin   bloating; obligant
bogle   globe
bogles   globes
Bogota   Tobago
bogs   gobs
bogy   boyg; go by
boh   hob
boil   lobi
boiled   bolide
boiler   reboil
boilers   reboils
boils   Blois
bok   kob
boko   book; Obok
bokos   books
boks   bosk; kobs
Bolbec   cobble
bolden   blonde; Döbeln
boldens   blondes
bolder   bordel
bole   lobe; Loeb

boles   lobes
bolide   boiled
Bols   lobs; slob
bolster   bolters; lobster
bolsters   lobsters
bolt   blot
bolters   bolster; lobster
bolting   biltong
bolts   blots
bolus   lobus
boma   ambo; M'Bao; Moab
bomas   ambos; Sambo
bombed   mobbed
bombing   mobbing
bon   nob
bondage   dogbane
bone   ebon
boned   Boden
boneless   noblesse
boner   borne
bongo   boong
bongos   boongs
boning   Ningbo
bonnie   Benoni
bonsai   Bosnia
bonus   bosun; bouns
bonzer   bronze
booby   yobbo
booh   hobo
book   boko; Obok
bookcase   casebook
bookcases   casebooks
bookies   booksie
book-oath   boat-hook
book-oaths   boat-hooks
books   bokos
booksie   bookies
booms   bosom
boong   bongo
boongs   bongos
boons   boson
boor   broo
boors   broos
boose   oboes
boost   boots
boot-jack   jackboot
boot-jacks   jackboots
boots   boost
boot-tree   beetroot
bor   orb; rob
bora   boar
boracic   braccio
boras   boars

borate boater
borated aborted; tabored
borates boaster; boaters
borating aborting; taboring
bordel bolder
bordello doorbell
bordellos doorbells
bore Boer; Ebro; robe
bored orbed; robed
boredom bedroom; broomed
borel blore
bores Boers; brose; robes; sober
boring orbing; robing
Boris biros
born Brno; Bron
borne boner
Borneo Oberon
Bornu bourn
bosche boches
bosh hobs
boshta bathos
boshter bothers
bosk boks; kobs
bos'n nobs; snob
Bosnia bonsai
bos'ns snobs
bosom booms
boson boons
boss sobs
bosses obsess
bossing obsigns
bostangi boasting
bosun bonus; bouns
Boswell bellows
bothering night-robe
bothers boshter
bots stob
Botsares boasters
bottled blotted
bottler blotter
bottlers blotters
bottling blotting
boules blouse; obelus
boult U-bolt
boulter blue-rot; trouble
boulters troubles
boults U-bolts
bounced buncoed
bouncing buncoing
bounder rebound; unrobed
bounders rebounds; suborned
bounding unboding
bouns bonus; bosun

bourgs Burgos
bourn Bornu
bourne unrobe
bournes unrobes
bourns suborn
Bowdler lowbred
bowel below; elbow
bowels elbows
bowers bowser; browse
bowery bowyer
bow-hands show band
bowl blow
bowled blowed
bowler blower
bowlers blowers
bowling blowing
bowls blows
bows swob
bowser bowers; browse
bowsers browses
bowyer bowery
boy yob
boyau bayou
boyg bogy; go by
boys sybo; yobs
bra bar; Rab
brabble babbler; blabber
brabbles babblers; blabbers
Brac crab
braccio boracic
brace acerb; caber; cabré
braced decarb
braces cabers
brackets back-rest
brad bard; drab
brads bards; drabs
brae bare; bear
braes bares; baser; bears; saber;
  sabre
brag garb; grab
brags garbs; grabs
Brahmi mihrab
braid Baird; rabid
braids disbar
brail libra
Braille liberal
brails libras
brain abrin; bairn; Brian
brains bairns
brainy binary
braise rabies; Serbia
braised air-beds; darbies; sea-bird
braises brassie

braize zeriba
brake baker; break
braked barked; debark
brakes bakers; basker; breaks
braking barking
bran barn
Brandeis brandies
brander Bernard
brandies Brandeis
Braque barque
bras bars
brasserie brassiere
brasseries brassieres
brassie braises
brassiere brasserie
brassieres brasseries
brast Barts; brats
brat Bart
brats Barts; brast
brattle battler; blatter
brattles battlers; blatters
braved adverb
brawled warbled
brawler warbler
brawlers warblers
brawling warbling
brawly byrlaw
brayed Red Bay
braze zebra
brazes zebras
brazier bizarre
breach Béchar; Rechab
bread ardeb; Bader; bared; beard;
  Breda; debar
bread-corn corn-bread
breaded bearded
breading bearding
breadnut turbaned
breads ardebs; beards; debars;
  sabred; serdab
break baker; brake
break in Bikaner; inbreak
breaking out outbreaking
break out outbreak
breaks bakers; basker; brakes
breaks in bearskin; inbreaks
breaks out outbreaks
break-up upbreak
break-wind wind-break
bream amber; embar
breams ambers; embars; Sambre
breast barest; baster; bestar; Tarbes
breasted betreads; debaters

breasts basters; bestars
breath bather; bertha
breathes Hartbees
breaths bathers; berthas
brecham becharm; chamber;
  chambré
brechams becharms; chambers
Breda ardeb; Bader; bared; beard;
  bread; debar
brede breed
bredes breeds
bree beer; bere
breed brede
breeds bredes
brees beers; beres
brehon Hebron
Brenda bander
Brescia ascribe
breve bever
breves bevers
Brian abrin; bairn; brain
bribed dibber; ribbed
bribing ribbing
bricole corbeil
bricoles corbeils
bridal labrid; ribald
bride Diber; rebid
brided bedrid; bidder; birded
brides debris; rebids
bridge begird
bridges begirds
Bridgeton Tonbridge
Bridie birdie
briding birding
bridle birled
bridles birsled
Brie bier; Ribe
brief fiber; fibre
briefed debrief
briefless fibreless
briefs fibers; fibres
briered berried
brigade abridge
brigaded abridged
brigades abridges
brigading abridging
brighten berthing
brindle blinder
brindles blinders
brined binder; inbred; rebind
brines nebris
brining inbring
brisance carbines

bristle blister	**Brusa** bursa
bristled driblets	**brush** shrub
bristles blisters	**brute** rebut; tuber
brisure bruiser; buriers	**brutes** buster; rebuts; tubers
brisures bruisers	**buat** abut; tabu; tuba
Britten bittern	**buats** abuts; tabus; tubas
Brno born; Bron	**bucked** beduck
broachers shore-crab	**buckets** bestuck
broad abord; board	**buckle** Lubeck
broadcaster rebroadcast	**buckler** bruckle
broadcasters rebroadcasts	**bud** dub
broaden bandore	**budder** redbud
broadens bandores	**budders** redbuds
broader boarder	**budge** debug
Broadmoor boardroom	**budges** debugs
broads abords; adsorb; boards	**buds** dubs
broadside sideboard	**buffer** rebuff
broadsides sideboards	**buffered** rebuffed
broadway wayboard	**buffering** rebuffing
broadways wayboards	**buffers** rebuffs
brogan Bangor; barong	**bugger** Brugge
brogans barongs	**bugle** bulge
broke out outbroke	**bugled** bludge; bulged
brome ombre	**bugler** bulger; burgle
Bron born; Brno	**buglers** bulgers; burgles
bronze bonzer	**bugles** bulges
broo boor	**bugling** bulging
brooked red-book	**builder** rebuild
broomed bedroom; boredom	**builders** rebuilds
brooms Sombor	**bulge** bugle
broomy byroom	**bulged** bludge; bugled
broos boors	**bulger** bugler; burgle
brose Boers; bores; robes; sober	**bulgers** buglers; burgles
broth throb	**bulges** bugles
broths throbs	**bulging** bugling
browse bowers; bowser	**bulse** blues
browses bowsers	**bummle** mumble
bruckle buckler	**bummled** mumbled
Brue Bure	**bummles** mumbles
Brugge bugger	**bummling** mumbling
bruin burin	**bun** nub
bruins burins	**buncoed** bounced
bruise buries; busier; rubies	**buncoing** bouncing
bruised burdies; bus-ride	**bunged** bedung
bruiser brisure; buriers	**bungle** blunge
bruisers brisures	**bungled** blunged
bruit Tibur	**bungler** blunger
brumal labrum; lumbar; umbral	**bunglers** blungers
brume umber; umbre	**bungles** blunges
Brunei rubine	**bungling** blunging
brunet bunter; burnet	**bunk** knub
brunets bunters; burnets; bursten	**bunked** debunk
brunt burnt	**bunks** knubs

buns   nubs; snub
bunted   but-end
bunter   brunet; burnet
bunters   brunets; burnets; bursten
bur   rub
buran   unbar; urban
burans   unbars
burble   lubber; rubble
burbles   lubbers; slubber
burd   drub
burden   burned; unbred
burdie   buried; rubied
burdies   bruised; bus-ride
burds   drubs
Bure   Brue
burg   grub
burgee   Gueber; Guebre
burgees   Guebers; Guebres
burgle   bugler; bulger
burgled   bludger
burgles   buglers; bulgers
Burgos   bourgs
burgs   grubs
buried   burdie; rubied
buriers   brisure; bruiser
buries   bruise; busier; rubies
burin   bruin
burins   bruins
burl   blur
burletta   rebuttal
burls   blurs; slurb
Burma   rumba; umbra
Burmese   embrues
burned   burden; unbred
burnet   brunet; bunter
burnets   brunets; bunters; bursten
Burnley   Leyburn
burnt   brunt
burs   rubs
bursa   Brusa
bursae   abuser
burse   rebus; suber
Burslem   lumbers; rumbles;
   slumber

bursten   brunets; bunters; burnets
bury   ruby
bus   sub
bush   hubs
bushels   blushes
bushier   Bushire
Bushire   bushier
busier   bruise; buries; rubies
busman   subman
bus-ride   bruised; burdies
bus-rides   disburse
buss   subs
bus station   substation
bus stations   substations
bust   buts; stub; tubs
busted   bedust; bestud; debuts
buster   brutes; rebuts; tubers
bustle   bluest; sublet; subtle
bustler   bluster; butlers; subtler
bustlers   blusters
busts   stubs
busy   buys
but   tub
butchers   Schubert
Bute   tube
Butea   beaut; taube; tubae
but-end   bunted
butlers   bluster; bustler; subtler
buts   bust; stub; tubs
buttered   rebutted
buttering   rebutting
buyer   Ebury
buys   busy
bwana   nawab
bwanas   nawabs
by-blow   wobbly
bye   bey
by-end   bendy
byes   beys
by-form   Formby
byrlaw   brawly
byroom   broomy
byte   ybet
bytes   Betsy

C

Caaba   abaca
cab   ABC
cabalism   balsamic
cabalist   basaltic
cabaret   bear-cat

cabarets   bear-cats
caber   acerb; brace; cabré
cabers   braces
cable   Caleb
cabob   bobac

caboc   bacco
cabré   acerb; brace; caber
cabs   scab
cachets   catches
cackled   clacked
cackler   clacker; crackle
cacklers   clackers; crackles
cackling   clacking
cacodyl   accoyld
caddie   Eddaic
cade   dace
cadent   canted; decant
cades   cased
cadet   acted
cadets   casted
cadge   caged
cadger   graced
cadi   acid
cadis   acids; asdic
cadre   acred; arced; cared; cedar;
   raced
cadres   cedars; sacred; scared
cads   scad
caduceus   caucused
Caen   acne; ance; cane
caestus   cuestas
cafe   face
cafes   faces
caged   cadge
Caher   chare; rache; reach
cahier   Archie
cahiers   cashier
Cahors   orachs
caiman   maniac
caimans   maniacs
Cain   Inca
caird   acrid; daric; Dirac
caisson   casinos; cassino
Caithness   asthenics
calamint   claimant
calamints   claimants
calcines   scenical
Calder   cradle; credal
Caleb   cable
Caledon   celadon
calendar   landrace
calendars   landraces
calender   encradle
calenders   encradles
calends   candles
calenture   crenulate
caliber   calibre
calibers   calibres

calibrate   bacterial
calibre   caliber
calibres   calibers
caliche   chalice
calico   accoil
califs   fiscal
caliper   replica
calipers   replicas; spiracle
caliphate   hepatical
caliver   clavier
calivers   claviers; visceral
calk   lack
calked   lacked
calker   lacker
calkers   lackers; slacker
calking   lacking
calks   lacks; slack
call-bird   bird-call
call-birds   bird-calls
caller   cellar; recall
callers   cellars; recalls; scleral
calligraphy   graphically
callosity   stoically
calls   scall
callus   sulcal
calm   clam
calmed   macled
calmer   Carmel; marcel
calmest   camlets
calms   clams
Calne   clean; lance
calories   Escorial
caloyers   coarsely
calp   clap
calque   claque
calques   claques
calumets   muscatel
calumnies   masculine
Calvary   cavalry
calve   cavel; clave
calver   carvel; claver
calvers   carvels; clavers
calves   cavels; claves; sclave
cam   mac
camber   cembra
cambered   embraced
cambering   embracing
cambers   cembras
cambrel   clamber
cambrels   clambers; scramble
came   acme; mace
camel   macle
camels   macles; mascle; mescal

camerated   demarcate; macerated
cameration   maceration
Cameron   Cremona; Menorca;
   romance
camion   manioc
camise   amices
camlets   calmest
camped   decamp
campers   scamper
campled   clamped
campling   clamping
camps   scamp
cams   macs
camus   caums; Musca; sumac
canaille   alliance
canaries   Cesarian
canaster   caterans
canceration   anacreontic
cancroid   draconic
Candia   Dacian
Candide   candied
candied   Candide
candies   incased
candle   lanced
candles   calends
cane   acne; ance; Caen
cane-chairs   saccharine
caned   dance
caneh   nache
canehs   naches
canephor   Cape Horn; chaperon
canephore   chaperone
canephores   chaperones
canephors   chaperons
canes   scena
cangue   uncage
cangues   uncages
canis   Incas; Sican
canister   scantier
canisters   scenarist
canker   Neckar
canners   scanner
canniest   ancients; instance
cannot   canton
canny   Nancy
canoe   ocean
canoed   acnode; deacon
canoeist   aconites
canoeists   cessation
canoes   oceans
canoness   sonances
canonises   ascension
canonist   contains; sanction

canonists   sanctions
canopies   caponise
cans   scan
canst   cants; scant
canted   cadent; decant
canter   carnet; creant; Cretan;
   nectar; recant; tanrec; trance
cantered   crenated; decanter;
   nectared; recanted
cantering   recanting
canters   carnets; Cretans; recants;
   tanrecs; trances
canthus   chaunts; staunch
canticles   lac insect
cantle   cental; lancet
cantles   centals; lancets
canto   acton; cotan; octan
canton   cannot
cantor   Carnot; carton; contra
cantors   cartons; contras
cantos   actons; Octans
cants   canst; scant
cantus   Tuscan
Canute   uncate
capable   pacable
cape   pace
caped   paced
Cape Horn   canephor; chaperon
capelin   panicle; pelican
capelins   panicles; pelicans
caper   crape; pacer; recap
capers   Casper; crapes; escarp;
   pacers; parsec; recaps; scrape;
   spacer
capes   Caspe; paces; scape; space
capillarity   piratically
caping   pacing
Capis   aspic; picas; spica
capitan   captain
capitans   captains
Capitol   coal-pit; optical; pit-coal;
   topical
caple   place
caples   places
capon   Copàn
caponise   canopies
Capote   toecap
Caprese   escaper; percase
Capri   carpi
capsular   scapular
capsulary   scapulary
capsule   specula
captain   capitan

captains capitans
caption paction; Pontiac
captioned pactioned
captioning pactioning
captions pactions
capuchin china cup
capuchins china cups
car arc
carat carta
carats cartas
carbines brisance
carbon corban
carbonise escribano
carbonises escribanos
carcinoma macaronic
cardecu accrued
cardecus accursed
carder Redcar
carders scarred
cardigan arcading
cardigans arcadings
care acer; acre; race
cared acred; arced; cadre; cedar; raced
careen enrace
careens caserne; enraces
cares acers; acres; carse; races; scare; scrae; sérac
caress carses; crases; scares; scraes; séracs
caret carte; cater; crate; react; recta; trace
carets cartes; caster; caters; crates; Cresta; reacts; recast; traces
cargoes corsage; socager
Carib baric; rabic
carina arnica; crania
carinate craniate
caring arcing; racing
cark rack
carked arcked; dacker; racked
carking arcking; racking
carks racks
carline en clair; Linacre
Carlist St. Clair
Carlos carols; claros; corals
Carluke caulker
Carmel calmer; marcel
Carmiel Almeric; claimer; miracle; reclaim
carmine Crimean; Mercian
carnage cranage
carneous nacreous

carnet canter; creant; Cretan; nectar; recant; tanrec; trance
carnets canters; Cretans; recants; tanrecs; trances
Carnot cantor; carton
Carnoustie cautioners
carob coarb; Cobar; cobra
carobs coarbs; cobras
caroche coacher
caroches coachers
carol claro; coral; Lorca
Carole coaler; oracle
caroli lorica
Carolina conarial
Caroline acrolein; Cornelia; creolian
carolled collared
carolling collaring
carols Carlos; claros; corals
caroms Marcos
carotin anticor; Cortina
carouse acerous
carp crap
carped craped; redcap
carpel parcel; placer
carpels clasper; parcels; placers; scalper
carpets precast; spectra
carpi Capri
carping craping
carps craps; scarp; scrap
carries scarier
carrot trocar
carrots trocars
cars arcs; scar
carse acers; acres; cares; races; scare; scrae; sérac
carses caress; crases; scares; scraes; séracs
carta carat
cartas carats
carte caret; cater; crate; react; recta; trace
carted crated; Dectra; redact; traced
cartel claret; rectal; tarcel
cartels clarets; scarlet; tarcels
carter arrect; crater; tracer
carters craters; tracers
cartes carets; caster; caters; crates; Cresta; reacts; recast; traces
Cartesian ascertain; sectarian
Cartesians ascertains; sectarians
cart-horse orchestra

cart-horses   orchestras
Cartier   cirrate; erratic
carting   tracing
carton   cantor; Carnot; contra
cartons   cantors; contras
cartoon   coranto; Cortona
cartoons   corantos; ostracon
carts   scart; scrat
carucate   accurate
carucates   Crustacea
carve   caver; crave; varec
carved   craved
carvel   calver; claver
carvels   calvers; clavers
carven   cavern; craven
carver   craver
carvers   cravers
carves   cavers; craves
carving   craving
carvings   cravings
Cary   racy
case   aces; aesc
casebook   bookcase
casebooks   bookcases
cased   cades
casein   incase
casern   cranes; rances
caserne   careens; enraces
cash   Chas.
cashed   chased
cashed in   inchased
Cashel   chelas; laches
cashes   chases; chasse
cashier   cahiers
cash in   chains
cashing   chasing
cashmere   marchese
casing   Signac
casinos   caisson; cassino
cask   sack
casked   sacked
casking   sacking
casks   sacks
Caspe   capes; paces; scape; space
Casper   capers; crapes; escarp;
   pacers; parsec; recaps; scrape;
   spacer
casque   sacque
casques   sacques
Cassel   scales
cassette   test-case
cassettes   test-cases
cassia   Isaacs

cassino   caisson; casinos
cassock   Cossack
cassocks   Cossacks
cast   acts; cats; scat
Castalian   Satanical
caste   cates; sceat
casted   cadets
caster   carets; cartes; caters; crates;
   Cresta; reacts; recast; traces
casters   actress; Castres; recasts
Castile   astelic; elastic; laciest;
   latices
cast-iron   Nicastro
castle   cleats; sclate
castles   sclates
castling   catlings
castor   actors; Castro; Croats; scrota;
   tarocs
cast out   outcast
castrated   Tadcaster
Castres   actress; casters; recasts
Castro   actors; castor; Croats; scrota;
   tarocs
casts   scats
casts out   outcasts
casual   causal
casually   causally
cat   act
catalogue   coagulate
catalogued   coagulated
catalogues   coagulates
cataloguing   coagulating
catchers   cratches
catches   cachets
catechism   schematic
categories   categorise
categorise   categories
category   grey-coat
cater   caret; carte; crate; react; recta;
   trace
caterans   canaster
catered   cedrate; created; reacted
caterer   retrace; terrace
caterers   retraces; terraces
cateress   Cerastes
catering   argentic; citrange;
   creating; reacting
caters   carets; cartes; caster; crates;
   Cresta; reacts; recast; traces
cates   caste; sceat
Cath   chat; tach
Cathy   yacht
Catilines   inelastic; sciential

cation   action; atonic
cations   actions; Scotian
catkins   catskin
catlings   castling
Cato   atoc; coat
Catrine   ceratin; certain; crinate;
  nacrite
cats   acts; cast; scat
cat-silver   verticals
catskin   catkins
cat's-tail   statical
catsup   upcast
catsups   upcasts
cattier   citrate
caucused   caduceus
caudle   cedula; Claude
cauld   Claud; ducal
caulker   Carluke
cauls   Lucas
caums   camus; Musca; sumac
causal   casual
causally   casually
cause   sauce
caused   sauced
causer   cesura; Creüsa; saucer
causers   cesuras; saucers;
  sucrase
causes   sauces
causing   saucing
caution   auction
cautionary   auctionary
cautioned   auctioned; education
cautioner   Cointreau
cautioners   Carnoustie
cautioning   auctioning
cautions   auctions
cavalry   Calvary
caveat   vacate
caveats   vacates
cavel   calve; clave
cavels   calves; claves; sclave
caver   carve; crave; varec
cavern   carven; craven
cavers   carves; craves
caviare   avarice
cavils   clavis; Slavic
Cavite   active
cavitied   vaticide
caws   scaw
Ceará   areca
ceasing   incages
Cebu   cube
Cebus   cubes

cedar   acred; arced; cadre; cared;
  raced
cedarn   craned; dancer; ranced
cedars   cadres; sacred; scared
cedi   dice; iced
cedis   dices
cedrate   catered; created; reacted
Cedrela   cleared; creedal; declare
Cedros   coders; credos; scored
cedula   caudle; Claude
ceil   ciel; lice
ceiled   cieled
ceiling   cieling; Lignice
ceilinged   diligence
ceils   ciels; Leics.; Sicel; slice
celadon   Caledon
celebrate   erectable
Celia   Alice; ileac
Celina   ancile; inlace
cellar   caller; recall
cellared   recalled
cellaring   recalling
cellars   callers; recalls; scleral
Celsius   sluices
cembra   camber
cembras   cambers
cementer   cerement
cementers   cerements
Cenis   since
cense   scene
censed   scened
censer   screen; secern
censers   screens; secerns
censes   scenes
censing   scening
censor   crones; oncers
censorial   Creolians
censual   launces; unlaces; unscale
cental   cantle; lancet
centals   cantles; lancets
centaur   untrace
centaurs   Etruscan; recusant;
  untraces
center   centre; recent; tenrec
centering   centreing
centerings   centreings
centers   centres; tenrecs
centiare   creatine; increate; iterance
centigram   cremating
cento   conte; Notec
centos   contes
centralise   interlaces
centre   center; recent; tenrec

centred credent; red cent
centreing centering
centreings centerings
centres centers; tenrecs
centroid Crediton; doctrine
centroids doctrines
cents scent
centurion continuer
centurions continuers
cephalometric petrochemical
Ceram crame; cream; Crema;
  macer; Merca
ceramet cremate; meercat
ceramets cremates; meercats
ceramist matrices
Cerastes cateress
cerate create; ecarté
cerates creates; secreta
ceratin Catrine; certain; crinate;
  nacrite
Ceratodus croustade; educators
cercus cruces
cere cree
cereal alerce
cereals rescale
cered creed
cerement cementer
cerements cementers
ceres crees; scree
ceresin sincere
Cereus ceruse; Creuse; recuse;
  rescue; secure
ceria Erica
cering cringe
ceriph cipher
ceriphs ciphers; spheric
cerite recite; tierce
cero core
ceros cores; corse; score
cerous course; crouse; Crusoe;
  source
cerris criers
certain Catrine; ceratin; crinate;
  nacrite
certes erects; resect; secret
certifiable rectifiable
certification rectification
certified rectified
certifier rectifier
certifiers rectifiers
certifies rectifies
certify rectify
certifying rectifying

certitude rectitude
certs crest
ceruse Cereus; Creuse; recuse;
  rescue; secure
cervices crescive
Cesarian canaries
Cesena encase; seance; Seneca
cessation canoeists
cession cosines; Oscines
Cestoda coasted
cestodes cosseted
Cestracion accretions
Ceti cite; tice
Ceuta acute
chaco coach
Chagres charges; creaghs
chagrin arching; charing
chain Chian; china
chained echidna
chainlet ethnical
chainman Chinaman
chainmen Chinamen
chains cash in
chain-store anchorites
chairs Charis; rachis
Chaldee Cheadle; leached
chalet thecal; Thecla
chalets latches; satchel
chalice caliche
cham mach
chamber becharm; brecham;
  chambré
chambered becharmed
chambering becharming
chambers becharms; brechams
chambré becharm; brecham;
  chamber
changed ganched
changes ganches
changing ganching
chant natch
chanter tranche
chanters snatcher, stancher;
  tranches
chants snatch; stanch
Chanute unteach
chape cheap; peach
chapel pleach
chaperon canephor; Cape
  Horn
chaperone canephore
chaperones canephores
chaperons canephors

chapiter patchier; phreatic
chaps Pasch
chapter patcher
chapters patchers
char arch; rach
characterless clear-starches
chare Caher; rache; reach
chared arched
chares arches; chaser; eschar;
  raches; search
charge creagh
charges Chagres; creaghs
charing arching; chagrin
chariot haricot
chariots haricots
Charis chairs; rachis
charisma archaism; machairs
Charles larches
charm march
charmed marched
charmer marcher
charmers marchers
charming marching
Charon anchor; archon; rancho
charpoy Corypha
chars crash
chart ratch
charters Chartres; starcher
Chartres charters; starcher
charts scarth; starch
chary Archy
Chas. cash
chase aches
chased cashed
chaser arches; chares; eschar;
  raches; search
chasers crashes; eschars
chases cashes; chasse
chasing cashing
chasse cashes; chases
chaste cheats; sachet; scathe; taches
chasten natches
chat Cath; tach
chattel latchet
chattels latchets
chatter ratchet
chatters ratchets
chaunt nautch
chaunters stauncher
chaunts canthus; staunch
chawing chinwag
chaws schwa
Cheadle Chaldee; leached

cheap chape; peach
cheat tache; teach; theca
cheater hectare; teacher
cheaters hectares, teachers
cheating teaching
cheats chaste; sachet; scathe; taches
check-in chicken
check-ins chickens
cheeps peches; speech
cheer reech
cheerly lechery
cheero choree; cohere; echoer;
  re-echo
cheers creesh
cheery reechy
cheiropterans terpsichorean
chela leach
chelas Cashel; laches
Chelsea leaches
chemical alchemic
chenar enarch
chenars ranches
chenille Hellenic
Cheops epochs
chesil chiels; chiles; chisel; elchis;
  Schlei
chest techs
Chester etchers; retches
chesty scythe
chetahs hatches
Chian chain; china
chicken check-in
chickens check-ins
chicle cliche
chider herdic
chiders herdics
chiel chile; elchi
chiels chesil; chiles; chisel; elchis;
  Schlei
Chiem chime; miche
childer chirled
chile chiel; elchi
Chilean Lachine
chiles chesil; chiels; chisel; elchis;
  Schlei
chillies ice-hills
chime Chiem; miche
chimed miched
chimes miches
chiming miching
chin inch
china chain; Chian
china cup capuchin

43

china cups   capuchins
Chinaman   chainman
Chinamen   chainmen
chine   niche
chined   inched; niched
chines   chinse; inches; niches
chining   inching; niching
chinrest   christen; citherns
chinrests   christens
chinse   chines; inches; niches
chinwag   chawing
chirled   childer
chirre   richer
chirt   crith
chirted   ditcher
chirts   Christ; criths
chisel   chesil; chiels; chiles; elchis;
   Schlei
chit   itch
chits   stich
chitters   stitcher
chivy   Vichy
chlorite   clothier
choice   echoic
choir   ichor
choirman   harmonic
choirs   orchis
choked   hocked
choker   hocker
chokers   hockers; shocker
choking   hocking
cholera   chorale
Cholet   clothe
choline   helicon
choltries   clothiers
choose   cohoes
chooser   soroche
chopin   phonic
chopines   Echinops
chopins   phonics
choral   lorcha
chorale   cholera
chore   ochre
chorea   Horace; ochrea; orache
choree   cheero; cohere; echoer;
   re-echo
chorees   coheres; echoers
chores   cosher; ochres
chorist   ostrich
chose   Soche
chou   ouch
chouse   ouches
choused   douches; hocused

chousing   hocusing
chout   couth; touch
chowder   cowherd
chrism   smirch
Christ   chirts; criths
christen   chinrest; citherns
christens   chinrests
chromates   stomacher
chrysolite   chrysotile
chrysotile   chrysolite
chum   much
churl   lurch
churn   runch
cider   cried; dicer; riced
cider-and   riddance
ciders   dicers; scried
cidery   dry ice
ci-devant   Vedantic
ciel   ceil; lice
cieled   ceiled
cieling   ceiling; Lignice
ciels   ceils; Leics; Sicel; slice
cigar   craig
cigars   craigs
cilia   iliac
Cilla   lilac
cinder   crined
cinders   discern; rescind
cinema   anemic; iceman
cineol   Nicole
Cinerama   American; in camera
cinereal   reliance
Cinna   Incan
cinque   quince
Cinto   tonic
cipher   ceriph
ciphers   ceriphs; spheric
circle   cleric
circles   clerics
ciré   eric; icer; rice
cirrate   Cartier; erratic
cirrose   corries; crosier
ciseleur   ciselure
ciselure   ciseleur
cist   cits; tics
cisted   edicts
cistern   cretins
cit   tic
citadel   deltaic; dialect; edictal
citadels   dialects
citatory   atrocity
cite   ceti; tice
cited   edict

cites   tices
cither   thrice
citherns   chinrest; christen
citrange   argentic; catering;
   creating; reacting
citranges   recasting
citrate   cattier
citrates   cristate; scattier
citreous   cries out; outcries
citric   critic
citrin   nitric
citrine   crinite; inciter
Citroen   noticer
citrus   rustic
cits   cist; tics
cive   vice
cives   vices
civet   evict
civets   evicts
clacked   cackled
clacker   cackler; crackle
clackers   cacklers; crackles
clacking   cackling
claes   laces; scale
claim   malic
claimant   calamint
claimants   calamints
claimed   decimal; declaim; medical
claimer   Almeric; Carmiel; miracle;
   reclaim
claimers   miracles; reclaims
Claire   éclair; lacier
Clairton   contrail
clam   calm
clamber   cambrel
clambers   cambrels; scramble
clamped   campled
clamping   campling
clams   calms
clanged   glanced
clanging   glancing
clans   Lancs.
clap   calp
claps   clasp; scalp
claque   calque
claques   calques
Clare   clear
Clares   clears; scaler; sclera
claret   cartel; rectal; tarcel
clarets   cartels; scarlet;
   tarcels
clarino   clarion; Locrian
clarinos   clarions; Locrians

clarion   clarino; Locrian
clarionet   crotaline
clarions   clarinos; Locrians
claro   caroli coral; Lorca
claros   Carlos; carols; corals
clasp   claps; scalp
clasped   scalped
clasper   carpels; parcels; placers;
   scalper
claspers   scalpers
clasping   scalping
clasps   scalps
classed   declass
clat   talc
clatters   scrattle
Claud   cauld; ducal
Claude   caudle; cedula
clave   calve; cavel
claver   calver; carvel
clavers   calvers; carvels
claves   calves; cavels; sclave
clavier   caliver
claviers   calivers; visceral
clavis   cavils; Slavic
clay   lacy
clayed   lac-dye
clay-marl   lacrymal
claymores   lacrymose
clay-pit   typical
clays   scaly
Clea   Alec; lace
clean   Calne; lance
cleaned   elanced; enlaced
cleaners   cleanser
cleaning   elancing; enlacing
cleans   lances; Senlac
cleanse   elances; enlaces; scalene
cleanser   cleaners
cleansers   clearness
clear   Clare
cleared   Cedrela; creedal; declare
clearest   treacles
clearness   cleansers
clear out   colature
clears   Clares; scaler; sclera
clear-starches   characterless
cleat   éclat; lacet
cleats   castle; sclate
cleeks   seckel
cleep   clepe
cleeps   clepes
clematis   climates
clement   Tlemcen

45

Cleo   cole
Cleon   clone; Colne
clepe   cleep
clepes   cleeps
cleric   circle
clerics   circles
cliché   chicle
clientage   genetical
clients   stencil
climates   clematis
climaxes   exclaims
clime   melic
clinker   crinkle
clinkers   crinkles
Clio   coil; loci
clipes   splice
clipper   cripple
clippers   cripples
clobber   cobbler
clobbers   cobblers
clocked   cockled
clocking   cockling
clod   cold
clodly   coldly
clodpoles   scolloped
clods   colds; scold
clogged   coggled
clogging   coggling
cloister   coistrel; cortiles; costlier
cloisters   coistrels
cloke   Locke
cloked   locked
cloking   locking
clone   Cleon; Colne
close   coles; socle
closed   dolces
closer   cresol
closes   socles
closest   closets
closet   clotes
closets   closest
close-up   couples; opuscle; upclose
close-ups   Scopelus; upcloses
closure   colures
clot   colt
clotes   closet
clothe   Cholet
clothier   chlorite
clothiers   choltries
clots   colts
clotter   crottle
cloud   could
clouding   Dulcigno

clous   locus
clouts   locust
Clovis   Volsci
clow   cowl
clows   cowls; scowl
cloy   coly
clue   luce
clues   cluse; luces
clumber   crumble
clumbers   crumbles
Clunes   uncles
cluse   clues; luces
cluster   culters; custrel; cutlers;
   relucts
clusters   custrels
clutch   cultch
clutched   declutch
Cnut   cunt
coach   chaco
coacher   caroche
coachers   caroches
coachmen   Comanche
co-agent   cognate
co-agents   cognates
coagulate   catalogue
coagulated   catalogued
coagulates   catalogues
coagulating   cataloguing
coal   Acol; cola
coaler   Carole; oracle
coalers   escolar; oracles; solacer
coalitionist   solicitation
coalitionists   solicitations
coal-pit   Capitol; optical; pit-coal;
   topical
coals   colas
coarb   carob; Cobar; cobra
coarbs   carobs; cobras
coarsely   caloyers
coarsest   coasters; Socrates
coast   Ascot; coats; costa; Tosca
coasted   Cestoda
coasters   coarsest; Socrates
coasting   agnostic; coatings
coastline   sectional
coat   atoc; Cato
coating   cotinga
coatings   agnostic; coasting
coats   Ascot; coast; costa; Tosca
coax   coxa
Coban   bacon; banco
Cobar   carob; coarb; cobra
cobble   Bolbec

cobbler   clobber
cobblers   clobbers
cobra   carob; coarb; Cobar
cobras   carobs; coarbs
cocaine   oceanic
cockled   clocked
cockling   clocking
cod   doc
code   coed; Doce
codein   coined; no dice
coder   cored; credo; decor
coders   Cedros; credos; scored
codes   coeds
codex   coxed
codille   collide; collied
codlings   scolding
coed   code; Doce
coeds   codes
coeternal   tolerance
coeval   alcove; Levoca
coevals   alcoves
co-exist   exotics
coffers   scoffer
coffs   scoff
coggled   clogged
coggling   clogging
cognate   co-agent
cognates   co-agents
cognation   contagion
cognise   coignes
cognition   incognito
cogs   scog
co-heir   heroic
co-heirs   heroics
cohere   cheero; choree; echoer;
    re-echo
coheres   chorees; echoers
cohoes   choose
coif   fico; foci
coign   incog
coignes   cognise
coil   Clio; loci
coiled   docile
coin   icon
coined   codein; no dice
coiner   orcein; orcine
coiners   crinose; cronies; sericon
coins   icons; scion; sonic
Cointreau   cautioner
coistrel   cloister; cortiles; costlier
coistrels   cloisters
cola   Acol; coal
colanders   Androcles

colas   coals
colation   location
colature   clear out
cold   clod
coldly   clodly
colds   clods; scold
cold tea   located
cole   Cleo
Colenso   console
coles   close; socle
Colin   Nicol
colitis   solicit
collapse   escallop
collapsed   scalloped
collapses   escallops
collapsing   scalloping
collared   carolled
collaring   carolling
collide   codille; collied
collie   ocelli
collied   codille; collide
collier   Corelli
colliers   orsellic
collinear   coralline
collops   scollop
collusive   colluvies
colluvies   collusive
Colne   Cleon; clone
colonialist   oscillation
colonialists   oscillations
colonies   colonise
colonise   colonies
coloured   decolour
colt   clot
colters   corslet; costrel
colts   clots
colures   closure
coly   cloy
Comanche   coachmen
comarb   crambo
combat   tombac
combers   Scomber
combo   coomb
combos   coombs
comedian   daemonic; demoniac
come out   outcome
comer   crome
comers   cromes
comes out   outcomes
comet   Comte
comforter   recomfort
comforters   recomforts
comics   cosmic

Comines incomes; mesonic
coming gnomic
comities semiotic
comity myotic
commercialist microclimates
commits Comtism
Como coom
compact accompt
compacts accompts
companied compendia
compare compear
compares compears; mesocarp
compear compare
compears compares; mesocarp
compeer compère
compeers compères
compendia companied
compère compeer
compères compeers
compile polemic
compiled complied
compiler complier
compilers compliers
compiles complies; polemics
complaint compliant
complexed decomplex
compliant complaint
complied compiled
complier compiler
compliers compilers
complies compiles; polemics
compounded decompound
compressed decompress
comsat mascot
comsats mascots
Comte comet
Comtism commits
Conan ancon
conarial Carolina
concerted concreted
concerti necrotic
concerting concreting
concertino concretion
concertinos concretions
concetti tectonic
concreates consecrate
concreted concerted
concreting concerting
concretion concertino
concretions concertinos
conder corned
conders corsned; scorned
conditioner recondition

conditioners reconditions
condoles consoled
condor cordon
condors cordons
conduits discount
condyles secondly
condylomatous monodactylous
cone once
cones Cosne; scone; sonce
conflate falconet
conflates falconets
confrère enforcer
confrères enforcers
confrérie reinforce
confréries reinforces
congas Gascon
congeries recognise
congested decongest
Congreve converge
congruity crying out; outcrying
conical laconic
conies cosine; oscine
conifer fir cone; inforce
conifers fir cones; forensic;
     forinsec; inforces
conine Connie
Coniston scontion
conk nock
conked nocked
conker reckon
conkers reckons
conking nocking
conks nocks
Connie conine
Conrad Dacron
consecrate concreates
conservant conversant
conservation conversation
conservational conversational
conservationist conversationist
conservationists conversationists
conservative conversative
conserve converse
conserved conversed
conserves converses
conserving conversing
Consett contest
considerate desecration
consigned seconding
consist tocsins
consolate stone-coal
console Colenso
consoled condoles

consoles coolness
consolidates disconsolate
consort crotons
conster cornets; cronets
constipate costean-pit
constipates costean-pits
constrainers contrariness
construe cornutes; counters;
   recounts; trounces
consume muscone
consumed mud-cones
contadine contained
contagion cognation
contained contadine
container crenation
containerised inconsiderate
containers crenations
contains canonist; sanction
conte cento; Notec
contenting contingent
contes centos
contest Consett
contingent contenting
continued unnoticed
continuer centurion
continuers centurions
contour cornuto; crouton
contours cornutos; croutons
contra cantor; Carnot; carton
contrail Clairton
contrariness constrainers
contras cantors; cartons
contravene covenanter
contravenes covenanters
contuses countess
converge Congreve
conversant conservant
conversation conservation
conversational conservational
conversationist conservationist
conversationists conservationists
conversative conservative
converse conserve
conversed conserved
converses conserves
conversing conserving
converter reconvert
converters reconverts
conveyer reconvey
conveyers reconveys
cool loco
cooled locoed
coolers creosol

coolest ocelots
cooling locoing
coolness consoles
cools locos
coom Como
coomb combo
coombs combos
cooms Cosmo
coop poco
coopers scooper
coops scoop
co-ordinate decoration
co-ordinates decorations
coost coots; scoot
coot toco
coots coost; scoot
Copàn capon
copartner procreant
copers corpse
copes copse; Pecos; scope
copied epodic
copiers persico
copse copes; Pecos; scope
copses scopes
copula cupola
copular cupolar
copulated cupolated
cor orc; roc
Cora arco; Orca; Roca
coral carol; claro; Lorca
coralline collinear
corals Carlos; carols; claros
coral-tree correlate
coral-trees correlates
coranto cartoon; Cortona
corantos cartoons; ostracon
corban carbon
corbeil bricole
corbeils bricoles
cordate redcoat
cordon condor
cordons condors
cords scrod
core cero
corea ocrea
cored coder; credo; decor
coreless recloses; sclerose
Corelli collier
corer crore
corers crores; scorer
cores ceros; corse; score
cork rock
corked docker; rocked

corker rocker
corkers rockers
corkier rockier
corkiest rockiest; stockier
corking rocking
corks rocks
cork-tree rocketer
cork-trees rocketers
corky rocky
corn-bread bread-corn
corned conder
Cornelia acrolein; Caroline; creolian
Cornelius reclusion
corners scorner
cornet cronet
cornets conster; cronets
corniche enchoric
corniness incensors
cornmeal amelcorn
corns scorn
cornus Cronus
cornute counter; recount; trounce
cornuted trounced
cornutes construe; counters; recounts; trounces
cornuting trouncing
cornuto contour; crouton
cornutos contours; croutons
corny crony
corona racoon
coronal Locarno
coronas racoons
coroner crooner
coroners crooners
coronet Cotrone
corps crops
corpse copers
corpses process
corpus croups
correlate coral-tree
correlates coral-trees
corries cirrose; crosier
cors orcs; rocs
corsage cargoes; socager
corsages socagers
corse ceros; cores; score
corselet electors; selector
corselets selectors
corses scores; scorse
corset Cortes; coster; escort; scoter; sector; Tresco
corseted escorted

corseting escorting
corsets costers; escorts; scoters; sectors
corslet colters; costrel
corslets costrels; crosslet
corsned conders; scorned
Cortes corset; coster; escort; scoter; sector; Tresco
cortiles cloister; coistrel; costlier
Cortina anticor; carotin
Cortona cartoon; coranto
coruscate accoutres; court case
coruscates court cases
corves covers
corvet covert; vector
corvets coverts; vectors
Corvinae Veronica
Corydon Croydon
Corypha charpoy
cos soc
cosec secco
cosher chores; ochres
cosine conies; oscine
cosines cession; Oscines
cosmic comics
Cosmo cooms
Cosne cones; scone; sonce
Cossack cassock
Cossacks cassocks
cosset estocs
cosseted cestodes
cost cots; scot
costa Ascot; coast; coats; Tosca
costean octanes
costean-pit constipate
costean-pits constipates
coster corset; Cortes; escort; scoter; sector; Tresco
costers corsets; escorts; scoters; sectors
cost-free scot-free
costing gnostic
costlier cloister; coistrel; cortiles
costrel colters; corslet
costrels corslets; crosslet
costs scots
cotan acton; canto; Octan
coteries esoteric
cotillion octillion
cotillions octillions
cotinga coating
cotlands Scotland
Cotrone coronet

cots   cost; scot
coudé   douce
could   cloud
counsel   uncloc?e
counsels   uncloses
counter   cornute; recount; trounce
countercharm   countermarch
countered   recounted
countering   recounting
countermarch   countercharm
counter-paled   counterplead
counterplead   counter-paled
counters   construe; cornutes;
   recounts; trounces
countess   contuses
countries   cretinous
counts   Tucson
couper   croupe; cuerpo; recoup
coupers   croupes; recoups
couples   close-up; opuscle; upclose
couplet   octuple
couplets   octuples
coupures   cupreous
course   cerous; crouse; Crusoe;
   source
coursed   scoured
courser   scourer
coursers   cursores; scourers
courses   Croesus; sources; sucrose
coursing   scouring
court   Turco
court case   accoutres; coruscate
court cases   coruscates
courted   eductor
courtesan   nectarous; outrances
courtiers   scrutoire
courts   scruto; Turcos
cousins   Socinus
couth   chout; touch
covenanter   contravene
covenanters   contravenes
covers   corves
covert   corvet; vector
coverts   corvets; vectors
coveting   Viet-Cong
cowers   escrow
cowherd   chowder
cowl   clow
cowls   clows; scowl
cowries   scowrie
cows   scow
coxa   coax
coxed   codex

crab   Brac
crabs   scrab
crackle   cackler; clacker
crackles   cacklers; clackers
cradle   Calder; credal
craft   fract
crafts   fracts
crags   scrag
craig   cigar
craigs   cigars
crake   creak
crakes   creaks; sacker; screak
cram   marc
crambo   comarb
crame   Ceram; cream; Crema;
   macer; Merca
crames   creams; macers; scream
crampit   ptarmic
crampits   ptarmics
crams   scram
cranage   carnage
crane   crena; nacre; rance
craned   cedarn; dancer; ranced
cranes   casern; rances
crania   arnica; carina
craniate   carinate
craning   rancing
crans   scran
Cranston   Scranton
crap   carp
crape   caper; pacer; recap
craped   carped; redcap
crapes   capers; Casper; escarp;
   pacers; parsec; recaps; scrape;
   spacer
craping   carping
craps   carps; scarp; scrap
crare   racer
crares   racers
crases   caress; carses; scares; scraes;
   séracs
crash   chars
crashes   chaser; eschars
crass   scars
cratches   catchers
crate   caret; carte; cater; react; recta;
   trace
crated   carted; Dectra; redact; traced
crater   arrect; carter; tracer
craters   carters; tracers
crates   carets; cartes; caster; caters;
   Cresta; reacts; recast; traces
Crato   actor; Croat; taroc

cravat Vratca
crave carve; caver; varec
craved carved
craven carven; cavern
craver carver
cravers carvers
craves carves; cavers
craving carving
cravings carvings
crawlers scrawler
crawls scrawl
craws scraw
crayoned deaconry
creagh charge
creaghs Chagres; charges
creak crake
creaks crakes; sacker; screak
cream Ceram; crame; Crema;
   macer; Merca
creamed amerced; racemed
creamers screamer
creaming amercing; Germanic;
   Mérignac
creams crames; macers; scream
creant canter; carnet; Cretan;
   nectar; recant; tanrec; trance
crease searce
creased searced
creases searces
creasing Grecians; searching
creatable traceable
create cerate; ecarté
created catered; cedrate; reacted
creates cerates; secreta
creatine centiare; increate; iterance
creating argentic; catering;
   citrange; reacting
creation reaction
creational laceration
creations reactions
creative reactive
creatively reactively
creativity reactivity
creator acroter; reactor
creators acroters; reactors
crèches screech
credal Calder; cradle
credent centred; red cent
credit direct; triced
credited directed
crediting directing
Crediton centroid; doctrine
creditor director

creditors directors
credits directs
credo coder; cored; decor
credos Cedros; coders; scored
cree cere
creed cered
creedal Cedrela; cleared; declare
creeds screed
creep crêpe
creeps crepes
crees ceres; scree
creesh cheers
Creil relic
Crema Ceram; crame; cream;
   macer; Merca
cremate ceramet; meercat
cremates ceramets; meercats
cremating centigram
cremation manticore
cremator Mercator
Cremona Cameron; Menorca;
   romance
crena crane; nacre; rance
crenated cantered; decanter;
   nectared; recanted
crenation container
crenations containers
crenulate calenture
creolian acrolein; Caroline;
   Cornelia
Creolians censorial
Creon crone; oncer
creosol coolers
crêpe creep
crêpes creeps
crescive cervices
cresol closer
Crespin pincers; princes
cresset resects; secrets
Cressida sidecars
crest certs
Cresta carets; cartes; caster; caters;
   crates; reacts; recast; traces
Cretan canter; carnet; creant;
   nectar; recant; tanrec; trance
Cretans canters; carnets; recants;
   tanrecs; trances
Crete erect; terce
cretinoid direction
cretinous countries
cretins cistern
cretism metrics
Creüsa causer; cesura; saucer

Creuse Cereus; ceruse; recuse; rescue; secure
crews screw
cribbles scribble
cried cider; dicer; riced
cried out outcried
criers cerris
cries erics; icers; seric
cries out citreous; outcries
Crimea Mercia
Crimean carmine; Mercian
crimeful merciful
crimeless merciless
criminate metrician
criminates metricians
crimps scrimp
crinate Catrine; ceratin; certain; nacrite
crinated Dicentra
crine nicer
crined cinder
cringe cering
crinite citrine; inciter
crinites inciters
crinkle clinker
crinkles clinkers
crinose coiners; cronies; sericon
cripes Persic; precis; prices; spicer
cripple clipper
cripples clippers
crises scries
crisp scrip
crispate picrates; practise
crispated practised
crispation ascription
crisps scrips
cristate citrates; scattier
crith chirt
criths chirts; Christ
critic citric
critters restrict; stricter
Croat actor; Crato; taroc
Croats actors; castor; Castro; scrota; tarocs
crochets crotches
crocus succor
Croesus courses; sources; sucrose
crome comer
cromes comers
crone Creon; oncer
crones censor; oncers
cronet cornet
cronets conster; cornets

cronies coiners; crinose; sericon
Cronos croons
Cronus cornus
crony corny
crooner coroner
crooners coroners
croons Cronos
crops corps
croquet rocquet
crore corer
crores corers; scorer
crosier cirrose; corries
crossed scorsed
crosser recross
crosses scorses
crossing scorsing
crosslet corslets; costrels
crotaline clarionet
crotals scrotal
crotches crochets
crotons consort
crottle clotter
croupe couper; cuerpo; recoup
crouped produce
crouper procure
croupers procures
croupes coupers; recoups
croups corpus
crouse cerous; course; Crusoe; source
croustade Ceratodus; educators
crouton contour; cornuto
croutons contours; cornutos
crowned decrown
crows scrow
Croydon Corydon
cru cur; ruc
cruces cercus
crud curd
cruddle curdled
crude cured
cruds curds
cruel lucre; ulcer
cruells cullers; sculler
cruels ulcers
cruelty cutlery
cruet cuter; eruct; truce
cruets cruset; Custer; eructs; rectus; truces
cruise crusie; curies
cruiser curries
cruisers scurries
cruises crusies; cuisser

cruives cursive
crumble clumber
crumbles clumbers
crumpets spectrum
crunodes unscored
crus curs; rucs; scur
crusades used cars
cruse cures; curse; sucre
cruses curses; cusser
cruset cruets; Custer; eructs; rectus; truces
crusie cruise; curies
crusies cruises; cuisser
Crusoe cerous; course; crouse; source
crust curst
Crustacea carucates
crustae curates
crustal curtals
crustier recruits
crusty curtsy
crutches scutcher
cruve curve
cruves curves
crying out congruity; outcrying
cry out outcry
Ctesiphon phonetics
cube Cebu
cubes Cebus
cubist cubits
cubits cubist
cuddles scuddle
cuds scud
cue écu
cued duce
cueist cuties
cuerpo couper; croupe; recoup
cues écus
cuesta acutes
cuestas caestus
cuffs scuff
cuisser cruises; crusies
Culdees seclude
Culebra curable
Culion uncoil
Cullera cure-all
cullers cruells; sculler
cullings sculling
cullions scullion
culls scull
cultch clutch
culter cutler; reluct

culters cluster; custrel; cutlers; relucts
cumbers scumber
cuneal launce; Lucena; unlace
Cuneo ounce
cunt Cnut
cupid pudic
cupidity pudicity
cupids cuspid; Sidcup
cupola copula
cupolar copular
cupolated copulated
cuppers scupper
cupreous coupures
cuprite picture
cups cusp; scup
cur cru; ruc
curable Culebra
curaçao curaçoa
curaçoa curaçao
curate acture
curates crustae
curbs scrub
curd crud
curdle curled
curdled cruddle
curdles scudler
curds cruds
cure ecru
cure-all Cullera
cured crude
cureless recluses
curer recur
curers curser; recurs
cures cruse; curse; sucre
curia auric
curial uracil; Uralic
curies cruise; crusie
curled curdle
curries cruiser
curs crus; rucs; scur
curse cruse; cures; sucre
curser curers; recurs
curses cruses; cusser
cursive cruives
cursores coursers; scourers
curst crust
curtail trucial
curtain turacin
curtals crustal
curtness encrusts
curtsy crusty
curve cruve

curves cruves
Cush such
cusk suck
cusks sucks
cusp cups; scup
cuspate teacups
cuspid cupids; Sidcup
cusser cruses; curses
Custer cruets; cruset; eructs; rectus; truces
custos scouts
custrel cluster; culters; cutlers; relucts
custrels clusters
cuter cruet; eruct; truce
cuties cueist
cut in incut; tunic

cutler culter; reluct
cutlers cluster; culters; custrel; reluct
cutlery cruelty
cutlet cuttle
cutlets cuttles; scuttle
cuts scut
cuts in tunics
cutters scutter
cuttings tungstic
cuttle cutlet
cuttles cutlets; scuttle
cyders descry
cylindrite indirectly
cylix xylic
Cyril lyric

D

da ad
dab bad
dabber barbed
dabbler rabbled
dabbles slabbed
dace cade
Dacian Candia
Dacians scandia
dacker arcked; carked; racked
Dacron Conrad
dad add
daddles saddled
dado Odda
dads adds
daemon Menado; moaned; Modane; Modena; nomade
daemonic comedian; demoniac
daemons monades; nomades
Daf fad
dafter farted; rafted
dag gad
dagger ragged
daggle lagged
daggles slagged
dago goad
dagoes dosage; sea-dog; sea-god
Dagon donga; gonad; Gonda
dagos gadso; goads
dags gads
dah had
dahs dash; shad
Dai aid; Ida

daidle laddie
daidles laddies
daiker raiked
Dail dali; dial; laid
dailies sedilia
daily Lydia
daimen Damien; demain; maiden; median; Medina
daimon domain
daimons domains; Madison
daintiest dittanies
Dairen Darien; rained; randie
dairies diaries
dairy diary
dairyman mainyard
dais aids; Dias; Sadi; said; Sida
Dakar Kadar
daker arked; drake; raked
dakers drakes
dal lad
dale deal; lade; lead; Leda
dales deals; lades; leads; slade
dalesman leadsman
dalesmen leadsmen
dali Dail; dial; laid
dalis Aldis; dials; slaid
Dallas sallad
dalle Della; ladle
dalles ladles
dallied dialled
dallier dialler; rallied
dalliers diallers

dallies sallied
dals lads
dam mad
dame Edam; made; mead
dames meads
Damien daimen; demain; maiden;
   median; Medina
damnatory mandatory
damned demand; madden
Damon monad; nomad
damper ramped
dampish phasmid
dams mads
damsel medals
damson monads; nomads
dan and
dance caned
dancer cedarn; craned; ranced
dances ascend
dander darned; narded
dandle landed
Dane Aden; dean; Edna
Danes Andes; deans; Desna;
   sedan; snead
danger gander; garden; ranged
dangers ganders; gardens
dangle angled; Glenda
dangled gladden
dangler gnarled
danglers glanders
dangles slanged
Daniel Aldine; alined; Delian;
   denial; lead-in; nailed
Danish sandhi
Danite detain; Taiden
Danites detains; instead; sainted;
   stained
danker darken; narked; ranked
dans sand
Dante anted
Dantean andante; at an end
dap pad
dapper rapped
dapple lapped; palped
dapples slapped
daps pads
darbies air-beds; braised; seabird
Darby bardy
dare ared; dear; eard; rade; read
dared adder; aredd; dread
dares dears; rased; reads
darg drag; Gard
darga Garda

dargs drags
dari arid; raid
daric acrid; caird; Dirac
Darien Dairen; rained; randie
daring gradin
Darius radius
darken danker; narked; ranked
darkle larked
darling larding
darn nard; rand
darned dander; narded
darnel aldern; enlard; lander
darner errand; Renard
darners errands; Randers
darning narding
darns nards; rands
dart drat; trad
darted traded
darter dartre; retard; tarred; trader
darters retards; starred; traders
darting trading
dartre darter; retard; tarred; trader
darts drats; strad
Darwen Andrew; dawner; wander;
   warden; warned
Darwin draw in; inward
das ads; sad
dash dahs; shad
dashed shaded
dasher shared
dashes sashed; shades
dashing shading
dassie asides
Datel dealt; delta; lated
date-line entailed; lineated
date-palm palmated
dater adret; rated; tared; trade;
   tread
daters adrets; stared; trades; treads
dates sated; stade; stead
date-sugar graduates
dato toad
datos toads
Datsun daunts
daturine indurate; ruinated;
   urinated
daub baud
daubed bedaub
dault adult
daults adults
daunted undated
daunts Datsun
Dave deva; vade; Veda

Davies advise; visaed
daw wad
dawd wadd
dawded wadded
dawdle waddle
dawdled waddled
dawdler drawled; waddler
dawdlers swaddler; waddlers
dawdles swaddle; waddles
dawdling waddling
Dawley yawled
dawn wand
dawner Andrew; Darwen; wander;
   warden; warned
dawnered wandered
dawnering wandering
dawners wanders; wardens
dawns wands
daws swad; wads
dawtie waited
dawties waisted
daze adze
dazes adzes
deacon acnode; canoed
deaconry crayoned
deacons acnodes
dead Edda
deadlier derailed
deadlock deck-load
deadlocks deck-loads
dead-set sedated; steaded
deaf fade
deafer feared
deafest defeats; feasted
deafly flayed
deal dale; lade; lead; Leda
dealed leaded
dealer leader
dealers leaders
dealing aligned; leading
dealings leadings
deals dales; lades; leads; slade
dealt Datel; delta; lated
dean Aden; Dane; Edna
deaner Dearne; earned; endear;
   neared
deaners endears
deanery renayed; yearned
deans Andes; Danes; Desna;
   sedan; snead
dear ared; dare; eard; rade; read
deare arede; eared; Reade
dearer reader; reared; reread

deares aredes; erased; Red Sea;
   reseda; seared
dearest derates; estrade; reasted
dearies reading
dearing areding; deraign; gradine;
   grained; reading
dearn Arden; Derna
Dearne deaner; earned; endear;
   neared
dears dares; rased; reads
dearth hatred; red-hat; thread
dearths hardest; hatreds; red-hats;
   threads; trashed
deary deray; rayed; ready; yeard
deasil aisled; ideals; ladies; sailed
death hated
deaths hasted; 'sdeath; tashed
deave evade
deaved evaded
deaves evades
deaving evading
deb bed
debar ardeb; Bader; bared; beard;
   bread; Breda
debark barked; braked
debars ardebs; beards; breads;
   sabred; serdab
debase sea-bed
debater berated; betread; rebated
debaters betreads; breasted
debates bestead
debating Nebit-Dag
debile belied; edible
debit betid; bidet
debited betided
debiting betiding
debitor orbited
debits bed-sit; bidets
debrief briefed
debris brides; rebids
debs beds
debtor betrod
debug budge
debugger begrudge; buggered
debuggers begrudges
debugs budges
debunk bunked
debut tubed
debuts bedust; bestud; busted
decal laced
decals scaled
decamp camped
decamps scamped

decant cadent; canted
decanter cantered; crenated; nectared; recanted
decants descant; scanted
decarb braced
decastere desecrate
decasteres desecrates
Decatur traduce
deceiver received
decide de-iced
decider decried
deciders descried
decigram grimaced
decimal claimed; declaim; medical
decimally medically
decimals declaims; medicals
decimate medicate
decimated medicated
decimates medicates
decimating medicating
decimation medication
decker recked
deck-load deadlock
deck-loads deadlocks
declaim claimed; decimal; medical
declaimer reclaimed
declaims decimals; medicals
declare Cedrela; cleared; creedal
declares rescaled
declass classed
declines licensed; silenced
declutch clutched
decollate ocellated
decolour coloured
decomplex complexed
decompound compounded
decompress compressed
decongest congested
decor coder; cored; credo
decoration co-ordinate
decorations co-ordinates
decree recede
decreed receded
decrees recedes; seceder
decrepit depicter
decrial radicel; radicle
decried decider
decries de-icers
decrown crowned
Dectra carted; crated; redact; traced
dedal addle; laded
dedans sadden; sanded
dedimus muddies

deduce deuced; educed
deduces seduced
Dee Ede
deem deme; Mede; meed
deems demes; Medes; meeds
deep peed
deepen peened
deeper De Pere; peered
deepest steeped
deeps speed
deer dere; dree; rede; reed
default faulted
defeats deafest; feasted
defend fended
defer freed
deferment fermented
defiant fainted
de fide defied
defied de fide
defiled fielded
defiler fielder
defilers fielders
defiling fielding
deflex flexed
deflorate floreated
deflower flowered; reflowed
deforces frescoed
deforest forested; fostered
deform formed
deformer reformed
defoul fouled
defray frayed
defrock frocked
defrost frosted
degarnish garnished
Degas gades
degust gusted
dehorn horned
dehort red-hot
dehorts shorted
de-iced decide
de-icers decries
deification edification
deified edified
deifies edifies
deify edify
deifying edifying
deign Nigde
deigns design; sdeign; signed; singed
deil eild; idle; lied
deils idles; sidle; slide
Deirdre derider; ridered

deism   dimes
deist   diets; dites; edits; id est; sited;
   St. Dié; stied; tides
deistic   diciest
deists   desist; sisted
delaine   Adeline; aliened
delapse   elapsed; pleased
delate   elated
Delaware   Weardale
delay   leady
delayer   layered; relayed
deles   Edsel; Leeds; seled
deletes   sleeted; steeled
deletion   entoiled
delf   fled
Delia   ailed; ideal
Delian   Aldine; alined; Daniel;
   denial; lead-in; nailed
delible   bellied
delicateness   delicatessen
delicatessen   delicateness
deligation   intaglioed
delight   lighted
delights   slighted
delimit   limited
deliver   livered; relived; reviled
deliverer   redeliver
deliverers   redelivers
delivers   desilver; silvered; slivered
Della   dalle; ladle
Delorme   remodel
Delos   doles; lodes; soled
Del Rio   roiled
delta   Datel; dealt; lated
deltaic   citadel; dialect; edictal
deltas   desalt; lasted; salted; slated;
   staled
delude   eluded
deluding   indulged; ungilded
delusion   insouled; unsoiled
demain   daimen; Damien; maiden;
   median; Medina
demains   maidens; medians;
   sideman
demand   damned; madden
demanded   maddened
demander   remanded
demanding   maddening
demands   maddens
demarcate   camerated; macerated
deme   deem; Mede; meed
demean   amende; amened
demeanour   enamoured

demeans   amendes
demerge   emerged
demerit   dimeter; Edremit; merited
demerits   dimeters
demersal   emeralds
demerse   emersed; redeems
demes   deems; Medes; meeds
demesnes   seedsmen
demi-god   Megiddo
demi-lance   endemical
demireps   premised; simpered
demise   Medise
demised   Medised; misdeed
demises   Medises
demising   Medising
demit   timed
demits   misted; stimed
demo   dome; Edom; mode
demoniac   comedian; daemonic
demos   domes; modes
demote   emoted
demount   mounted
demounts   mudstone
demur   mured
demurred   murdered
demurrer   murderer
demurrers   murderers
demurring   murdering
den   end; Ned
denarius   Eridanus; unraised
denary   yarned
denatures   sauntered
dene   Eden; need
denes   dense; needs
Denia   Adeni; Andie; Diane; Edina
denial   Aldine; alined; Daniel;
   Delian; lead-in; nailed
denials   lead-ins; snailed
denied   indeed
denier   nereid; reined
deniers   nereids
denies   seined
denim   mined
Denis   dines; snide
Denison   ondines
Dennis   sinned
denominate   emendation
denotes   Tenedos
denounce   enounced
dens   ends; send; sned
dense   denes; needs
denser   sender
densimeter   determines

density destiny
dent tend
dentated attended
dentation intonated
dented tended
dentex extend
denting tending
dentist stinted
Denton tendon
dents stend; tends
dentures sederunt; underset; undesert
denude dudeen; Dundee
denudes dudeens
denunciate enunciated
Denver nerved; vender; Verden
deny dyne
Deo doe; ode
deodar adored
depart parted; prated; petard; traped
departs petards
depasture depurates
depend pended
De Pere deeper; peered
depicter decrepit
depilate epilated; pileated
depletes steepled
depone opened
depones spondee
deport de trop; ported
deports sported
depose epodes; speedo
deposes speedos
deposit dopiest; posited; topside
depositor droopiest
deposits side-post; topsides
depot opted; poted; toped
depots despot; posted; stoped
deprave pervade
depraved pervaded
depraves pervades
depraving pervading
depress pressed; spersed
depurates depasture
deraign areding; dearing; gradine; grained; reading
deraigns gradines; readings
derail laired; Lérida; railed; relaid
derailed deadlier
derails sideral
derange angered; en garde; enraged; grandee; grenade

deranged gardened
deranges grandees; grenades
deranging gardening
derates dearest; estrade; reasted
derating gradient; red giant; treading
deration ordinate; rationed; Rodentia
deray deary; rayed; ready; yeard
derayed yearded
deraying readying; yearding
derays yeards
dere deer; dree; rede; reed
dered dreed
deres drees; redes; reeds; Seder
Derg dreg
derham harmed
derider Deirdre; ridered
derides desired; resided
dering dinger; engird; girned; ringed
derision Ironside
derive reived; revied; rieved
derives deviser; De Vries; diverse; revised
derma ad rem; armed; dream
dermal marled; medlar
dern rend
Derna Arden; dearn
derns rends
derris driers; reirds; riders; sirred
Derry dryer; Ryder
der Tag grated; targed
dervish shrived
desalt deltas; lasted; salted; slated; staled
descant decants; scanted
descend scended
descent scented
describe escribed
descried deciders
description predictions
descry cyders
desecrate decastere
desecrates decasteres
desecration considerate
desert deters; rested
desertion detersion
deserts dessert; tressed
deserve severed
desiccant accidents
design deigns; sdeign; signed; singed

designed sdeigned
designer energids; resigned
designing sdeigning
designs sdeigns
desilver delivers; silvered; slivered
desire eiders; reside
desired derides; resided
desirer Dreiser; serried
desires resides
desiring residing; ringside
desist deists; sisted
desk keds
desman amends; menads
desmans madness
Desna Andes; Danes; deans; sedan; snead
despair aspired; diapers; praised
despairing diaperings
despise pedesis
despiser disperse; Perseids; presides
despisers disperses
despites side-step
despoil diploes; dipoles; peloids; soliped; spoiled
despoils solipeds
despot depots; posted; stoped
dessert deserts; tressed
desserts stressed
d'Estaing sedating; steading
Desterro resorted; rostered
destiny density
desulphur sulphured
detail dilate; tailed
details dilates
detain Danite; Taiden
detainer retained
detains Danites; instead; sainted; stained
detent netted; tented
deter treed
deterge greeted
determines densimeter
deters desert; rested
detersion desertion
detest tested
dethrones shortened
detort rotted
detour douter; outred; red out; routed; toured
detours dourest; douters; outreds; rousted
detrain tan-ride; trade-in; trained

detrains strained; tan-rides
Detroit dottier
de trop deport; ported
deuce educe
deuced deduce; educed
deuces educes
Deurne endure; enured
deus dues; Duse; sued; used
deva Dave; vade; Veda
devaluate evaluated
devas saved; vades; Vedas
devest vested
Devi dive; vied
deviates sedative
devil lived; vilde
devils slived
devise sieved; viséed
deviser derives; De Vries; diverse; revised
devisers disserve; dissever
devisor devoirs; visored; voiders
devitrify fervidity
devoid voided
devoir voider
devoirs devisor; visored; voiders
devolve evolved
devote vetoed
De Vries derives; deviser; diverse; revised
dew wed
Dewali wailed
dewan awned; waned
dewani wained
Dewar wader; wared
De Wet tweed
Dewey weedy
dewiness wideness
dews weds
dey dye
deys dyes; syed
Dhar hard
dhole holed
dhurrie hurried
diabetes beadiest
diadem maided
diagnose agonised; San Diego
dial Dail; dali; laid
dialect citadel; deltaic; edictal
dialects citadels
dialled dallied
dialler dallier; rallied
diallers dalliers
dials Aldis; dalis; slaid

diamante animated
diametric matricide
Diana Aidan; naiad
Diane Adeni; Andie; Denia; Edina
diaper paired; pardie; repaid
diaperings despairing
diapers aspired; despair; praised
diaries dairies
diary dairy
Dias aids; dais; Sadi; said; Sida
diastema Adamites
diaster asterid; astride; disrate;
    staired; tirades
diasters asterids; disaster; disrates
diastyle steadily
diatoms mastoid
dib bid
dibber bribed; ribbed
Diber bride; rebid
dibs bids
dice cedi; iced
diced Eddic
Dicentra crinated
dicer cider; cried; riced
dicers ciders; scried
dices cedis
diciest deistic
dickens snicked
dicker ricked
dictates acid test
didder ridded
diddle lidded
diddler riddled
didoes diodes
die ide
dieb bide
dies Ides; side
dies back backside
diesel elides; sedile; seiled
diesels idlesse
diet dite; edit; tide; tied
dieted edited
dieting editing; ignited
dietitian initiated
diets deist; dites; edits; id est; sited;
    St. Dié; stied; tides
differ riffed
dig gid
digester estridge
digesters estridges
digestions disgestion
digests disgest
digger rigged

dignity tidying
digonal loading
dika kadi
dikas kadis
diker irked
dikers risked
dikes skied
dilate detail; tailed
dilates details
dilatory adroitly; idolatry
diligence ceilinged
dilly idyll
diluent untiled
diluted luddite
dim mid
dimble limbed
dime idem
dimer mired; rimed
dimerous soredium
dimes deism
dimeter demerit; Edremit; merited
dimeters demerits
dimmer rimmed
dimness missend
dimple limped
din Ind; nid
dinar drain; Drina; Indra; nadir
dinars drains; nadirs
dindles slidden
dine Enid; nide
diner Indre
diners rinsed
dines Denis; snide
dinger dering; engird; girned;
    ringed
dingers engirds
dingle elding; engild; gilden
dingles engilds; singled
dingo doing
dingy dying
dink kind
dinks kinds
dinnle linden; linned
dinnles lindens
Dino Odin
dins sind
dint tind
dinted tinded
dinting tinding
dints tinds
diode Dodie
diodes didoes
diopter dioptre

diopters dioptres; dipteros;
    proteids; riposted
dioptre diopter
dioptres diopters; dipteros;
    proteids; riposted
dioptric tripodic
diploe dipole
diploes despoil; dipoles; peloids;
    soliped; spoiled
dipole diploe
dipoles despoil; diploes; peloids;
    soliped; spoiled
dipper ripped
Diptera pirated
dipteros diopters; dioptres;
    proteids; riposted
Dirac acrid; caird; daric
dire Reid; ride
direct credit; triced
directed credited
directing crediting
direction cretinoid
directions discretion
directives discretive
director creditor
directors creditors
directs credits
direr drier; reird; rider
direst driest; stride
dirge gride; ridge
dirges grides; grised; ridges
dirhams Midrash
dirled riddle
dirts strid
Dis Sid
disable baldies
disappear appraised
disaster asterids; diasters; disrates
disbar braids
disburse bus-rides
discern cinders; rescind
discerned rescinded
discerning rescinding
discerns rescinds
disconsolate consolidates
discount conduits
discounter introduces; reductions
discover divorces
discoverer rediscover
discoverers rediscovers
discreet discrete
discreetly discretely
discreetness discreteness

discrepant predicants
discrete discreet
discretely discreetly
discreteness discreetness
discretion directions
discretive directives
discriminator doctrinairism
disease seaside
disgest digests
disgestion digestions
disgown dowsing
dished eddish
dishes hissed
dishevel she-devil
dishevels she-devils
dishing hidings; shindig
dishonest hedonists
disinter inditers
disk kids; skid
disks skids
Disney Sidney
dispel lisped; spiled
disperse despiser; Perseids;
    presides
disperses despisers
dispone spinode
dispones spinodes
disport tripods
disprove provides
disrate asterid; astride; diaster;
    staired; tirades
disrates asterids; diasters; disaster
dissenter residents; tiredness
disserve devisers; dissever
disserves dissevers
dissever devisers; disserve
dissevers disserves
dissolute solitudes
disuse issued
dita adit
ditas adits; staid
ditcher chirted
dite diet; edit; tide; tied
dited tided
dites deist; diets; edits; id est; St.
    Dié; sited; stied; tides
dittanies daintiest
diva avid; Vida
divan Dvina; viand
divans viands
dive Devi; vied
diver drive; rived; Verdi
diverge grieved

divers drives
diverse derives; deviser; De Vries; revised
diverts strived
dives vised
diviner drive-in
diviners drive-ins
divorces discover
Dnieper repined
Dniester inserted; resident; sintered
do od
Döbeln blonde; bolden
doc cod
Doce code; coed
docile coiled
docker corked; rocked
dockets stocked
doctrinairism discriminator
doctrine centroid; Crediton
doctrines centroids
dod odd
dodger red-dog
dodgers gorsedd
Dodie diode
dods odds
doe Deo; ode
doer Doré; Oder; re-do; rode; roed
doers dorse; rodes; rosed
does dose; odes
doesn't Donets; Ostend; stoned
dog god
dogate dotage; togaed
dogbane bondage
dog-bite bigoted
dogger gorged
dog-leg logged
dog-legs slogged
dogs gods
dog-watch watch-dog
doh hod
doing dingo
doings dosing
dolces closed
dole lode
dolerite loitered
doles Delos; lodes; soled
dolia Idola
doline indole; Leonid
dolines Leonids; sondeli
dolium Idolum
dolly Lloyd
dolman almond; old man

dolmans almonds
dolmen old men
dolt told
Dom mod
domain daimon
domains daimons; Madison
domal modal
dome demo; Edom; mode
domes demos; modes
dominate nematoid
dominates Maidstone
domination admonition
dominative admonitive
dominator admonitor
dominators admonitors
domineers modernise
don nod
Donar adorn
donate atoned; nodate
donates onstead
donator odorant; tornado
done node
done in ondine
Donet noted; toned
Donets doesn't; Ostend; stoned
donga Dagon; gonad; Gonda
dongas gonads
Donne end-on; on end
donor doorn; rondo
donors doorns; rondos
dons nods; snod
donsie Edison; noised; onside; side-on
donuts stound
doom mood
dooms dsomo; moods; Sodom
Doone Odeon
door ordo; rood
doorbell bordello
doorbells bordellos
doorman madroño
doormen morendo
doorn donor; rondo
doorns donors; rondos
doors Ordos; roods; sordo
dope oped
doper pedro; pored; roped
dopers pedros; prosed
dopes posed; spode
dopier period
dopiest deposit; posited; topside
doping pongid
dor ord; rod

Dora Odra; road
Doras dorsa; roads; Rodas; sorda
Doré doer; Oder; re-do; rode; roed
doree erode
dorees erodes
Dorian inroad; ordain
dormant mordant
dormie moider
dormies misdoer; moiders
dorp drop; prod
dorps drops; prods; sprod
dors ords; rods; sord
dorsa Doras; roads; Rodas; sorda
dorse doers; rodes; rosed
dorsel drôles; solder; resold
dorsels rodless; solders
dorser orders
dorses dosser; sordes
Dorset sorted; stored; strode
Dorsten rodents; snorted
dort trod
dosage dagoes; sea-dog; sea-god
dosages sea-dogs; sea-gods
dose does; odes
doseh hosed; shoed
dosing doings
doss dsos; sods
dosser dorses; sordes
dossil solids
dost dots; tods
dot tod
dotage dogate; togaed
dotes tosed
doting tin god
dots dost; tods
dottier Detroit
dottle lotted
dottles slotted
doubles bloused
doubter obtrude; outbred; redoubt
doubters obtrudes; redoubts
douce coudé
douches choused; hocused
dour duro; Ordu
dourer ordure
dourest detours; douters; outreds;
     rousted
dourness resounds; sounders
douser roused; soured
douter detour; outred; red out;
     routed; toured
douters detours; dourest; outreds;
     rousted

dover drove; roved
dovers droves
dovetail violated
dowel lowed
dowelling well-doing
dowels slowed; sowled
dower rowed
dowers dowser; drowse; worsed
dowlas woalds
downa adown
dowry rowdy; wordy
dowse sowed
dowser dowers; drowse; worsed
dowsers drowses
dowsing disgown
dozen zoned
drab bard; brad
drabs bards; brads
draconic cancroid
Draconis sardonic
draconites redactions
drafter redraft
drafters redrafts
drag darg; Gard
dragée agreed; geared
draggle gargled; raggled
drag-net granted
dragon Gondar
drags dargs
drail laird; Liard
drails lairds
drain dinar; Drina; Indra; nadir
drainage gardenia
drainers serranid
drains dinars; nadirs
drake arked; daker; raked
drakes dakers
dramas madras
drap pard; prad
drape padre; pared; raped;
     repad
draped padder; parded; Praded
drapers sparred
drapes padres; parsed; rasped;
     repads; spared; spread
drapier parried
draps pards; prads
drat dart; trad
drats darts; strad
drave raved; Revda; Varde
draw ward
drawback backward
drawbacks backwards

drawer redraw; reward; warder; warred
drawers redraws; rewards; warders
draw in Darwin; inward
drawing warding
drawled dawdler; waddler
draw on onward
draws sward; wards
draws in inwards
draws on onwards
dray adry; yard
drays yards
dread adder; aredd; dared
dreads adders; sadder
dream ad rem; armed; derma
dreaming margined; mid-range; Niger Dam
dreamer rearmed
dree deer; dere; rede; reed
dreed dered
dreeing energid; reeding; reigned
drees deres; redes; reeds; Seder
dreg Derg
Dreiser desirer; serried
Dresden reddens
dresser redress
drey dyer; Ryde; yerd
dreys dyers; yerds
drib bird
driblets bristled
dribs birds
drier direr; reird; rider
driers derris; reirds; riders; sirred
dries rides; sider; sired
driest direst; stride
Drin rind
Drina dinar; drain; Indra; nadir
drive diver; rived; Verdi
drive-in diviner
drive-ins diviners
drives divers
drogue gourde; rogued; rouged
drogues gourdes; groused
droguet grouted
drôle older
drôles dorsel; resold; solder
drolling lordling
drolly lordly
dromes smored
drone ronde
droned nodder
drones rondes; snored; sorned

drongo Gordon; Grodno
droopiest depositor
drop dorp; prod
drops dorps; prods; sprod
Drosera adorers
dross sords
drove dover; roved
droves dovers
drow word
drows sword; words
drowse dowers; dowser; worsed
drowses dowsers
drub burd
drubs burds
drugged grudged
drugging grudging
drumbeat umbrated
drumble rumbled
drupe duper; Dupré; perdu; prude; pured
drupel purled
drupes dupers; perdus; prudes; pursed
druse dures
druses duress
dryer Derry; Ryder
dry ice cidery
dso sod
dsomo dooms; moods; Sodom
dsos doss; sods
dual auld; laud; udal
dub bud
dubs buds
ducal cauld; Claud
duce cued
ducker rucked
dudeen denude; Dundee
dudeens denudes
duds sudd
duel dule
duels dulse; slued
dues deus; Duse; sued; used
duetto touted
duffel duffle; luffed
duffer ruffed
duffle duffel; luffed
dugong gun dog
dugongs gun dogs
Dulcigno clouding
dule duel
dulse duels; slued
duma maud
Dumas adsum; mauds

dumpier umpired
dumple lumped; plumed
dumples slumped
Dunbar Durban
dunces secund
Dundee denude; dudeen
dune nude; unde
dunes nudes
dungaree underage; ungeared
Dunmore mourned
duo Oud; udo
duodenal unloaded
duper drupe; Dupré; perdu; prude; pured
dupers drupes; perdus; prudes; pursed
dupes pseud; spued
duple puled; upled
Dupré drupe; duper; perdu; prude; pured
duramen manured; maunder; unarmed
Durban Dunbar
dure rude; rued; urdé
dured udder
Düren runed; under; úrned
Dürer ruder
dures druse
duress druses

during ungird
durmast mustard
durn rund
durns runds
duro dour; Ordu
durst turds
Duse deus; dues; sued; used
dust stud
duster rusted
dusters trussed
dusts studs
dusty study
Dvina divan; viand
dwale lawed; waled; weald
dwales swaled
dwine Edwin; widen; wined
dwined winded
dwines widens; Widnes
dwining winding
dye dey
dyed eddy
dyer drey; Ryde; yerd
dyers dreys; yerds
dyes deys; syed
dying dingy
dynamo Monday
dynamos Mondays
Dyson synod

E

ea ae
each ache
eager agree; eagre
eaglet Galtee; gelate; legate; teagle; telega
eaglets legates; teagles; telegas
eagre agree; eager
eagres agrees; grease
Ealing genial; linage
ean ane; Ena; nae
eanling aneling; leaning; nealing
eanlings leanings
eans sane; sean; Sena
ear are; era
eard ared; dare; dear; rade; read
earfuls refusal
earing gainer; graine; regain; regina
earings erasing; gainers; regains; searing; Seraing; seringa

earl lare; lear; râle; real
earless leasers; sealers
earliest ateliers
earls Arles; lares; laser; lears; reals; seral
early layer; relay
earn Arne; nare; near; Rena
earned deaner; Dearne; endear; neared
earner nearer
earnest eastern; nearest
earnests assenter; sarsenet
earning engrain; grannie; nearing
earnings engrains; grannies
earns nares; nears; saner; snear
earring angrier; grainer; rearing
earrings grainers
ears ares; arse; eras; rase; sear; sera
earst arets; aster; astre; rates; reast; resat; stare; strae; tares; tears; teras

earth Harte; hater; heart; Herat; rathe; Thera; thrae
earthborn abhorrent
earthed hearted; red-heat
earthen hearten; Teheran
earth-fed fathered
earthiness heartiness
earthing hearting; ingather
earthling haltering; lathering
earthly heartly
earthquake heartquake
earths haters; hearts; Sarthe; sheart
earth-shaped heart-shaped
earthy hearty
earwitness wateriness
eas sae; sea
easel lease
easels eassel; leases
easing agnise
eassel easels; leases
eassil aisles; laisse; lassie
east eats; sate; seat; seta; taes; teas
easted seated; sedate; teased
easter arêtes; eaters; reates; reseat; saeter; teaser; Teresa
Easter egg segregate
Easter eggs segregates
easterling generalist
easterlings generalists
eastern earnest; nearest
easters reseats; saeters; teasers; tessera
easting Gastein; genista; ingates; ingesta; seating; tangies; teasing; tsigane
eastings giantess
eastlin elastin; entails; salient; slàinte; staniel
eastling Galenist; genitals; stealing
eastlings Galenists
eastlins salients; staniels
Easton atones; Seaton
easy eyas; yeas
eat ate; eta; tae; tea
eater arête; reate; Taree
eaters arêtes; easter; reates; reseat; seater; teaser; Teresa
eath hate; heat; thae; Thea
eating ingate; tangie
eats east; sate; seat; seta; taes; teas
eavesdrops overpassed; passed over

ebbing Big Ben
ebon bone
Ebro Boer; bore; robe
Ebury buyer
ecarté cerate; create
Echidna chained
Echinops chopines
echoer cheero; choree; cohere; re-echo
echoers chorees; coheres
echoic choice
echt etch; tech
éclair Claire; lacier
eclat cleat; lacet
economies economise
economise economies
écritoires escritoire
ecru cure
écu cue
écus cues
Edam dame; made; mead
Eday yead
Edda dead
Eddaic caddie
Eddic diced
eddish dished
eddy dyed
Ede Dee
Eden dene; need
edentata antedate
Edenton tenoned
Edgar Gerda; grade; raged
edger greed
edges sedge
edginess seedings
Edgware ragweed; wagered
edible belied; debile
edict cited
edictal citadel; deltaic; dialect
edicts cisted
edification deification
edified deified
edifies deifies
edify deify
edifying deifying
edile elide
Edina Adeni; Andie; Denia; Diane
Edirne denier; nereid; reined
Edison donsie; noised; onside; side-on
edit diet; dite; tide; tied
edited dieted
editing dieting; ignited

edition   tenioid
editions   sedition
editor   rioted; tie-rod; triode
editors   roisted; rosited; sortied·
    steroid; storied; tie-rods; triodes
editress   resisted
edits   deist; diets; dites; id est; sited;
    St. Dié; stied; tides
Edna   Aden; Dane; dean
Edom   demo; dome; mode
Edremit   demerit; dimeter; merited
Edsel   deles; Leeds; seled
education   auctioned; cautioned
educators   Ceratodus; croustade
educe   deuce
educed   deduce; deuced
educes   deuces; seduce
eductions   seduction
eductor   courted
eductors   seductor
Edward   warded
Edwin   dwine; widen; wined
eel   lee
eelgrass   gearless; largesse
eels   else; lees; seel; sele; slee
eel-set   Steele
e'en   née
e'er   ere
eery   eyre
eft   fet
efts   fets
eftsoons   festoons
egad   aged; gade; gaed
eger   gree
egers   grees; grese; Segre; serge
egest   geste
egests   gestes
eggar   agger
eggars   aggers; sagger; seggar
eggler   legger
egglers   leggers
eggy   yegg
eglantine   inelegant
ego   geo
egocentric   geocentric
egos   goes
egress   greses
egret   greet
egrets   greets
eh   he
Eibar   Beira; Beria
eident   endite
eiders   desire; reside

eidograph   ideograph
eidographs   ideographs
eighth   height
eigne   genie
eignes   genies; seeing
eik   Ike; kie
eild   deil; idle; lied
eilding   eliding
Eire   Erie
eisel   Elsie; esile
Eisk   sike
ekes   seek; skee
e-la   ale; lea
Elam   alme; Elma; lame; leam;
    Lema; male; meal
élan   lane; lean; Lena
elance   enlace
elanced   cleaned; enlaced
elances   cleanse; enlaces; scalene
elancing   cleaning; enlacing
eland   laden; lande
elanet   lateen; La Tène
elapid   aliped; paidle; Pleiad
elapids   alipeds; lapides; paidles;
    palsied; Pleiads
Elaps   lapse; leaps; pales; peals;
    pleas; salep; sepal; spale; speal
elapse   asleep; please; sapele
elapsed   delapse; pleased
elapses   pleases
elapsing   pleasing
El Arish   hailers
elastic   astelic; Castile; laciest;
    latices
elastin   eastlin; entails; salient;
    slàinte; staniel
elate   telae
elated   delate
elater   relate; Tralee
elaterid   retailed
elaterin   entailer; treenail
elaters   Laertes; relates; stealer
elates   steale; stelae; teasel
Elath   ethal; lathe
elating   atingle; gelatin; genital
elation   toenail
Elba   Abel; able; albe; bael; bale;
    blae; Labe
elbow   below; bowel
elbow   bowel
Elbrus   rubles
Elche   leech
elchi   chiel; chile

elchis chesil; chiels; chiles; chisel; Schlei
eld led
eldin lined
elding dingle; engild; gilden
Eldred reddle
elections selection
electors corselet; selector
Electra treacle
elects select
elegies elegise
elegise elegies
elegist elegits
elegits elegist
elfishness fleshiness
Elgar glare; lager; large; regal; Relga
Elgin ingle; ligne; Nigel
Eli lei; lie
Elian alien; aline; anile; liane
Elias aisle
elide edile
elides diesel; sedile; seiled
eliding eilding
Eliot toile
Elis isle; leis; lies; seil; sile
elision lionise
elisor lories; oilers; oriels; Serlio
elitism El Misti; limiest; limites
elk lek
elks leks; Selk
Ella leal
Ellis lisle
ells sell
elm lem
Elma alme; Elam; iame; leam; Lema; male; meal
Elman leman; Lemna
Elmer merel; merle
Elmina maline; menial
Elmira mailer
El Misti elitism; limiest; limites
elms lems
elmy Lyme; ylem
elogist logiest
Elohist hostile
eloins esloin; insole; lesion; Sileno
elops lopes; olpes; poles; slope
Elsa ales; leas; sale; seal; slae
else eels; lees; seel; sele; slee
Elsevier relieves
Elsie eisel; esile

elsin lenis; liens; lines; nelis; Niles; silen
elsins silens
Elstow lowest; owlets; towels
elt let; tel
Eltham hamlet; Thelma
elts lest; lets; tels
Eluard lauder
eluded delude
eluding indulge
elution outline
elvan levan; navel; venal
Elvas laves; salve; selva; slave; vales; valse
elver lever; revel
elvers levers; revels
elves Veles
Elvis evils; levis; lives; slive; veils
Ely ley; lye
elytra lyrate; realty
em me
emanate enemata; manatee
emanates manatees
emanating manganite
Emba beam; bema
embar amber; bream
embars ambers; breams; Sambre
embay beamy; maybe
emboil bemoil; emboli; mobile
emboiled bemoiled
emboiling bemoiling
emboils bemoils; mobiles
emboli bemoil; emboil; mobile
embraced cambered
embracing cambering
embrues Burmese
emend Mende
emendation denominate
emendator Notre Dame
emeralds demersal
emerged demerge
emersed demerse; redeems
emes Esme; mese; seem; semé; smee
emigrants mastering; St. Germain; streaming
emigrate remigate
emigrated remigated
emigrates remigates
emigrating remigating
emigration remigation
émigré regime
émigrés regimes

Emil   lime; mile
emir   meri; mire; riem; rime
emirate   meatier
emirates   steamier
emirs   mitres; miser; Reims; riems;
    rimes
emit   item; mite; time
emits   items; metis; mites; smite;
    stime; times
Emma   Mame
Emmaus   summae
emoted   demote
empanel   emplane
empanels   emplanes
empathic   emphatic
emperors   premorse
emphasis   misshape
emphatic   empathic
empire   epimer
Empire gown   empowering
empires   emprise; epimers;
    imprese; premise; spireme
emplane   empanel
emplanes   empanels
emplaster   palm trees
emplastron   Palmerston
empowering   Empire gown
emprise   empires; epimers;
    imprese; premise; spireme
emprises   impreses; premises;
    spiremes
emption   pimento
emu   meu
emus   meus; muse
en   ne
Ena   ane; ean; nae
enable   baleen
enactors   ancestor; Escatrón
enacts   ascent; secant; stance
en ami   amine; animé; Maine;
    Menai; minae
enamoured   demeanour
enarch   chenar
enarm   Marne; namer
enarmed   amender; meander;
    renamed
enarming   renaming
enarms   namers
encase   Cesena; seance; Seneca
encases   seances
encashed   enchased
encashes   enchases
encashing   enchasing

encharm   märchen
enchase   achenes
enchased   encashed
enchases   encashes
enchasing   encashing
enchoric   corniche
en clair   carline; Linacre
enclasp   spancel
enclasps   spancels
enclave   valence
enclaves   valences
enclouds   unclosed
encodes   seconde
encores   necrose
encradle   calender
encradles   calenders; esclandre
Encratism   miscreant
encrusts   curtness
encurtain   runcinate; uncertain
end   den; Ned
endarch   ranched
endart   ardent; ranted; red ant
endarting   integrand
endarts   red ants; stander
endear   deaner; Dearne; earned;
    neared
endearing   engrained; grenadine
endears   deaners
endemical   demi-lance
endews   Sweden
end-game   manèged
ending   ginned
endite   eident
enditing   indigent
endive   envied; veined
endlang   England
endodermis   modernised
end-on   Donne; on end
endorsable   banderoles; bandoleers
endow   nowed; owned; Woden
endower   re-endow
endowers   re-endows
endows   snowed
end-papers   snappered
ends   dens; send; sned
endure   Deurne; enured
endures   ensured
enduringly   underlying
end use   ensued
endwise   sinewed
enemas   enseam; seamen
enemata   emanate; manatee
enemy   Yemen

energic generic
energid reigned
energids designer; resigned
energised reseeding
energy greeny; Ygerne
enervate venerate
enervated venerated
enervates venerates
enervating venerating
enervation veneration
enerve veneer
enerves veneers
enew ween
enewed weened
enewing weening
enews sewen; weens
Enfield enfiled
enfiled Enfield
enfire ferine; Fernie; fineer; infere;
  refine
enfired refined
enfires fineers; refines
enfiring infringe; refining
enfold fondle
enfolds fondles
enforcer confrère
enforcers confrères
enforest softener
enforests softeners
enframe freeman
enframed freedman
en garde angered; derange;
  enraged; grandee; grenade
engild dingle; elding; gilden
engilds dingles; singled
engird dering; dinger; girned;
  ringed
engirds dingers
England endlang
Englander Greenland
English shingle
englobed belonged
englobing belonging
englut gluten
engores Negroes
engrail aligner; learing; nargile;
  realign; reginal
engrailed Geraldine; realigned
engrailing realigning
engrailment realignment
engrailments realignments
engrails aligners; realigns;
  Salinger; sanglier; seal-ring

engrain earning; grannie; nearing
engrained endearing; grenadine
engrains earnings; grannies
engram german; manger; ragmen
engrams germans; mangers
engrave avenger
engraves avengers
Enid dine; nide
enigma gamine
enigmas gamines; seaming
enigmatist estimating
enisle ensile; nelies; senile; Silene
enisled ensiled; linseed
enisles ensiles
enisling ensiling
enlace elance
enlaced cleaned; elanced
enlaces cleanse; elances; scalene
enlacing cleaning; elancing
en l'air larine; linear; nailer
enlard aldern; darnel; lander
enlards landers; slander; snarled
enlarge general; gleaner
enlargement Greenmantle
enlarges generals; gleaners
enlight lighten
enlighted lightened
enlighting lightening
enlights lightens
enlist inlets; listen; silent; tinsel
enlisted listened
enlister Leinster; listener; re-enlist
enlisters listeners; re-enlists
enlisting listening
enlists listens; tinsels
en masse enseams
Enna Anne
Ennis nines
enodal loaned
enol leno; Leon; lone; Noel
enormous nemorous
Enos eons; noes; nose; ones; sone
enosis essoin; noesis; noises;
  ossein; sonsie
enounced denounce
enow Owen
en prise erepsin; repines
enquires squireen
enrace careen
enraces careens; caserne
enrage genera
enraged angered; derange; en
  garde; grandee; grenade

enraging   angering
enrapt   arpent; entrap; panter; parent; trepan
enrich   richen
enriched   richened
enriching   richening
enring   ginner
enrings   ginners
enrol   loner; Lorne; nerol
enrols   loners
ens   sen
ensate   sateen; senate; steane
enseam   enemas; seamen
enseams   en masse
enshroud   unhorsed
ensigns   sensing
ensilage   lineages
ensile   enisle; nelies; senile; Silene
ensiled   enisled; linseed
ensiles   enisles
ensiling   enisling
enslave   leavens
enslaves   vaneless
ensnared   Andersen
ensnares   nearness
ensnarl   lanners
ensue   Neuse
ensued   end use
ensure   enures
ensured   endures
entailed   date-line; lineated
entailer   elaterin; treenail
entailers   treenails
entails   eastlin; elastin; salient; slàinte; staniel
entasis   Saintes; sestina; Staines; tansies; tisanes
enter   rente; terne; treen
entera   neater; rateen
enterer   re-enter; terrene
enterers   re-enters; resenter; terrenes
enteric   enticer
enters   Ernest; nester; rentes; resent; Sterne; tenser; ternes
entia   Taine; tinea
enticer   enteric
entirely   lientery
entires   entries; Steiner; Teniers; trenise
entirety   eternity
entitling   inletting
entoiled   deletion

entomic   Metonic
entozoic   enzootic
entrail   Latiner; latrine; ratline; reliant; retinal; trenail
entrails   Latiners; latrines; ratlines; trenails
entrances   renascent
entrap   arpent; enrapt; panter; parent; trepan
entraps   arpents; panters; parents; pastern; trepans
entreat   ratteen; ternate
entreats   ratteens
entries   entires; Steiner; Teniers; trenise
entropium   importune
entrust   nutters; test run
entrusts   test runs
enumeration   mountaineer
enunciated   denunciate
enured   Deurne; endure
enures   ensure
envied   endive; veined
envier   Nièvre
enviers   inverse; versine; Viersen
envies   neives; nieves
envious   niveous; veinous
enwrap   pawner
enwraps   pawners; spawner
enzootic   entozoic
eon   Neo; Noe; one
eonism   Miseno; monies; Simeon; Simone
eons   Enos; noes; nose; ones; sone
eorl   lore; Orel; orle; role
eorls   Leros; loser; orles; Osler; roles; soler; Sorel
eosin   noise
Epacris   Serapic
eparch   preach
eparchies   parcheesi
eparchy   preachy
epha   heap
ephod   hoped
ephor   hoper
epic   pice
epical   plaice; plicae
epics   spice
epidermal   impearled; impleader
epigon   pigeon
epigons   pigeons
epigram   primage
epilate   pileate

epilated depilate; pileated
epimer empire
epimers empires; emprise; imprese; premise; spireme
Epinal alpine; penial; pineal
Epirus uprise
episcopal Pepsi-Cola
epistler peltries; reptiles
epochs Cheops
epodes depose; speedo
epodic copied
epos opes; peso; pose
épris peris; piers; pries; prise; ripes; speir; spire
Epsom mopes; poems; pomes
epulotic poultice
equals squeal
equators quaestor
equip pique
equips piques
er re
era are; ear
eras ares; arse; ears; rase; sear; sera
erased aredes; deares; Red Sea; reseda; seared
erasing earings; gainers; regains; searing; Seraing; seringa
Erasmus amusers; masseur; mausers
Erastian artesian; resinata
erasures reassure
Erato orate
erbium imbrue
ere e'er
erect Crete; terce
erectable celebrate
erection neoteric
erections resection; secretion
erects certes; resect; secret
eremital Lemaître; matériel; real-time
erepsin en prise; repines
erethism etherism
Erewhon nowhere; whereon
erf ref
Erfurt returf
erg Reg
ergo goer; gore; ogre
ergon Genro; goner; Negro
ergot Roget
Erhard harder
eric ciré; icer; rice
Erica ceria

erics cries; icers; seric
Eridanus denarius; unraised
Erie Eire
Erin in re; rein; Reni
eringo ignore; Origen; region
Eris reis; rise; sire
eristical realistic
Erith their
Eritrean rain-tree; retainer
Eritreans rain-trees; retainers; ternaries
Erivan ravine; vainer; Vanier
erks serk; sker
erne Rene
ernes sneer
Ernest enters; nester; rentes; resent; Sterne; tenser; ternes
Ernestine internees
Ernie Irene
Ernst rents; stern; terns
erode doree
erodes dorees
eroding Gironde; groined; ignored; negroid; redoing
Eros ores; roes; rose; sore
eroticism isometric; meroistic
errand darner; Renard
errands darners; Randers
errant ranter
erratic Cartier; cirrate
erratum maturer
erring ringer
errs serr
Erse seer; sere
erst rest; rets
eruct cruet; cuter; truce
eructs cruets; cruset; Custer; rectus; truces
erupted reputed
erupting reputing
eruptions pertusion
erupts purest
erven nerve; never; Vener; Verne
eryngo groyne
escallop collapse
escallops collapses
escaper Caprese; percase
escarp capers; Casper; crapes; pacers; parsec; recaps; scrape; spacer
escarps parsecs; scrapes; spacers
Escatrón ancestor; enactors

eschar arches; chares; chaser; raches; search
eschars chasers; crashes
escheat teaches
esclandre calenders; encradles
escolar coalers; oracles; solacer
escolars lacrosse; solacers
Escorial calories
escort corset; Cortes; coster; scoter; sector; Tresco
escorted corseted
escorting corseting
escorts corsets; costers; scoters; sectors
escribano carbonise
escribanos carbonises
escribed describe
escritoire écritoires
escroc soccer
escrow cowers
Esher herse; sheer
esile eisel; Elsie
esker reeks; skeer
eskers skeers
esloin eloins; insole; lesion; Sileno
esloins insoles; lesions; lioness
Esme emes; mese; seem; semé; smee
esne seen
Esneh sheen
esnes Essen; sense
esoteric coteries
espalier pearlies
Esperanto personate
espousal sepalous
espouser repoussé
esprit priest; Pteris; ripest; sprite; stripe; tripes
espy Spey; sype
esquire queries
esse sees
Essen esnes; sense
Essex sexes
essive sieves
essoin enosis; noesis; noises; ossein; sonsie
essoins session
estate tea-set; testae
estates tea-sets
estating tangiest
Este Sète; tees
ester reest; reset; steer; stere; teers; terse; trees

esters reests; resets; steers; steres
Esth hest; Seth; shet
Esther ethers; Hester; threes
estimating enigmatist
estocs cosset
Eston notes; onset; seton; stone; Tenos; tones
estop poets; potes; stoep; stope; topes
estops posset; stoeps; stopes
Estoril estriol; loiters; toilers
estover overset
estrade dearest; derates; reasted
estradiol idolaters
estrange grantees; greatens; reagents; segreant; sergeant
estranges greatness; sergeants
estray reasty; stayer; yarest
estrays stayers
estreat restate
estreats restates
estrepe steeper
estreped pestered
estreping perstinge; pestering; Presteign
estrich richest
estridge digester
estridges digesters
estriol Estoril; loiters; toilers
estro roset; rotes; store; tores; torse
estrous oestrus; ousters; sourest; souters; tousers; trouses; tussore
estrum muster; stumer
estrus russet; tusser
esurient retinues; reunites
eta ate; eat; tae; tea
et. al. late; leat; tael; tale; teal; tela
etalon lean-to
etalons lean-tos
etc. tec
etch echt; tech
etchers Chester; retches
eten nete; tene
etens steen; teens; tense
eternal teleran
eternity entirety
eth het; the
ethal Elath; lathe
ethanol Athlone
ethe thee
Ethel Lethe
ether there; three
etherism erethism

ethers Esther; Hester; threes
ethicist itchiest; theistic
ethnical chainlet
ethnics sthenic
ethologic theologic
ethological theological
ethologist theologist
ethologists theologists
ethology theology
ethos shote; those
ethyl lythe
etna ante; Aten; neat; Tean
etnas antes; nates; Nesta; Senta; stane; stean; Teans
Eton note; tone
étourdi outride
étrier reiter; retire
étriers reiters; retires; retries; terries
Etruscan centaurs; recusant; untraces
Etruscans recusants
Etta tate; teat
ettles settle
etuis suite
etyma matey; meaty
eugh huge
euro roué
euros roués; rouse
Eva ave; vae
evade deave
evaded deaved
evades deaves
evading deaving
evaluated devaluate
Evan nave; Neva; vane; vena
evanishes heaviness
Evans avens; naves; Sevan; vanes
eve vee
Evelyn evenly
evenly Evelyn
evens Neves; seven
events Steven
ever veer
evert revet
everts revest; revets
eves vees
evets Steve
evict civet
evicts civets; Vectis
evidents invested
evil Levi; live; veil; vile; vlei
evilly lively; vilely

evilness vileness
evils Elvis; levis; lives; slive; veils; vleis
evince Venice
evites stieve
evolved devolve
Ewan anew; wane; wean
ewe wee
ewer were
ewers sewer; sweer; Weser
ewes swee; wees
ewest sweet
Ewing winge
ewk Kew
ewt tew; wet
ewts stew; tews; west; wets
exacter excreta
exalt latex
exam Xema
example exempla
except expect
excepted expected
excepting expecting
excepts expects
excides excised
excised excides
excitation intoxicate
excitor xerotic
excitors exorcist
exclaims climaxes
excreta exacter
exeem exeme
exeems exemes
exeme exeem
exemes exeems
exempla example
exerting genetrix
exertions exsertion
exerts exsert
exiles ilexes
exist exits; sixte
exists sexist
exits exist; sixte
exon oxen
exorcist excitors
exotics co-exist
expect except
expected excepted
expecting excepting
expects excepts
expires prexies
explain axle-pin
explains axle-pins

exporter re-export
exporters re-exports
exsert exerts
exsertion exertions
extend dentex
extension in extenso
extirpates sexpartite
extra taxer

extras astrex; taxers
eyas easy; yeas
eyed yede; yeed
eyelids seedily
eyra aery; Ayer; yare; year
eyras sayer; years
eyre eery
Ezra raze

F

face cafe
facer farce
facers farces
faces cafes
factional falcation
factor forçat
factories factorise
factorise factories
factors forçats
facula faucal
fad Daf
fade deaf
faeries arefies; freesia; sea-fire
Faeroes Faroese
faery arefy; Freya
fag-end fanged
faience fiancée
failed afield
fain Ifan; naif
faint Fanti
fainted defiant
fairness sanserif
fairs fiars
faithless flashiest
faker freak
fakers freaks
fakir Kafir
fakirs friska; Kafirs
fa-la alfa
falcation factional
falcon flacon
falconet conflate
falconets conflates
falcons flacons
fallout outfall
false feals; fleas; leafs
falser farles; flares; flaser
falsest fatless
Falster falters
faltered reflated
faltering reflating

falters Falster
falx flax
fameless self-same
famine infame
famines infames
fancier Francie
fancies fascine; fiancés
fanged fag-end
fangle flange
fangles flanges
fannies Fenians
Fanti faint
far fra
farce facer
farces facers
fardel Alfred; flared
fare fear; frae
fared Freda
fares farse; fears; safer
farfel raffle
farle feral; flare
farles falser; flares; flaser
farmed framed
farmer framer
farmers framers
farming framing
farmost formats
faro Afro
Faroese Faeroes
farrier Ferrari
farse fares; fears; safer
fart raft
farted dafter; rafted
farter rafter
farters rafters
farting ingraft
farts rafts
fascine fancies; fiancés
fast fats
fasten nefast; Stefan
fastener fenestra

77

fastens fatness
faster afters; strafe
Fastnet fattens
fat aft
fate feat
fates feast; feats; festa
fathered earth-fed
fathers shafter
fatless falsest
fatness fastens
fats fast
fatso softa
Fats Waller waterfalls
fattens Fastnet
fattrels flatters
faucal facula
faulted default
faults flatus
faunist fustian
fauns Fusan; snafu
feal flea; leaf
fealed leafed
fealing finagle; leafing
feals false; fleas; leafs
fealty featly
fear fare; frae
feared deafer
fears fares; farse; safer
feast fates; feats; festa
feasted deafest; defeats
feaster afreets; sea-fret
feasts safest
feat fate
feather terefah
featly fealty
feats fates; feast; festa
febrile Félibre
feebly bee-fly
feeder feered; reefed
feeding feigned
feel flee
feeling fine leg; fleeing
feels flees
feer fere; free; reef
feered feeder; reefed
feering feigner; freeing; reefing
feers feres; frees; reefs
feet fête
feigned feeding
feigner feering; freeing; reefing
feints finest; infest
Félibre febrile
felinity finitely

Felis files; flies; 'slife
felsite lefties
felt left
females alms-fee
feminal inflame
fen nef
fended defend
fenestra fastener
Fenians fannies
Fenris infers
fens nefs
feodal foaled; loafed
feral farle; flare
fere feer; free; reef
feres feers; frees; reefs
feria afire
ferine enfire; Fernie; fineer; infere;
   refine
ferly flyer
fermented deferment
Fermo forme; Frome
Fernie enfire; ferine; fineer; infere;
   refine
Ferrari farrier
ferrous furores
ferule refuel
ferules refuels
fervidity devitrify
festa fates; feast; feats
fester freest
festoons eftsoons
fet eft
fetal aleft
fête feet
fets efts
feuds fused
feutre refute
feutres refutes
fiancée faience
fiancés fancies; fascine
fiars fairs
fiber brief; fibre
fibers briefs; fibres
fibre brief; fiber
fibreless briefless
fibres briefs; fibers
fickled flicked
fickling flicking
fico coif; foci
Fidel field; filed
fidget gifted
fie Ife
fief fife

field Fidel; filed
fielded defiled
fielder defiler
fielders defilers
fielding defiling
field notes fieldstone
fieldstone field notes
fiend fined
fiendish finished
fierce Recife
fiery reify
fife fief
fig gif
fighter freight
fighters freights
figurate fruitage
filar flair; frail
file Leif; lief; life
filed Fidel; field
filer flier; lifer; rifle
filers fliers; lifers; rifles
files Felis; flies; 'slife
filets itself; stifle
filler refill
fillers refills
filter lifter; trifle
filters lifters; stifler; trifles
filtration flirtation
finagle fealing; leafing
finale al fine
finder friend
finders friends
fine neif; nife
fined fiend
fineer enfire; ferine; Fernie; infere;
　refine
fineers enfires; refines
fine leg feeling; fleeing
finer infer
fines neifs
finest feints; infest
finger fringe
fingers fringes
finished fiendish
finitely felinity
Finke knife
fino foin; info
fir Rif
fir cone conifer; inforce
fir cones conifers; forensic;
　forinsec; inforces
fire Frei; reif; rife
fire-back backfire

fire-backs backfires
fired fried
firelight flightier
fires fries; serif
firs fris
first frist; frits; rifts
firth frith
firths friths; shrift
fiscal califs
fisher sherif
fishers sherifs
fissure fussier
fist fits; sift
fisted sifted
fisting sifting
fists sifts
fitness infests
fits fist; sift
fitter titfer
fitters titfers
fizzing gin-fizz
flacon falcon
flacons falcons
flair filar; frail
flame fleam
flames fleams
flaneur funeral
flaneurs funerals
flange fangle
flanges fangles
flare farle; feral
flared Alfred; fardel
flares falser; farles; flaser
flaser falser; farles; flares
flashback half-backs
flashiest faithless
flashy fly ash
flatirons frost-nail
flatters fattrels
flatus faults
flax falx
flayed deafly
flea feal; leaf
fleam flame
fleams flames
fleas false; feals; leafs
flecker freckle
fleckers freckles
fled delf
flee feel
fleeing feeling; fine leg
fleer refel
fleers refels

flees feels	**foal** loaf; Olaf
Flemish himself	**foaled** feodal; loafed
flesh shelf	**foaling** loafing
flesher herself	**foals** loafs; sol-fa
fleshiness elfishness	**foci** coif; fico
fleshy shelfy	**fodder** forded
flexed deflex	**foetor** footer; refoot; tofore
flicked fickled	**Fogo** goof
flicking fickling	**foin** fino; info
flier filer; lifer; rifle	**foister** forties
fliers filers; lifers; rifles	**Foligno** fooling; loofing
flies Felis; files; 'slife	**fonder** Fronde
fling out flouting	**fondle** enfold
flirtation filtration	**fondled** Flodden
flirted trifled	**fondler** forlend
flirting trifling	**fondlers** forlends
flit lift	**fondles** enfolds
flits lifts	**fool** loof
float aloft; flota	**fooled** loofed
floater floreat; refloat	**fooling** loofing
floaters forestal; refloats	**fools** loofs
Flodden fondled	**footer** foetor; refoot; tofore
flog golf	**for** fro
flood of old	**foramen** foreman
floreat floater; refloat	**forcat** factor
floreated deflorate	**forçats** factors
florid Ilford	**forces** fresco
flota aloft; float	**forded** fodder
flounder unfolder	**fordo** Frodo
flounders unfolders	**fore** orfe
flour fluor	**foredo** roofed
flouting fling out	**forelies** free-soil
flouts Loftus	**foreman** foramen
flow fowl; wolf	**foremast** mort-safe
flowed fowled; wolfed	**foremasts** mort-safes
flower fowler; reflow; wolfer	**fore-mean** fore-name
flowered deflower; reflowed	**fore-means** fore-names; freemason
flowering reflowing	**fore-name** fore-mean
flowers fowlers; reflows; wolfers	**fore-names** fore-means; freemason
flowery rye-wolf	**forenight** fothering
flowing fowling; wolfing	**forensic** conifers; fir cones;
flows fowls	forinsec; inforces
flue fuel	**foresight** gift horse
fluent unfelt	**forest** fortes; foster
flues fuels	**forestage** fosterage
fluor flour	**forestal** floaters; refloats
flushing lung-fish	**forested** deforest; fostered
fluster fluters; restful	**forester** fosterer
fluters fluster; restful	**foresters** fosterers
flutinas inflatus	**foresting** fostering
fly ash flashy	**forests** fosters
flyer ferly	**forge** gofer
fly rail frailly	**forges** gofers

forinsec   conifers; fir cones;
  forensic; inforces
forlend   fondler
forlends   fondlers
torm   from
formalin   informal
formats   farmost
forme   Fermo; Frome
formed   deform
former   reform
formers   reforms
Formica   aciform
formulae   fumarole
for sale   loafers
Forst   forts; frost
fortes   forest; foster
forth   froth
forties   foister
forts   Forst; frost
forward   froward
forwardness   frowardness
forwards   frowards
foster   forest; fortes
fosterage   forestage
fostered   deforest; forested
fosterer   forester
fosterers   foresters
fostering   foresting
fosters   forests
fothering   forenight
fouled   defoul
founder   refound
founders   refounds
foundling   unfolding
fouter   foutre
fouters   foutres
foutre   fouter
foutres   fouters
fowl   flow; wolf
fowled   flowed; wolfed
fowler   flower; reflow; wolfer
fowlers   flowers; reflows; wolfers
fowling   flowing; wolfing
fowls   flows
fra   far
fract   craft
fracts   crafts
frae   fare; fear
frail   filar; flair
frailly   fly rail
fraise   sea-fir
fraises   sea-firs
framed   farmed

framer   farmer
framers   farmers
framing   farming
Francio   fancier
frayed   defray
freak   faker
freaks   fakers
freckle   flecker
freckles   fleckers
Freda   fared
free   feer; fere; reef
free-bench   beech-fern
freebie   beefier
freed   defer
freedman   enframed
freeing   feering; feigner; reefing
freeman   enframe
freemason   fore-means; fore-names
freer   refer
frees   feers; feres; reefs
freesia   arefies; faeries; sea-fire
free-soil   forelies
freest   fester
Frei   fire; reif; rife
freight   fighter
freights   fighters
frenetic   reinfect
fresco   forces
frescoed   deforces
fresher   refresh
fret   reft
fretful   truffle
fretsaw   wafters
Freya   arefy; faery
fried   fired
friend   finder
friends   finders
fries   fires; serif
fringe   finger
fringes   fingers
fris   firs
friseur   frisure; surfier
friska   fakirs; Kafirs
frist   first; frits; rifts
frisure   friseur; surfier
frith   firth
friths   firths; shrift
frit   rift
frits   first; frist; rifts
fro   for
frocked   defrock
Frodo   fordo
from   form

Frome Fermo; forme
Fronde fonder
froren frorne
frorne froren
frost Forst; forts
frosted defrost
frost-nail flatirons
froth forth
frounced unforced
froward forward
frowardness forwardness
frowards forwards
fruitage figurate
frumenty furmenty
fuel flue
fuels flues
fulmar armful

fulmars armfuls
fumarole formulae
fumble beflum
fumbles beflums
funeral flaneur
funerals flaneurs
funfair ruffian
funfairs ruffians
furbisher refurbish
furmenty frumenty
furnisher refurnish
furores ferrous
furs surf
Fusan fauns; snafu
fused feuds
fussier fissure
fustian faunist

G

gab bag
gabardine bargained
gabbler grabble
gabblers grabbles
gabion bagnio
gabions bagnios
gable bagel; belga
gables bagels; belgas
Gabon obang
gabs bags
gad dag
gadder graded
gade aged; egad; gaed
gades Degas
gadget tagged
gadgets stagged
gads dags
gadso goads
gae age
gaed aged; egad; gade
Gael gale; geal; Gela
Gaels gales; geals
gaes ages; sage
Gail gila; glia
gaillard galliard
gaillards galliards
gain agin; Agni; Gina
gainer earing; graine; regain;
  regina
gainers earings; erasing; regains;
  searing; seringa
gainly laying

gainsays assaying
gainst giants; sating
gair ragi
gaiter triage
gaiters agister; sea-girt; stagier;
  strigae; triages
gaits agist
gal lag
gala alga
Galahad Ala Dagh
gale Gael; geal; gela
galea algae
Galen angel; angle; genal; glean
galena alnage; Angela; anlage;
  lagena
Galenic angelic; anglice
Galenical angelical
Galenist eastling; genitals;
  stealing
Galenists eastlings
gales Gaels; geals
galilees legalise
Galle legal
galleon allonge
galleons allonges
galleries allergies
gallery allergy; largely; regally
galliard gaillard
galliards gaillards
galling gingall
galore gaoler
gals lags; slag

Galtee eaglet; gelate; legate; teagle; telega
Galwegians Glaswegian
gam mag
gambler gambrel
gamblers gambrels
gambrel gambler
gambrels gamblers
game mage
game-bird Ambridge
gamed madge
gamely gleamy; mygale
gamer marge; regma
gamers marges
gamete metage
gametes Maesteg; metages
gamier imager; maigre; mirage
gamin Ngami
gamine enigma
gamines enigmas; seaming
gaming gigman
gamma magma
gammer gramme
gammers grammes
gams mags
gan nag
ganched changed
ganches changes
ganching changing
gander danger; garden; ranged
ganders dangers; gardens
gane Agen; gean; gena
ganged nagged
ganger grange; nagger
gangers granges; naggers
ganging nagging
ganister angriest; astringe; gantries; granites; inert gas; ingrates; reasting
gant gnat; tang
ganted tanged
ganting tanging
gantries angriest; astringe; ganister; granites; inert gas; ingrates; reasting
gants angst; gnats; stang; tangs
gaol goal; Olga
gaoled age-old; old age
gaoler galore
gaols goals; Lagos
gap Pag
gape page; peag
gaped paged

gaper grape; parge
gapers gasper; grapes; parges; sparge
gapes Gaspé; pages
gaping paging
gaps gasp
gar rag
garb brag; grab
garbe barge; begar; Berga
garbed badger; barged
garbes barges
garbing barging
garbler Arlberg
garbs brags; grabs
Gard darg; drag
Garda darga
garden danger; gander; ranged
Gardena Grenada
gardened deranged
gardener garnered
gardenia drainage
gardening deranging
gardens dangers; ganders
Gardner grander
gare gear; Gera; rage
garget tagger
gargle lagger; raggle
gargled draggle; raggled
gargles laggers; raggles
gargling raggling
garment margent; ragment
garments margents; ragments
garner ranger
garnered gardener
garners rangers
garnet argent
garnets Sargent; Stanger; strange
garni agrin; grain
garnish sharing
garnished degarnish
Garonne Argonne
garotter garrotte
garotters garrottes
garret garter; grater
garreted gartered; regrated; Tredegar
garrets garters; graters
garrotte garotter
garrottes garotters
gars Gras; rags
garter garret; grater
gartered garreted; regrated; Tredegar

gartering   regrating
garters   garrets; graters
garvie   Argive; rivage
garvies   Argives; rivages
Gary   gray
gas   sag
Gascon   congas
gases   sages
gash   hags; shag
gasp   gaps
Gaspé   gapes; pages
gasper   gapers; grapes; parges;
   sparge
gaspers   sparges
gas-rings   grassing
Gastein   easting; genista; ingates;
   ingesta; seating; tangies; teasing;
   tsigane
Gaston   Sontag; tangos; tongas
gat   tag
gate   geat
gates   geats; stage
gats   stag; tags
Gatun   gaunt
Gaul   gula
Gauls   gusla
Gaumont   Montagu
gaums   magus
gaunt   Gatun
gauntries   signature
gaurs   Argus; sugar
gave   Vega
gavel   Gävle
Gävle   gavel
gayer   yager
gayest   stagey
gazer   graze
gazers   grazes
geal   Gael; gale; Gela
geals   Gaels; gales
gean   Agen; gane; gena
geans   Agnes; genas; Senga
gear   gare; Gera; rage
geared   agreed; dragée
gearless   eelgrass; largesse
gears   rages; sager; sarge
geat   gate
geats   gates; stage
Geel   glee
gee-string   greetings
Geiger   Reggie
geist   geits
geits   geist

gel   leg
Gela   Gael; gale; geal
gelate   eaglet; Galtee; legate; teagle;
   telega
gelatin   atingle; elating; genital
gelatine   legatine
gelation   legation
geld   gled
gelder   ledger
gelders   ledgers; sledger
gelding   niggled
geldings   sniggled
gelds   gleds
gelid   glide
gels   legs
gem   Meg
geminates   magnesite; magnetise
gena   Agen; gane; gean
genal   angel; angle; Galen; glean
genas   Agnes; geans; Senga
genera   enrage
general   enlarge; gleaner
generalist   easterling
generalists   easterlings
generals   enlarges; gleaners
generate   green tea; renegate;
   teenager
generates   renegates; teenagers
generic   energic
genetical   clientage
genetrix   exerting
geneva   avenge
genial   Ealing; linage
genie   eigne
genies   eignes; seeing
genista   easting; Gastein; ingates;
   ingesta; seating; tangies; teasing;
   tsigane
genital   atingle; elating; gelatin
genitals   eastling; Galenist; stealing
genitival   vigilante
Genoa   agone; Onega
genre   green
genres   greens
Genro   ergon; goner; Negro
gentiles   sleeting; steeling
genuine   ingénue
geo   ego
geocentric   egocentric
Gera   gare; gear; rage
Geraint   granite; ingrate; Tangier;
   tearing
Gerald   glared

Geraldine engrailed; realigned
Gerard grader; regard
gerbe grebe
gerbes grebes
Gerda Edgar; grade; raged
gerent regent
gerents regents
Germain reaming
german engram; manger; ragmen
germane Mangere
Germanic amercing; creaming;
  Mérignac
Germans engrams; mangers
germinal maligner; malinger
germinates magnetiser
Gerona onager; orange
Gervas graves
gest gets; tegs
Gestapo postage
geste egest
gestes egests
get teg
gets gest; tegs
ghost Goths
ghoul lough
ghouls loughs; slough
giant tangi
giantess eastings
giants gainst; sating
gib big
gibbons sobbing
gibing biggin
gid dig
gif fig
gifted fidget
gift horse foresight
gigman gaming
gila Gail; glia
Gilan Laing; liang; ligan; linga
gild glid
gilded glided
gilden dingle; elding; engild
gilder girdle; glider; lidger; ridgel
gilders girdles; gliders; grisled;
  lidgers; ridgels
gilding gliding
gilt glit
Gina agin; agni; gain
gin-fizz fizzing
gingall galling
ginger nigger
gingers niggers; snigger
gingle niggle

gingles niggles; sniggle
gink king
ginks kings
ginned ending
ginnel Lingen
ginner enring
ginners enrings
gins sing; snig
gin-sling singling; slinging
gin trap parting; prating; traping
gip pig
gips pigs
girandole negroidal; reloading
girasole seraglio
gird grid
girdle gilder; glider; lidger; ridgel
girdled glidder; griddle
girdles gilders; gliders; grisled;
  lidgers; ridgels
girds grids
Giresun reusing
girkins griskin; risking
girlond lording
girn grin; ring
girned dering; dinger; engird;
  ringed
girning ringing
girns grins; rings
Giro Gori
giron groin
Gironde eroding; groined; ignored;
  negroid; redoing
girons grison; groins; rosing;
  Signor
girt grit; trig
girth grith; right
Girton roting; trigon
girts grist; grits; strig; trigs
Girvan raving
gist tigs
gite tige
gites tiges
gittern retting
gju jug
gjus jugs
glacier gracile
gladden dangled
glairin lairing; railing
glanced clanged
glancing clanging
glanders danglers
glans slang
glare Elgar; lager; large; regal; Regla

glared　Gerald
glares　lagers; regals
Glaswegian　Galwegians
glaum　algum; almug; mulga
glaums　mulgas
gleamy　gamely; mygale
glean　angel; angle; Galen; genal
gleaner　enlarge; general
gleaners　enlarges; generals
gleans　angels; angles
gled　geld
glede　gleed; ledge
gledes　gleeds; ledges; sledge
gledge　legged
gleds　gelds
glee　Geel
gleed　glede; ledge
gleeds　gledes; ledges; sledge
gleeman　mélange
glees　leges
Glenda　angled; dangle
glia　Gail; gila
glibness　blessing
glid　gild
glidder　girdled; griddle
glide　gelid
glided　gilded
glider　gilder; girdle; lidger; ridgel
gliders　gilders; girdles; grisled;
　lidgers; ridgels
gliding　gilding
glinted　tingled
glinting　tingling
glisten　singlet; tingles
glistens　singlets
glister　gristle
glit　gilt
gloater　legator; Ortegal
gloaters　legators
gloating　goatling
globe　bogle
globes　bogles
Glos.　logs; slog
gloss　slogs
glossing　goslings
glover　grovel
glovers　grovels
glue　gule; luge
glued　luged
gluer　gruel; luger
gluers　gruels; lugers
glues　gules; luges
gluing　luging

gluten　englut
Glynis　lysing; singly
gnar　gran; rang
gnarled　dangler
gnash　hangs
gnashing　hangings
gnat　gant; tang
gnats　angst; gants; stang; tangs
gnaw　wang
gnawed　Gwenda
gnaws　swang; wangs
gneiss　singes
gnomic　coming
gnomonic°　oncoming
gnostic　costing
gnu　gun
gnus　guns; snug; sung
Goa　ago
goad　dago
goads　dagos; gadso
goal　gaol; Olga
goals　gaols; Lagos
goat　Göta; toga
goatling　gloating
goats　togas
gob　bog
goblin　lobing
gobs　bogs
go by　bogy
god　dog
godets　stodge
godling　lodging
godlings　lodgings
godly　goldy
gods　dogs
godso　goods
goer　ergo; gore; ogre
goers　gores; gorse; ogres; Sergo;
　soger
goes　egos; sego
goes by　bogeys
gofer　forge
gofers　forges
goglet　toggle
goglets　toggles
goiter　goitre
goitre　goiter
Golan　along; Logan; longa
golden　longed
goldy　godly
golf　flog
gonad　Dagon; donga; Gonda
gonads　dongas

Gonda   Dagon; donga; gonad
Gondar   dragon
goner   ergon; Genro; Negro
goners   Negros
Gonvil   loving; voling
goods   godso
goof   Fogo
goop   pogo
goral   algor; argol; largo
Gordian   adoring; gradino; roading
Gordon   drongo; Grodno
gore   ergo; goer; ogre
gores   goers; gorse; ogres; Sergo; soger
gorged   dogger
Gori   Giro
goring   gringo
gorse   goers; gores; ogres; Sergo; soger
gorsedd   dodgers
gory   Györ; orgy
gosh   hogs; shog
goslings   glossing
got   tog
Göta   goat; toga
Goths   ghost
gourde   drogue; rogued; rouged
gourdes   drogues; groused
gouts   gusto
Goya   yoga
grab   brag; garb
grabble   gabbler
grabbles   gabblers
graben   banger
grabens   bangers
grabs   brags; garbs
graced   cadger
gracile   glacier
graddan   grandad
grade   Edgar; Gerda; raged
graded   gadder
grader   Gerard; regard
graders   regards
gradient   derating; red giant; treading
gradients   red giants
gradin   daring
gradine   areding; dearing; deraign; grained; reading
gradines   deraigns; readings
grading   niggard
gradino   adoring; Gordian; roading

graduates   date-sugar
gradus   guards
Graeme   meagre
Graham   Armagh
grail   argil; Lairg
grain   agrin; garni
graine   earing; gainer; regain; regina
grained   areding; dearing; deraign; gradine; reading
grainer   angrier; earring; rearing
grainers   earrings
grains   rasing; Sangir
grainy   raying
graith   aright
gramme   gammer
grammes   gammers
gran   gnar; rang
Granados   Sangrado
grandad   graddan
grandam   grandma
grandee   angered; derange; en garde; enraged; grenade
grandees   deranges; grenades
grander   Gardner
grandiose   organdies; organised
grandma   grandam
grange   ganger; nagger
granges   gangers; naggers
granite   Geraint; ingrate; Tangier; tearing
granites   angriest; astringe; ganister; gantries; inert gas; ingrates; reasting
grannie   earning; engrain; nearing
grannies   earnings; engrains
granted   drag-net
grantee   greaten; reagent
grantees   estrange; greatens; reagents; segreant; sergeant
granter   regrant
granters   regrants
grape   gaper; parge
grapes   gapers; gasper; parges; sparge
graphically   calligraphy
graphology   logography
Gras   gars; rags
grasp   sprag
grasped   sparged
grasper   sparger
graspers   spargers
grasping   sparging

grasps sprags
grassing gas-rings
grate great; Greta; targe; terga
grated der tag; targed
grater garret; garter
graters garrets; garters
grates Greats; stager; targes
grating targing
gratis striga
graves Gervas
gray Gary
grayling ragingly
graze gazer
grazes gazers
grease agrees; eagres
great grate; Greta; targe; terga
greaten grantee; reagent
greatens estrange; grantees;
  reagents; segreant; sergeant
greater regrate
greatness estranges; sergeants
Greats grates; stager; targes
grebe gerbe
grebes gerbes
Grecians creasing; searcing
gree eger
greed edger
green genre
Greene renege
greened reneged
greening reneging
greenish sheering
Greenland Englander
Greenmantle enlargement
greens genres
green tea generate; renegate;
  teenager
greeny energy; Ygerne
grees egers; grese; Segre; serge
greet egret
greeted deterge
greetings gee-string
greets egrets
gremlin merling; mingler
gremlins merlings; minglers
Grenaa Reagan
Grenada Gardena
grenade angered; derange; en
  garde; enraged; grandee
grenades deranges; grandees
grenadier rereading
grenadine endearing; engrained
grese egers; grees; Segre; serge

greses egress
Greta grate; great; targe; terga
grey gyre
grey-coat category
greys gyres
grid gird
griddle girdled; glidder
gride dirge; ridge
grided ridged
grides dirges; grised; ridges
griding ridging
grids girds
grieved diverge
grimaced decigram
grin girn; ring
grinder regrind
grinders regrinds
gringo goring
grinned rending
grins girns; rings
grip prig
grips prigs; sprig
gris rigs
grised dirges; grides; ridges
griskin girkins; risking
grisled gilders; girdles; gliders;
  lidgers; ridgels
grison girons; groins; rosing;
  Signor
grist girts; grits; strig; trigs
gristle glister
grit girt; trig
grith girth; right
grits girts; grist; strig; trigs
groan argon; Ongar; orang; organ
groans orangs; organs; Sargon;
  sarong
groat argot
groats argots
Grodno drongo; Gordon
groin giron
groined eroding; Gironde; ignored;
  negroid; redoing
groining ignoring
groins girons; grison; rosing;
  Signor
groma Margo
groser rogers
groove overgo
grounded underdog
groundless groundsels
groundsels groundless
grouper regroup

groupers regroups
groupies pirogues
grouse orgues; rogues; rouges;
   rugose
groused drogues; gourdes
grouted droguet
grouty yogurt
grovel glover
grovels glovers
grown wrong
groyne eryngo
grub burg
grubs burgs
grudge rugged
grudged drugged
grudging drugging
gruel gluer; luger
gruels gluers; lugers
grunted trudgen
grunts strung
guards gradus
Gueber burgee; Guebre
Guebers burgees; Guebres
Guebre burgee; Gueber
Guebres burgees; Guebers
guerdon undergo; ungored
Guiana iguana
guiser regius
gula Gaul
gulden lunged
gule glue; luge
gules glues; luges
gullies ligules
gulp plug
gulps plugs

guly ugly
gum mug
gums mugs; smug
gun gnu
gun dog dugong
gun dogs dugongs
guns gnus; snug; sung
gunsel lunges
gunshot noughts; shotgun
gunshots shotguns
gunter gurnet; urgent
gunters gurnets
gup pug
gur rug
gurgle lugger
gurgles luggers; slugger
gurnet gunter; urgent
gurnets gunters
gush hugs
gusla Gauls
gust guts; tugs
Gustave vaguest
gusted degust
gusto gouts
gusty gutsy
gut tug
guts gust; tugs
gutsy gusty
guy yug
Gwenda gnawed
Györ gory; orgy
gyrated tragedy
gyre grey
gyres greys

H

ha ah
habitat Tabitha
habited Thebaid
hackles shackle
hacks shack
had dah
haddocks shaddock
Hades heads; shade
hadji jihad
hadjis jihads
haeres hearse
hafts shaft
hags gash; shag
hailed halide

hailers El Arish
hair-net inearth
hair-nets inearths
hairs arish; Shari
Halden Handel; handle
hale heal; Leah
haled heald
hales halse; heals; leash; selah;
   shale; sheal
half-backs flashback
halide hailed
haling Hlaing
halloo holloa
hallows shallow

halls shall
halma almah; hamal
halos shoal; shola; solah
Hals lash
halse hales; heals; leash; selah;
  shale; sheal
halsed lashed
halses hassle; lashes; shales;
  sheals
halsing lashing
halt lath
halted lathed
halter lather; thaler
haltered lathered
haltering earthling; lathering
halters harslet; Herstal; lathers;
  slather
halting Althing; lathing
halts laths; shalt; Stahl
halve Havel
hamal almah; halma
hambles shamble
Hamburg Murghab
hame ahem; Mahé
hames shame; Shema
Hamites atheism
hamlet Eltham; Thelma
hammal mahmal
hammers shammer
hams mash; sham
hamster amherst
hamsters amhersts
Handel Halden; handle
hander harden
handers hardens
handle Halden; Handel
handles handsel
handless handsels
hand-outs thousand
hands shand
handsel handles
handsels handless
handy Haydn
hangar arghan
hangings gnashing
hang-out to-hunga
hangover overhang
hangovers overhangs
hangs gnash
hank ankh; Kahn; khan
hanker harken
hankered harkened
hankering harkening

hankers harkens
hanks ankhs; khans; shank
Hans Nash; shan
hanse ashen; Shane
Hants. shan't; snath
hap pah
hapless plashes
haps hasp; pash; Shap
haram marah
hard Dhar
harden hander
hardens handers
harder Erhard
hardest dearths; hatreds; red-hats;
  threads; trashed
hardier harried
hards shard
hard up purdah
hardy Hydra
hare hear; Hera; rhea
hared heard
hareld harled; herald
harelds heralds
harems masher; shamer
hares hears; rheas; share; shear
haricot chariot
haricots chariots
harken hanker
harkened hankered
harkening hankering
harkens hankers
harks shark
harled hareld; herald
Harlem Mahler; Ramleh
harlot Lothar
harmed derham
harmonic choirman
harmonical monarchial
harmonicas maraschino
harms marsh
harpers sharper
harp on orphan
harps sharp
harps on orphans
harried hardier
Harris arrish; shirra; sirrah
harshest thrashes
harslet halters; Herstal; lathers;
  slather
hart rath; tahr; thar
Hartbees breathes
Harte earth; hater; heart; Herat;
  rathe; Thera; thrae

harts   raths; tahrs; thars; trash
harvest   thraves
has   ash
has-been   banshee
has-beens   banshees
hash   shah
haslet   lathes; Shelta; Thales
haslets   Hasselt; hatless
hasp   haps; pash; Shap
hasped   pashed; phased; shaped
hasping   pashing; phasing; shaping
Hasselt   haslets; hatless
hassle   halses; lashes; shales; sheals
hassled   slashed
hassles   slashes
hassling   lashings; slangish;
    slashing
hast   hats; tash
haste   ashet; hates; heats
hasted   deaths; 'sdeath; tashed
hasten   Athens; snathe; sneath;
    thanes
hastener   heartens
hastens   snathes; sneaths
hastes   ashets; tashes
hastier   sheriat
hasting   tashing
Hastings   stashing
hatches   chetahs
hate   eath; heat; thae; Thea
hated   death
hater   earth; Harte; heart; Herat;
    rathe; Thera; thrae
haters   earths; hearts; Sarthe;
    'sheart
hates   ashet; haste; heats
hating   a'thing
hatless   haslets; Hasselt
hatred   dearth; red-hat; thread
hatreds   dearths; hardest; red-hats;
    threads; trashed
hats   hast; tash
hatter   threat
hatters   rathest; shatter; threats
haunt   unhat
haunter   unearth
haunters   unearths
hauntings   unhasting
haunts   sunhat; unhats; Ushant
haut   Utah
Havel   halve
havens   Hesvan; shaven
havers   shaver

haves   shave; sheva
hawm   wham
hawms   shawm; whams
haws   shaw; wash
hawser   washer; whares
hawsers   swasher; washers
hay   yah
Haydn   handy
hayed   heady
hays   ashy; shay
hazel   Zahle
he   eh
header   adhere; hedera
headers   adheres; sheared
headings   sheading
headlamps   lampshade
heads   Hades; shade
heady   hayed
heal   hale; Leah
heald   haled
heals   hales; halse; leash; selah;
    shale; sheal
heap   epha
heaps   Pesah; phase; shape
hear   hare; Hera; rhea
heard   hared
hearer   rehear
hearers   rehears; shearer
hearings   shearing
hears   hares; rheas; share;
    shear
hearse   haeres
heart   earth; Harte; hater; Herat;
    rathe; Thera; thrae
hearted   earthed; red-heat
hearten   earthen; Teheran
heartens   hastener
heartiness   earthiness
hearting   earthing; ingather
heartly   earthly
heartquake   earthquake
hearts   earths; haters; Sarthe;
    'sheart
heart-shaped   earth-shaped
heartsome   horsemeat
hearty   earthy
heat   eath; hate; thae; Thea
heater   aether; hereat; reheat
heaters   reheats; Theresa
heaths   sheath
heats   ashet; haste; hates
heaves   sheave
heaviness   evanishes

heavy   Yahve
Hebron   brehon
hectare   cheater; teacher
hectares   cheaters; teachers
hector   rochet; tocher; troche
hectored   tochered
hectoring   tochering
hectors   rochets; tochers; torches;
   troches
hedera   adhere; header
Hedon   honed
hedonists   dishonest
heeding   neighed
heel   hele
heeler   reheel
heelers   reheels
heels   heles; sheel
height   eighth
heinous   in-house
heir   hire
heirless   relishes
heirs   hires; shier; shire
heist   shite; sithe; Thiès
heists   shiest; shites; sithes; Theiss;
   thesis
hele   heel
heles   heels; sheel
helices   lichees
helicon   choline
Hellenic   chenille
hellers   sheller
hells   shell
helot   hotel; thole
helots   hostel; hotels; tholes
helves   shelve
he-man   maneh
hems   mesh; Shem
Henri   Rhein; Rhine
hens   nesh
hent   then
hepar   phare; raphe
hepatic   aphetic
hepatical   caliphate
hep-cats   patches
heptads   spathed
her   reh; rhe
Hera   hare; hear; rhea
herald   hareld; harled
heralds   harelds
Herat   earth; Harte; hater; heart;
   rathe; Thera; thrae
herdic   chider
herdics   chiders

herds   sherd; shred
hereat   aether; heater; reheat
herein   inhere; Rheine
Herman   Arnhem
hermit   mither
hermits   mithers
hernial   inhaler
herniated   inearthed
hero   hoer; Ohre; rheo
Herod   horde
heroic   co-heir
heroics   co-heirs
heron   Horne; Rhone
herons   rhones; Senhor
herpes   Hesper; pheers; sphere
hers   rhes
herse   Esher; sheer
herself   flesher
herses   sheers
Herstal   halters; harslet; lathers;
   slather
Herts.   Resht; tehrs
Hesper   herpes; pheers; sphere
hesperid   perished; shred-pie
hesperids   shred-pies
Hess   shes
Hessen   sheens; sneesh
hest   Esth; Seth; shet
Hester   Esther; ethers; threes
Hesvan   havens; shaven
het   eth; the
hetman   anthem
hetmans   anthems
hewer   where
hewing   whinge
hewings   shewing; whinges
hewn   when
hews   shew
hibernate   inbreathe
hibernated   inbreathed
hibernates   inbreathes
hibernating   inbreathing
hide   hied
hides   shied
hidings   dishing; shindig
hied   hide
hight   thigh
hights   thighs
hikers   shriek; shrike
hikes   sheik
hills   shill
hilt   lith
hilts   liths

himself Flemish	**Hogmanay** mahogany
hinders shrined	**hogs** gosh; shog
hindlegs shingled	**hoister** shortie
hing nigh	**hold up** uphold
hint Nith; thin	**hold-ups** upholds
hinting in-thing	**holed** dhole
hints thins	**holes** She'ol
hip phi	**holiday** hyaloid
hippos popish; shippo	**holloa** halloo
hips pish; ship	**Holst** holts; sloth
hipsters thripses	**holster** hostler
hipt pith	**holsters** hostlers
Hiram ihram	**holt** loth
hire heir	**holts** Holst; sloth
hires heirs; shier; shire	**homage** ohmage
hirsel hirsle; relish	**homeliest** lithesome
hirsels hirsles	**Homer** horme
hirsle hirsel; relish	**Homeric** moriche
hirsles hirsels	**honed** Hedon
his ish	**hones** hosen; shone
hisn shin; sinh	**honest** Sethon; Stheno
Hispar parish; raphis; Shairp	**honestly** on the sly
hissed dishes	**hoo** oho
hist hits; shit; sith; this; Tshi	**hooks** shook
hists shits	**hoop** pooh
Hitler lither	**hoot** Otho; toho
hits hist; shit; sith; this; Tshi	**hooters** shooter; soother
hitter tither	**hoots** shoot; sooth; Sotho
hitters tithers	**hop** poh
hivers shiver; shrive	**hoped** ephod
hives shive	**hoper** ephor
Hlaing haling	**hopers** ephors; posher
ho oh	**Hopi** Ipoh
hoard Rhoda	**hoplites** isopleth
hoarse ashore	**hoppers** shopper
hoast Athos; hosta; oaths; shoat	**hoppings** shopping
hoasts hostas; shoats; Thasos	**hops** posh; shop; soph
hoaxed oxhead	**Horace** chorea; ochrea; orache
hob boh	**horde** Herod
hobo booh	**hordes** horsed; Rhodes; shoder;
hobs bosh	shored
hocked choked	**horme** Homer
hocker choker	**hormone** moorhen
hockers chokers; shocker	**hormones** moorhens
hocking choking	**horn** Hron
hocks shock	**Horne** heron; Rhone
hocused choused; douches	**horned** dehorn
hocusing chousing	**hornet** Horten; throne
hod doh	**hornets** shorten; thrones
hods shod	**horns** shorn
hoer hero; Ohre; rheo	**Hornsea** Senhora
hoers horse; shoer; shore	**horrent** norther
hoes hose; shoe	**Horsa** Orsha

horse   hoers; shoer; shore
horsed   hordes; Rhodes; shoder; shored
horsemeat   heartsome
horses   shoers; shores
horsing   shoring
horst   short
horsts   shorts
Horta   Thora; Torah
Horten   hornet; throne
Hortensia   Senhorita
Horus   hours
hose   hoes; shoe
hosed   doseh; shoed
hosen   hones; shone
hoses   shoes
host   hots; shot; tosh
hosta   Athos; hoast; oaths; shoat
hostas   hoasts; shoats; Thasos
hosted   toshed
hostel   helots; hotels; tholes
hostile   Elohist
hosting   toshing
hostler   holster
hostlers   holsters
hot   tho'
hotel   helot; thole
hotels   helots; hostel; tholes
hotel suite   silhouette
hotel suites   silhouettes
hots   host; shot; tosh
hot tap   top hat
hot taps   top hats
hotter   tother
hotting   tonight
hounds   Hudson; unshod
hours   Horus
houseboat   boathouse
houseboats   boathouses
housework   workhouse
hovels   shovel
hovers   shover; shrove
hoves   shove
how   who
however   whoever
howlet   thowel
howlets   thowels

Hron   horn
hubs   bush
Hudson   hounds; unshod
huers   usher
hug   ugh
huge   eugh
Hughes   sheugh
hugs   gush
humidor   mid-hour; rhodium
humidors   mid-hours
hump   umph
humps   sumph
hums   mush
Huns   shun
hunt   Thun
hunters   shunter
huntress   shunters
hunts   shunt
hups   push
hurdle   hurled
hurled   hurdle
Hurons   onrush
hurried   dhurrie
hurries   rushier
hurst   hurts
hurt   ruth; thru; Thur
hurtful   ruthful
hurtfully   ruthfully
hurting   ungirth; unright
hurtle   Luther
hurtles   hustler; Thurles
hurtless   hustlers; ruthless
hurtlessly   ruthlessly
hurtlessness   ruthlessness
hurts   hurst
hustle   sleuth
hustler   hurtles; Thurles
hustlers   hurtless; ruthless
hustles   sleuths
hustling   sunlight
huts   shut; thus; tush
Hyads   shady
hyaloid   holiday
Hydra   hardy
hydrate   thready
hydrous   shroudy
hypnotic   pythonic

I

Iain   inia
Ian   ani

Ian Smith   isthmian
iatric   Tricia

Ibadan indaba
Iberians Siberian
Icarian Arician
icecap ipecac
iced cedi; dice
ice-hills chillies
Iceland inlaced
iceman anemic; cinema
icepack pack-ice
icepan in pace
icepans inscape; pincase
icer ciré; eric; rice
icers cries; erics; seric
ices sice
ichor choir
iciness incises
ickers scrike; sicker
Icod odic
icon coin
iconolater relocation
icons coins; scion; sonic
Ida aid; Dai
ide die
idea aide
idea'd aided
ideal ailed; Delia
idealisers serialised
idealism miladies
idealistic italicised
idealizers serialized
ideals aisled; deasil; ladies; sailed
ideas aides; aside; Sadie
ideation taenioid
idem dime
identic incited
ideograph eidograph
ideographs eidographs
ides dies; side
id est deist; diets; dites; edits; sited;
    St. Dié; stied; tides
idiots Idoist
idle deil; eild; lied
idler riled
idlers slider
idles deils; sidle; slide
idlesse diesels
idlest listed; silted; tildes
Idoist idiots
idol lido; Lodi; olid
Idola dolia
idolater tailored
idolaters estradiol
idolatry adroitly; dilatory

Idolum dolium
idols Isold; lidos; silo'd; sloid; soldi;
    solid
idyll lilly
Ifan fain; naif
Ife fie
ignaro oaring; origan
ignaros Signora; soaring
ignited dieting; editing
igniter tiering; tigrine
igniters resiting; strigine
ignorant Tir na n-Og
ignore eringo; Origen; region
ignored eroding; Gironde; groined;
    negroid; redoing
ignores regions; Signore
ignoring groining
iguana Guiana
ihram Hiram
Ike eik; kei
Ilagan agnail; Anglia
ileac Alice; Celia
Ilesha Sheila
ilexes exiles
Ilford florid
iliac cilia
ilk'a kail; Kali; Lika
Ilkley likely
ill Lil
Illinois illision
illision Illinois
ill-nature tellurian
ills sill
illudes ill-used; sullied
ill-used illudes; sullied
ill-uses sullies
illy lily; yill
Ilmen limen; Milne
I'm mi
imager gamier; maigre; mirage
imagers mirages
imaginer migraine
imaginers migraines
imam maim
imams maims; miasm
imarets Artemis; maestri; maister;
    misrate; semitar; St. Marie
imbed bedim
imbeds bedims
imbrue erbium
imbrues imburse
imburse imbrues
imitancy intimacy

immersed simmered
immersing simmering
impaled implead
impanel maniple
impanels maniples
imparl primal
impart armpit
impartial primatial
imparts armpits
impaste pastime
impastes pastimes
impearl lempira; palmier
impearled epidermal; impleader
impeding impinged
impels Milspe; simple
impetus imputes
impinged impeding
implate palmiet
implates palmiest; palmiets;
  petalism; septimal
implead impaled
impleader epidermal; impearled
impleads misplead
implored impolder
implores pelorism; sperm-oil
impolder implored
impones peonism
importers misreport
imports tropism
importune entropium
importuned minute-drop
imposer promise; semi-pro
imposers promises; semi-pros
impost impots
impots impost
imprecated mercaptide
imprecates spermaceti
impregnate permeating
impresari primaries
imprese empires; emprise;
  epimers; premise; spireme
impreses emprises; premises;
  spiremes
impress Persism; premiss; simpers
impresses premisses
impressibility permissibility
impressible permissible
impression permission
impressive permissive
impressively permissively
impressiveness permissiveness
imprest permits
imprints misprint

imps simp
impugners presuming
impugns spuming
impure umpire
imputes impetus
inaction nicotian
inane Annie
inapt paint; patin; pinta
inaptly ptyalin
inarched Red China
inarm Marin; minar
inarmed adermin; Amerind
inarms minars
inbreak Bikaner; break in
inbreaks bearskin; breaks in
inbreathe hibernate
inbreathed hibernated
inbreathes hibernates
inbreathing hibernating
inbred binder; brined; rebind
inbreed bendier
inbring brining
Inca Cain
incages ceasing
in camera American; Cinerama
Incan Cinna
in care Racine
Incas canis; Sican
incase casein
incased candies
incenses niceness
incensors corniness
incept pectin
inceptions inspection
inceptors inspector
incessant instances
incest insect; nicest; scient
inch chin
inchased cashed in
inchases Anchises
inched chined; niched
inches chines; chinse; niches
inching chining; niching
incised indices
incises iciness
incisure sciurine
incited identic
inciter citrine; crinite
inciters crinites
include nuclide
includes nuclides; unsliced
incog coign
incognita actioning

incognito cognition
incomers sermonic
incomes Comines; mesonic
inconsiderate containerised
incorporate procreation
increase resiance
increases scenarise
increate centiare; creatine; iterance
incudes incused; induces
incur runic
incused incudes; induces
incut cut in; tunic
Ind din; nid
indaba Ibadan
indeed denied
indent intend; tinned
indented intended
indenter interned
indenting intending
indents intends
India Aidin
indicate actinide
indicates actinides
indices incised
Indies inside
indigent enditing
indirectly cylindrite
indiscreet indiscrete; iridescent
indiscreetly indiscretely
indiscreetness indiscreteness
indiscrete indiscreet; iridescent
indiscretely indiscreetly
indiscreteness indiscreetness
indite tineid
inditers disinter
indole doline; Leonid
indoors Sondrio; sordino
Indore ironed
indorse rosined; sordine
Indra dinar; drain; Drina; nadir
Indre diner
induces incudes; incused
indues undies
indulge eluding
indulged deluding; ungilded
indurate daturine; ruinated;
  urinated
Indus nidus
inearth hair-net
inearthed herniated
inearths hair-nets
inelastic Catilines; sciential
inelegant eglantine

inerm miner
inert inter; nitre; Terni; trine
inert gas angriest; astringe;
  ganister; gantrico, granules;
  ingrates; reasting
Ines sine
in esse Neisse; seines
in extenso extension
Inez zein
infame famine
infamed ad finem
infames famines
infarct infract
infarction infraction
infarctions infractions
infarcts infracts
infefts stiffen
infer finer
infere enfire; ferine; Fernie; fineer;
  refine
inferring infringer
infers Fenris
infest feints; finest
infests fitness
infidel infield
infield infidel
inflame feminal
inflamer rifleman
inflatus flutinas
info fino; foin
inforce conifer; fir cone
inforces conifers; fir cones;
  forensic; forinsec
informal formalin
informer reinform; reniform
informers reinforms
infract infarct
infraction infarction
infractions infarctions
infracts infarcts
infringe enfiring; refining
infringer inferring
ingate eating; tangie
ingates easting; Gastein; genista;
  ingesta; seating; tangies; teasing;
  tsigane
ingather earthing; hearting
ingénue genuine
ingénues unseeing
ingest signet; tinges
ingesta easting; Gastein; genista;
  ingates; seating; tangies; teasing;
  tsigane

ingests signets
ingle Elgin; ligne; Nigel
ingles lignes; seling; single
ingot tigon
ingots stingo; tigons; tosing
ingraft farting; rafting
ingrafts strafing
ingrain raining
ingram arming; margin
ingrate Geraint; granite; Tangier;
  tearing
ingrates angriest; astringe;
  ganister; gantries; granites; inert
  gas; reasting
ingredients tenderising
Ingres reigns; renigs; resign;
  signer; singer
ingress resigns; signers; singers
Ingrid riding
ingroup pouring; rouping
ingrowth throwing; Worthing
ingrum muring
inhaler hernial
inhere herein; Rheine
in-house heinous
inia Iain
initiated dietitian
ink kin
ink-bag baking
ink-bags basking
inkers sinker
inkle Klein; liken
inkled kilned; kindle; linked
inkles likens; silken
inkling kilning; linking
inklings sling ink; slinking
inks kins; sink; skin
Inkster stinker; tinkers
inlace ancile; Celina
inlaced Iceland
in-laws Salwin
inlayer nailery
inlets enlist; listen; silent; tinsel
inletting entitling
in love love-in
inmate tamine
inmates Samnite
inmost monist
innate tinean
inners sinner
innings inn-sign; sinning
innovate venation
inn-sign innings; sinning

inoculates inosculate
inoculations inosculation
inorb robin
inorbs robins
inosculate inoculates
inosculation inoculations
in pace icepan
inphase in shape
in re Erin; rein; Reni
inro iron; Rion
inroad Dorian; ordain
inroads ordains
inros irons; ornis; rosin
ins nis; sin
insane sienna
insatiable banalities
inscape icepans; pincase
insculp sculpin; unclips
insculps sculpins
inseam Amiens; amines; mesian
inseams samisen
insect incest; nicest; scient
insecure sinecure
insert inters; sinter; Strine; trines
inserted Dniester; resident;
  sintered
inserting sintering
inserts sinters
inset neist; set in; stein; tines
insets sets in; steins; Tessin
in shape inphase
inside Indies
insight shiting
insigne seining
insinuate annuities
insisted tidiness
insole eloins; esloin; lesion; Silone
insoles esloins; lesions; lioness
insouled delusion; unsoiled
inspect incepts; pectins
inspection inceptions
inspector inceptors
inspire pirnies; spinier
instal Latins; Stalin
instance ancients; canniest
instances incessant
instanter transient
instar santir; Sintra; strain; trains
instars santirs; strains
instate satinet
instates nastiest
instead Danites; detains; sainted;
  stained

instep spinet; step-in
insteps spinets; step-ins
in store orients; stonier; triones
insular urinals
insult sunlit
insulted unlisted
insulter lustrine
insure inures; rusine; ursine
insurer ruiners
insures sunrise
insurgent unresting
intaglio ligation; taglioni
intaglioed deligation
intake take-in
intakes take-ins
integer teering; treeing
integers reesting; steering; streigne
integral alerting; altering; relating;
   triangle
integrand endarting
integration orientating
intend indent; tinned
intended indented
intending indenting
intends indents
inter inert; nitre; Terni; trine
interests resistent; triteness
intergrade retreading
interim mintier; termini
interims minister
interlace lacertine; reclinate
interlaces centralise
interlope repletion
intern tinner
interned indenter
internees Ernestine
interns tinners
interoceptors retrospection
interosculates sansculotterie
interpage repeating
interpreter reinterpret
interpreters reinterprets
interrogatives tergiversation
inters insert; sinter; Strine; trines
in-thing hinting
intimacy imitancy
into not-I
intonated dentation
intoner ternion
intoners ternions
intones Sonnite; tension
intoxicate excitation
intra Nitra; riant; train; Trani

intradoses adroitness
in-tray Tyrian
in-trays Tyrians
intreat iterant; nattier; nitrate;
   tartine; tertian
intreating intrigante
intreats nitrates; straiten; tartines
intrigante intreating
introduce reduction
introduces discounter; reductions
intrude turdine; untired; untried
intruders unstirred
inundates unsainted; unstained
inure urine
inured ruined
inures insure; rusine; ursine
inuring ruining
inust suint; Tunis; units
invader ravined
invaders sandiver
Invar ravin
inveagler revealing
inveigler relieving
inverse enviers; versine; Viersen
inverses versines
invert virent
inverts striven; Ventris
invested evidents
inviter vitrine
inviters vitrines
inward Darwin; draw in
inwards draws in
ions Sion
ipecac icecap
Ipoh Hopi
Ira air; ria
irade aider; aired; redia
irades aiders; raised
Iran airn; Nair; rain; rani
irate terai
Irene Ernie
irides irised
iridescent indiscreet; indiscrete
irised irides
irked diker
irks kris; risk
iron inro; Rion
Iron Age origane
ironed Indore
ironer Renoir
ironic oniric
irons inros; ornis; rosin
Ironside derision

Irtysh shirty; thyrsi
Irun ruin
Irving riving; virgin
Irwell willer
is si
Isaacs cassia
Isar airs; Asir; rias; sair; sari
Isengrim remising
ish his
Isla ails; Lias; Lisa; sail; sial
Islam limas; mails; malis; Milas;
   salmi; Simla
isle Elis; leis; lies; seil; sile
isleman malines; menials; seminal
isles seils; siles
islet istle; steil; stile; teils; tiles
islets steils; stiles
isms miss
Isna anis; Nias; Nisa; sain; Sian
Isold idols; lidos; silo'd; sloid; soldi;
   solid
Isolde siloed; soiled
Isolt Solti; toils
isometric eroticism; meroistic
isopleth hoplites
isosceles solecises
isotherm moithers; Stroheim
Ispra pairs; Paris; Parsi
Israel sailer; serail; serial
Israelite realities

issuant sustain
issue Susie
issued disuse
issuer uresis
issues Suisse
isthmian Ian Smith
istle islet; steil; stile; teils; tiles
it ti
ita ait; tai
italicised idealistic
Italy laity
itas aits; Asti; sati; sita
itch chit
itches theics
itchiest ethicist; theistic
item emit; mite; time
items emits; metis; mites; smite;
   stime; times
iterance centiare; creatine; increate
iterant intreat; nattier; nitrate;
   tartine; tertian
iterate ariette
iterates ariettes; treaties; treatise
its sit; tis
itself filets; stifle
Ivan vain; vina
Ives vies; vise
ivresse revises
Iyar airy
iynx nixy

J

jackboot boot-jack
jackboots boot-jacks
jack-pines jack-snipe
jack-snipe jack-pines
jaded Jedda
Jaén Jane; Jean; Jena
jalouse jealous
jambul jumbal
jambuls jumbals
Jane Jaén; Jean; Jena
Jansen Nsanje
japes jaspe
jar raj
Jason Jonas
jaspe japes
jasy jays
Jat taj
jato jota
jaunt junta; Tunja

jaunts juntas
jays jasy
jealous jalouse
Jean Jaén; Jane; Jena
Jedda jaded
jeered jereed
Jena Jaén; Jane; Jean
jereed jeered
jerkin jinker
jerkins jinkers
jest jets
jetons jetson
jets jest
jetson jetons
jihad hadji
jihads hadjis
jingoist joisting
jinker jerkin
jinkers jerkins

joiner rejoin
joiners rejoins
joisting jingoist
Jonas Jason
jota jato
jotun junto
jotuns juntos
Juanita Tijuana
Judaic Judica
Judica Judaic

jug gju
jugs gjus
jumbal jambul
jumbalo jambuls
junta jaunt; Tunja
juntas jaunts
junto jotun
juntos jotuns
just juts
juts just

K

kabob bobak
Kabul baulk
Kàdar Dakar
kades asked
kadi dika
kadis dikas
kae kea
kaes Aske; keas; sake
Kafir fakir
Kafirs fakirs
Kahn ankh; hank; khan
kail ilk'a; kali; laik; Lika
kails kalis; laiks; Laski; skail
kaim kami; maik
kaims kamis; maiks; smaik
Kaiser Raikes
kale lake; leak
kales lakes; leaks; slake
kali ilk'a; kail; laik; Lika
kalis kails; laiks; Laski; skail
kame make
kames makes
kami kaim; maik
kamis kaims; maiks; smaik
Kano kaon
kans sank
kant tank
kants stank; tanks
kaon Kano
karat Katar
Karen anker; naker; nerka
Karens ankers; nakers
Karl lark
Kars arks; Sark
karst karts; stark; strak
karts karst; stark; strak
kasher shaker
Kashing shaking
Kaspar parkas

Kassel slakes
kat tak
Katar karat
Kate keta; take; teak
kats skat; taks; task
Katy kyat
Kay yak
kayle leaky
kayo oaky; okay
kayoed okayed
kayoing okaying
kayos okays
kea kae
Kean Kena
Kearny yanker
keas Aske; kaes; sake
Keats skate; Skeat; stake; steak;
    takes; teaks
Kedah kheda
keds desk
keel Klee; leek
keelers sleeker
keels leeks; sleek
keen knee
keens knees; skene; Sneek
keep peek; peke
keeping peeking
keeps peeks; pekes; Speke
kegs skeg
kei eik; Ike
keir kier
keirs kiers; skier
Keltic tickle
kemi mike
ken nek
Kena Kean
Kendal ankled
kens neks
Keos okes; skeo; soke

kepi   kipe; pike
kepis   kipes; pikes; Pisek; spike
keps   skep
Kerman   Marken
kesar   asker; rakes; reaks; saker;
  skear
kesars   askers; sakers; skears
keta   Kate; take; teak
Kew   ewk
key   kye
keynotes   keystone
keys   Skye; syke; yesk
keystone   keynotes
khan   ankh; hank; Kahn
khans   ankhs; hanks; shank
kheda   Kedah
kibe   bike
kibes   bikes
kids   disk; skid
Kiel   like
kier   keir
kiers   keirs; skier
Kilbride   bird-like
kiley   kylie
kileys   kylies
kills   skill
kiln   Klin; link
kilned   inkled; kindle; linked
kilning   inkling; linking
kilns   links; slink
kin   ink
kinas   Nasik
kind   dink
kindle   inkled; kilned; linked
kinds   dinks
kine   Nike
king   gink
kingpin   pink gin; pinking
kingpins   pink gins
kings   ginks
kins   inks; sink; skin
kipe   kepi; pike
kipes   kepis; pikes; Pisek; spike
kippers   skipper
kips   skip
kirn   rink
kirns   rinks
kiss   skis
kisser   skiers
kist   kits; skit
kitchen   thicken
kitchened   thickened
kitchener   thickener

kitcheners   thickeners
kitchening   thickening
kitchens   thickens
kite   tike
kites   skite; tikes
kits   kist; skit
kitsch   thicks
Klan   lank
Klee   keel; leek
Klein   inkle; liken
Klin   kiln; link
knaps   spank
knar   kran; nark; rank
knars   krans; narks; ranks; skran;
  snark
knawel   wankle
knee   keen
knees   keens; skene; Sneek
knife   Finke
knit   tink
knits   skint; stink; tinks
knitter   trinket
knitters   trinkets
knops   knosp
knosp   knops
knots   stonk
knower   wroken
knows   snowk
knub   bunk
knubs   bunks
koa   oak; oka
koas   oaks; okas; soak
kob   bok
kobs   boks; bosk
kolo   look
kolos   looks; Sokol
Koper   poker; proke
Koran   Akron; krona
koto   toko; took
kotos   stook
kran   knar; nark; rank
krans   knars; narks; ranks; skran;
  snark
kreese   seeker
kreeses   seekers
kris   irks; risk
krona   Akron; Koran
Kroo   rook
Kroos   rooks
Krus   rusk
Kurt   Turk
kyat   Katy
kye   key

kylie   kiley
kylies   kileys
Kyoto   Tokyo

kyte   tyke
kytes   skyte; tykes

L

laager   alegar
laagers   Alsager
lab   alb
Laban   Alban; banal
Labe   Abel; able; albe; bael; bale;
   blae; Elba
label   be-all; Bella
labiate   Baalite
labiates   Baalites; satiable
labile   alible; Belial; Biella; liable
labis   bails; basil
labrador   larboard
labret   albert; tabler
labrets   alberts; blaster; stabler;
   tablers
labrid   bridal; ribald
labrum   brumal; lumbar; umbral
labs   albs; slab
laburnum   alburnum
lac-dye   clayed
lace   Alec; Clea
laced   decal
lace-man   Maclean; manacle
laceration   creational
lacertine   interlace; reclinate
laces   claes; scale
lacet   cleat; éclat
lacey   Yecla
laches   Cashel; chelas
Lachine   Chilean
lacier   Claire; éclair
laciest   astelic; Castile; elastic;
   latices
laciness   sanicles
lacing   Anglic
lac insect   canticles
lack   calk
lacked   calked
lacker   calker
lackers   calkers; slacker
lacking   calking
lacks   calks; slack
Laclos   locals
laconic   conical
lacrosse   escolars; solacers
lacrymal   clay-marl

lacrymose   claymores
lacteous   osculate
lactose   alecost; locates; scatole;
   talcose
lacy   clay
lad   dal
ladder   Aldred; larded; raddle
ladders   raddles; saddler
laddie   daidle
laddies   daidles
lade   dale; deal; lead; Leda
laded   addle; dedal
laden   eland; lande
lades   dales; deals; leads; slade
ladies   aisled; deasil; ideals; sailed
Ladin   Linda
Ladino   laid on; Olinda
ladle   dalle; Della
ladles   dalles
lads   dals
lady   yald
Laertes   elaters; relates; stealer
lag   gal
lagena   alnage; Angela; anlage;
   galena
lager   Elgar; glare; large; regal;
   Regla
lagers   glares; regals
lagged   daggle
lagger   gargle; raggle
laggers   gargles; raggles
lagniappe   appealing
lagoon   Loango
Lagos   gaols; goals
La Grange   langrage
lags   gals; slag
lagunes   Angelus
laid   Dail; dali; dial
laid on   Ladino; Olinda
laik   ilk'a; kail; kali; Lika
laiks   kails; kalis; Laski; skail
lain   anil; nail
Laing   Gilan; liang; ligan; linga
lair   aril; liar; lira; rail; rial
laird   drail; Liard
lairds   drails

laired   derail; Lérida; railed; relaid
Lairg   argil; grail
lairing   glairin; railing
lairs   liars; liras; rails; rials
laisse   aisles; eassil; lassie
laisses   lassies
laity   Italy
lake   kale; leak
lakelets   skeletal
lakes   kales; leaks; slake
Lalin   all in
lam   mal
lama   alma
lamas   almas
lamb   balm
lambaste   blastema
lambed   ambled; balmed; bedlam;
   beldam; blamed
Lambeth   the Lamb
lambing   ambling; balming;
   blaming
lambkins   lambskin
lambs   balms
lambskin   lambkins
lame   alme; Elam; Elma; leam;
   Lema; male; meal
lamed   medal
lamely   mellay
lameness   maneless; nameless;
   salesmen
lament   mantel; mantle; mental
lamenting   alignment
laments   mantels; mantles
lamer   Ramle
lames   almes; leams; males; meals;
   Salem; samel; Selma
lamest   metals; samlet
lamina   animal; manila
laminar   railman
laminas   animals
lamination   antimonial; antinomial
laming   lingam; malign
lamp   palm
lampas   plasma
lamped   palmed
Lampeter   palm-tree
lamping   palming
lamps   palms; plasm; psalm
lampshade   headlamps
lams   alms; slam
lana   Alan; anal; nala
Lanai   liana
Lancaster   ancestral

lance   Calne; clean
lanced   candle
lancer   rancel
lancers   rancels
lances   cleans; Senlac
lancet   cantle; cental
lancets   cantles; centals
Lancs.   clans
lande   eland; laden
landed   dandle
lander   aldern; darnel; enlard
landers   enlards; slander; snarled
Landes   sendal
Landor   Arnold; lardon; Roland;
   Ronald
landrace   calendar
landraces   calendars
lane   élan; lean; Lena; neal
lanes   leans; neals; slane
Lanett   latent; latten; talent
langrage   La Grange
languid   lauding
langur   Lurgan
lank   Klan
lanker   rankle
lanners   ensnarl
Laon   loan; Nola
Laos   also; sola
Lao-tse   osteal
lap   alp; pal
Lapeer   leaper; repeal
lapel   Pella
lapides   alipeds; elapids; paidles;
   palsied; Pleiads
lapis   pails; spial
La Porte   prolate
Lapp   palp; plap
lapped   dapple; palped
lapper   rapple
lappers   rapples; slapper
lappies   applies
lapping   palping
Lapps   palps; plaps
laps   Alps; pals; salp; slap
lapse   Elaps; leaps; pales; peals;
   pleas; salep; sepal; spale; speal
lapsed   pedals; pleads
lapses   sepals; spales; speals
lapsing   palings; sapling
lapwings   spawling
larboard   labrador
larches   Charles
larded   Aldred; ladder; raddle

larding   darling
lardon   Arnold; Landor; Roland; Ronald
lardoon   Orlando
lardy   lyard; Rydal
lare   earl; loar, tale; real
Laredo   loader; ordeal; reload
lares   Arles; earls; laser; lears; reals; seral
large   Elgar; glare; lager; regal; Regla
largely   allergy; gallery; regally
largesse   eelgrass; gearless
largo   algor; argol; goral
lariat   Altair; atrial; latria
lariats   Al Sirat
larine   en l'air; linear; nailer
lark   Karl
larked   darkle
Larne   learn; renal
larum   mural; rumal
larums   murals; rumals
Larus   sural; Urals
larva   arval; lavra
larval   vallar
Las Bela   salable
lascar   rascal; sacral; scalar
lascars   rascals; scalars
laser   Arles; earls; lares; lears; reals; seral
lash   Hals
lashed   halsed
lasher   ashler
lashers   ashlers; slasher
lashes   halses; hassle; shales; sheals
lashing   halsing
lashings   hassling; slangish; slashing
Laski   kails; kalis; laiks; skail
lass   sals
lasses   salses
lassie   aisles; eassil; laisse
lassies   laisses
lasso   solas
lassoer   oarless
last   lats; salt; slat
lasted   deltas; desalt; salted; slated; staled
laster   alerts; alters; artels; ratels; salter; slater; staler; stelar; tarsel
lasters   artless; salters; slaters; tarsels

lasting   anglist; salting; slating; staling
lastly   saltly
lasts   saltoj slats
Las Vegas   salvages
latches   chalets; satchel
latchet   chattel
latchets   chattels
late   et al.; leat; tael; tale; teal; tela
lated   Datel; dealt; delta
lateen   elanet; La Tène
laten   leant
La Tène   elanet; lateen
latent   Lanett; latten; talent
later   alert; alter; ratel; taler
latest   stealt
latex   exalt
lath   halt
lathe   Elath; ethal
lathed   halted
lather   halter; thaler
lathered   haltered
lathering   earthling; haltering
lathers   halters; harslet; Herstal; slather
lathes   haslet; Shelta; Thales
lathing   Althing; halting
laths   halts; shalt; Stahl
latices   astelic; Castile; elastic; laciest
Latiner   entrail; latrine; ratline; reliant; retinal; trenail
Latiners   entrails; latrines; ratlines; trenails
Latinise   alienist; litanies
Latinises   alienists
Latins   instal; Stalin
latish   tahsil
latitude   altitude
latitudes   altitudes
latitudinal   altitudinal
latitudinarian   altitudinarian
latitudinous   altitudinous
Latona   atonal
latria   Altair; atrial; lariat
latrine   entrail; Latiner; ratline; reliant; retinal; trenail
latrines   entrails; Latiners; ratlines; trenails
Latrobe   bloater
lats   last; salt; slat
latten   Lanett; latent; talent
latter   rattle; tatler

lattice tactile
Latvia avital
Latvian valiant
laud auld; dual; udal
lauder Eluard
lauding languid
lauds Aldus; udals
launce cuneal; Lucena; unlace
launces censual; unlaces; unscale
launch nuchal; unchal
launder Arundel; lurdane; rundale
launders lurdanes
Laura aural
laurel allure
laurels allures
Laurens ulnares
lava Alva; aval; Vaal
lavages salvage
lavas vasal
lave leva; vale; veal; vela
laveer leaver; reveal
laveers leavers; reveals; several
laver ravel; Reval; velar
lavers ravels; salver; serval; slaver;
  versal
laves Elvas; salve; selva; slave;
  vales; valse
lavisher shrieval
lavra arval; larva
law awl
lawed dwale; waled; weald
Lawes swale; sweal; wales; weals
lawing waling
lawk walk
lawks walks
lawned Walden
laws awls; slaw
lawyer warely
laxer relax
layer early; relay
layered delayer; relayed
layering relaying; yearling
layers relays; slayer
laying gainly
laymen meanly; namely
layover overlay
layovers overlays
lays slay
laze zeal
lazed Zelda
lea ale; e-la
leach chela
leached Chaldee; Cheadle

leaches Chelsea
lead dale; deal; lead; Leda
leaded dealed
leaden aneled; leaned; nealed
leader dealer
leaders dealers
lead-in Aldine; alined; Daniel;
  Delian; denial; nailed
leading aligned; dealing
leadings dealings
lead-ins denials; snailed
leads dales; deals; lades; slade
leadsman dalesman
leadsmen dalesmen
leady delay
leaf feal
leafed fealed
leafing fealing; finagle
leafs false; feals; fleas
Leah hale; heal
leak kale; lake
leaking linkage
leaks kales; lakes; slake
leaky kayle
leal Ella
leam alme; Elam; Elma; lame;
  Lema; male; meal
leams almes; lames; males; meals;
  Salem; samel; Selma
lean élan; lane; Lena; neal
Leander learned
leaned aneled; leaden; nealed
leaning aneling; eanling; nealing
leanings eanlings
leans lanes; neals; slane
leant laten
lean-to etalon
lean-tos etalons
leap pale; peal; pela; plea
leaped pealed
leaper Lapeer; repeal
leapers pleaser; relapse; repeals
leaping pealing
leaps Elaps; lapse; pales; peals;
  pleas; salep; sepal; spale; speal
leapt lepta; palet; pelta; petal; plate;
  pleat
lear earl; lare; râle; real
lea-rigs Algiers
learing engrail; nargile; realign;
  reginal
learn Larne; renal
learned Leander

learns ransel
learnt altern; antler; rental; ternal
lears Arles; earls; lares; laser; reals;
   coral
leas ales; Elsa; sale; seal; slae
lease easel
leased sealed
leaser resale; sealer; Searle
leasers earless; sealers
leases easels; eassel
leash hales; halse; heals; selah;
   shale; sheal
leashing shealing
leasing linages; sealing
least leats; slate; Stael; stale; steal;
   stela; taels; tales; teals; tesla
leat et al.; late; tael; tale; teal; tela
leather tar-heel
leathers tar-heels
leats least; slate; Stael; stale; steal;
   stela; taels; tales; teals; tesla
leavens enslave
leaver laveer; reveal
leavers laveers; reveals; several
leaves sleave
leavings Svengali
Leavis Aviles; valise
lebensraum mensurable
Lebu blue
lechery cheerly
led eld
Leda dale; deal; lade; lead
ledge glede; gleed
ledger gelder
ledgers gelders; sledger
ledges gledes; gleeds; sledge
lee eel
leech Elche
leeches Scheele
Leeds deles; Edsel; seled
leek keel; Klee
leeks keels; sleek
leer lere; reel
leered reeled
leeriest steelier
leering reeling
leers leres; reels
leery Leyre
lees eels; else; seel; sele; slee
leets sleet; steel; stele
left felt
lefties felsite
leg gel

legal Galle
legalise galilees
legalist stillage; tillages
legalists stillages
legate eaglet; Galtee; gelate; teagle;
   telega
legates eaglets; teagles; telegas
legatine gelatine
legation gelation
legator gloater; Ortegal
legators gloaters
leges glees
legged gledge
legger eggler
leggers egglers
legislator allegorist
legislators allegorists
leg-man mangel; mangle
Legnago agelong
legs gels
lei Eli; lie
Leics. ceils; ciels; Sicel; slice
Leif file; lief; life
Leinster enlister; listener; re-enlist
leir lier; lire; riel; rile
leirs liers; riels; riles; siler
leis Elis; isle; lies; seil; sile
leister sterile
leisters tireless
Leith lithe
Leitrim limiter
lek elk
leks elks; Selk
Lely yell
lem elm
Lema alme; Elam; Elma; lame;
   leam; male; meal
Lemaître eremital; matériel;
   real-time
leman Elman; Lemna
lemans Anselm; mensal
lemming Memling
Lemna Elman; leman
Lemnos lemons; melons; solemn
lemon melon
lemons Lemnos; melons; solemn
lemony myelon
lempira impearl; palmier
lems elms
Lena élan; lane; lean
lenders slender
Lenin linen
Leningrad enlarding

lenis elsin; liens; lines; nelis; Niles; silen
leno enol; Leon; lone; Noel
lenses lessen
lenticel lenticle
lenticels lenticles
lenticle lenticel
lenticles lenticels
lentil lintel
lentils lintels
lentisk tinkles
lento olent; Olten
Leon enol; leno; lone; Noel
Leonid doline; indole
Leonids dolines; sondeli
leopard paroled
leper repel
lepers repels
lepid piled; plied
lepra paler; parle; pearl; repla
leprous sporule
lepta leapt; palet; pelta; petal; plate; pleat
lere leer; reel
leres leers; reels
Lérida derail; laired; railed; relaid
Lerins liners
Leros eorls; loser; orles; Osler; roles; soler; Sorel
lesion eloins; esloin; insole; Silone
lesions esloins; insoles; lioness
lessen lenses
lessened needless
Lessing singles
lessons sonless
lessor losers; solers
lest elts; lets; tels
Lester relets; streel
Lesvos solves
let elt; tel
Lethe Ethel
let rip triple
lets elts; lest; tels
letters settler; sterlet; trestle
Lettish lithest; thistle
leva lave; vale; veal; vela
levan elvan; navel; venal
levanter relevant
Levantine Valentine
Le Vau uveal; value
levees sleeve
lever elver; revel
levers elvers; revels

Levi evil; live; veil; vile; vlei
levin liven
levirate relative
levis Elvis; evils; lives; slive; veils; vleis
Levoča alcove; coeval
lewd weld
lewder welder
Lewes sewel; sweel; weels; Wesel
lewis weils; wiels; wiles
ley Ely; lye
Leyburn Burnley
Leyden needly
Leyre leery
leys lyes; lyse; sley
liability alibility
liable alible; Belial; Biella; labile
Liam lima; mail; mali
liana Lanai
lianas Salian; salina
liane alien; aline; anile; Elian
lianes aliens; alines; saline; Selina; silane
liang Gilan; Laing; ligan; linga
liar aril; lair; lira; rail; rial
Liard drail; laird
liars lairs; liras; rails; rials
liart trail; trial
Lias ails; Isla; Lisa; sail; sial
liberal Braille
libra brail
librae bailer
libras brails
librate Alberti; triable
lice ceil; ciel
license selenic; silence
licensed declines; silenced
licenser reclines; silencer
licensers silencers
licenses silences
licensing silencing
lichees helices
licker rickle
lickers rickles; slicker
licks slick
Licosa social
lidded diddle
lidger gilder; girdle; glider; ridgel
lidgers gilders; girdles; gliders; grisled; ridgels
lido idol; Lodi; olid
lidos idols; Isold; silo'd; sloid; soldi; solid

lids   sild; slid
lie   Eli; lei
lied   deil; eild; idle
lieder   relied
lief   file; Leif; life
liefer   relief
lien   line; Neil; Nile
liens   elsin; lenis; lines; nelis;
   Niles; silen
lientery   entirely
lier   leir; lire; riel; rile
lierne   reline
liernes   relines
liers   leirs; riels; riles; siler
lies   Elis; isle; leis; seil; sile
Liestal   tailles; tallies
liever   relive; revile
Liévres   relives; reviles; servile
life   file; Leif; lief
lifer   filer; flier; rifle
lifers   filers; fliers; rifles
lift   flit
lifter   filter; trifle
lifters   filters; stifler; trifles
lifts   flits
ligan   Gilan; Laing; liang; linga
ligate   aiglet; taigle
ligated   taigled
ligates   aiglets; taigles
ligating   taigling
ligation   intaglio; taglioni
ligations   taglionis
liger   Rigel
lighted   delight
lighten   enlight
lightened   enlighted
lightening   enlighting
lightens   enlights
lighter   relight
lighters   relights; slighter
lightness   nightless
ligne   Elgin; ingle; Nigel
lignes   ingles; seling; single
Lignice   ceiling; cieling
lignin   lining
lignose   lingoes
ligroin   roiling
ligules   gullies
Lika   ilk'a; kail; kali; laik
like   Kiel
likely   Ilkley
liken   inkle; Klein
likens   inkles; silken

liker   Rilke
likes   Sikel
Lil   ill
lllac   Cilla
lilacs   Scilla
lilt   till
lilted   tilled
lilting   tilling
lilts   still; tills
lily   illy; yill
lima   Liam; mail; mali
limas   Islam; mails; malis; Milas;
   salmi; Simla
limbate   timbale
limbed   dimble
lime   Emil; mile
limen   Ilmen; Milne
limens   Semlin; simnel
limes   miles; slime; smile
limestone   milestone
limiest   elitism; El Misti; limites
limited   delimit
limiter   Leitrim
limites   elitism; El Misti; limiest
limitary   military
limned   milden; Mindel
limner   merlin; Milner
limners   merlins
limp   plim
limped   dimple
limper   prelim
limpers   prelims; simpler
limpest   limpets; Mt. Siple
limpets   limpest; Mt. Siple
limps   plims
lin   nil
Linacre   carline; en clair
linage   Ealing; genial
linages   leasing; sealing
Linares   nailers
Linda   Ladin
Lindau   unlaid
linden   dinnle; linned
lindens   dinnles
line   lien; Neil; Nile
lineages   ensilage
linear   en l'air; larine; nailer
lineated   dateline; entailed
lined   eldin
linen   Lenin
liners   Lerins
lines   elsin; lenis; liens; nelis; Niles;
   silen

line-up   lupine; up-line
line-ups   lupines; spinule; up-lines
linga   Gilan; Laing; liang; ligan
lingam   laming; malign
lingel   lingle
Lingen   ginnel
lingers   slinger
lingle   lingel
lingoes   lignose
lings   sling
lingual   lingula
lingula   lingual
lining   lignin
link   kiln; Klin
linkage   leaking
linked   inkled; kilned; kindle
linking   inkling; kilning
links   kilns; slink
linned   dinnle; linden
lino   lion; loin; noil
linos   lions; loins; noils
linseed   enisled; ensiled
lintel   lentil
lintels   lentils
lion   lino; loin; noil
lionel   niello; O'Neill
lionels   niellos
lioness   esloins; insoles; lesions
lionesses   noiseless
lionise   elision
lionises   oiliness
lions   linos; loins; noils
Lipa   pail; Pali; pila
liparite   reptilia
lip-read   predial
lips   lisp; slip
liquate   tequila
lira   aril; lair; liar; rail; rial
liras   lairs; liars; rails; rials
lire   leir; lier; riel; rile
Lisa   ails; Isla; Lias; sail; sial
lisle   Ellis
Lismore   moilers
lisp   lips; slip
lisped   dispel; spiled
lisper   perils; Perlis; pilers; pliers
lisping   spiling
lisps   slips
Lissa   sails; Silas; sisal
list   silt; slit
listed   idlest; silted; tildes
listen   enlist; inlets; silent; tinsel
listened   enlisted

listener   enlister; Leinster; re-enlist
listeners   enlisters; re-enlists
listening   enlisting
listens   enlists; tinsels
lister   litres; tilers
listing   silting
lists   silts; slits
lit   til
Lita   alit; Atli; tail; tali
litanies   alienist; Latinise
lith   hilt
lithe   Leith
lither   Hitler
lithesome   homeliest
lithest   Lettish; thistle
litho   tholi
liths   hilts
litotes   toilets; T. S. Eliot
litre   relit; tiler
litres   lister; tilers
litter   tilter; titler
litters   slitter; stilter; testril; tilters;
    titlers
littoral   tortilla
littorals   tortillas
live   evil; Levi; veil; vile; vlei
lived   devil; vilde
lively   evilly; vilely
liven   levin
livens   Sliven; snivel
liver   livre; rivel
livered   deliver; relived; reviled
livers   livres; rivels; silver; sliver
livery   verily
lives   Elvis; evils; levis; slive; veils;
    vleis
livre   liver; rivel
livres   livers; rivels; silver; sliver
Lleyn   Nelly
Lloyd   dolly
load   alod; odal
loader   Laredo; ordeal; reload
loaders   ordeals; reloads; sea-lord
loading   digonal
loads   alods; odals
loaf   foal; Olaf
loafed   feodal; foaled
loafers   for sale
loafing   foaling
loafs   foals; sol-fa
loamier   Morelia
loams   salmo
loan   Laon; Nola

loaned enodal
loaner Lorena; reloan
loaners orleans; reloans; Salerno
Loango lagoon
loans salon; sloan; solan; Solna
loath lotah
loather rat-hole
loathers rat-holes
loathly tally-ho
lobate oblate
lobated bloated
lobation oblation
lobbied bilobed
lobbies bilboes
lobe bole; Loeb
lobes boles
lobi boil
lobing goblin
lobose sobole
lobs Bols; slob
lobster bolster; bolters
lobsters bolsters
lobules soluble
lobus bolus
locals Laclos
Locarno coronal
locate Alecto
located cold tea
locates alecost; lactose; scatole;
  talcose
location colation
loci Clio; coil
Locke cloke
locked cloaked
locking cloking
loco cool
locoed cooled
locoing cooling
locos cools
Locrian clarino; clarion
Locrians clarinos; clarions
locus clous
locust clouts
lode dole
lodes Delos; doles; soled
lodge ogled
lodging godling
lodgings godlings
Lodi idol; lido; olid
Loeb bole; lobe
loess loses; sloes; soles
loftier trefoil
Loftus flouts

Logan along; Golan; longa;
  NALGO
loge ogle
loges ogles; segol
logged dog-leg
loggers slogger
logiest elogist
logography graphology
logs Glos.; slog
loin lino; lion; noil
loins linos; lions; noils
Loire oiler; oriel
Loiret loiter; toiler
Lois oils; silo; soil; soli
loiter Loiret; toiler
loitered dolerite
loiters Estoril; estriol; toilers
Lomé mole
loment melton; molten
lone enol; leno; Leon; Noel
loner enrol; Lorne; nerol
loners enrols
longa along; Golan; Logan;
  NALGO
longed golden
longships sploshing
Looe oleo
loof fool
loofed fooled
loofing Foligno; fooling
loofs fools
looing olingo
look kolo
looked out outlooked
looking out outlooking
lookout outlook
lookouts looks out; outlooks
looks kolos; Sokol
looks out lookouts; outlooks
loom mool
looms mools; sloom
looniest oilstone
loons snool; Solon
loop polo; pool
looped poodle; pooled
loopers spooler
looping pooling
loops pools; sloop; spool
loos Oslo; solo
loose oleos; soole
loosed oodles; sooled
looses sooles
loosing olingos; sooling

loot tool
looted Toledo; tooled
looter Loreto; rootle; tooler
looters rootles; toolers
looting tooling
loots lotos; stool; tools
lope olpe; Opel; pole
loped poled
lopes elops; olpes; poles; slope
loping poling
lopper propel
loppers propels
lops slop
loran Arlon; Lorna
Lorca carol; claro; coral
lorcha choral
lorchas scholar
lording girlond
lordling drolling
lordly drolly
lore eorl; Orel; orle; role
Lorena loaner; reloan
Loreto looter; rootle; tooler
Loretta retotal
lorica caroli
loricates sectorial
lories elisor; oilers; oriels; Serlio
loris roils
L'Orme morel
Lorna Arlon; loran
Lorne enrol; loner; nerol
lose Ösel; sloe; sole
loser eorls; Leros; orles; Osler;
   roles; soler; Sorel
losers lessor; solers
loses loess; sloes; soles
losing soling
loss sols
lost lots; slot; St. Lô
lot Olt
lota alto; tola
lotah loath
lote tole
lotes toles
loth holt
Lothar harlot
Loti toil
lotos loots; stool; tools
lots lost; slot; St. Lô
lotted dottle
Lottie toilet
lotus louts; Soult
loud ludo

louden nodule; Oundle
loudens nodules
louder loured
loudest tousled
lough ghoul
loughs ghouls; slough
lounder roundel; roundle
lounders roundels; roundles
loured louder
louse ousel; Seoul
loused souled
louses ousels; soleus
lousy Louys
lout tolu; Toul
louts lotus; Soult
louver louvre; velour
louvers louvres; velours
louvre louver; velour
louvres louvers; velours
Louys lousy
love vole
loved voled
love-in in love
lovely volley
lovers solver
loves slove; solve; voles
loving Gonvil; voling
low owl
lowbred Bowdler
lowed dowel
lower owler; rowel
lowers owlers; rowels; slower
lowery owlery
lowest Elstow; owlets; towels
lows owls; slow; sowl
loyal alloy
lubber burble; rubble
lubbers burbles; slubber
Lubeck buckle
lucarne nuclear; unclear
Lucas cauls
luce clue
Lucena cuneal; launce; unlace
luces clues; cluse
Lucian Alcuin; Lucina; uncial
Lucina Alcuin; Lucian; uncial
lucre cruel; ulcer
luddite diluted
ludo loud
luffed duffel; duffle
luge glue; gule
luged glued
luger gluer; gruel

lugers gluers; gruels
luges glues; gules
lugger gurgle
luggers gurgles; slugger
luging gluing
lugs slug
lumbar brumal; labrum; umbral
lumber rumble
lumbers Burslem; rumbles;
    slumber
lumen Melun
lump plum
lumped dumple; plumed
lumpen plenum
lumper replum; rumple
lumpers rumples
lumping pluming
lumps plums; slump
lumpy plumy
lums slum
Luna ulan; ulna
lunar ulnar; urnal
lunarist Luristan
lunatics sultanic
lunettes unsettle
lunged gulden
lunges gunsel
lung-fish flushing
lungs slung
luniest utensil
lupine line-up; up-line
lupines line-ups; spinule; up-lines
lurch churl
lurdane Arundel; launder; rundale
lurdanes launders
lure rule
lured ruled
lures rules
Lurgan langur
luring ruling

Luristan lunarist
lush shul; Suhl
lust slut
luster lustre; luters; result; rustle;
    sutler; ulster
lusters lustres; results; rustles;
    sutlers; ulsters
lusting singult
lustre luster; luters; result; rustle;
    sutler; ulster
lustred rustled; strudel
lustres lusters; results; rustles;
    sutlers; ulsters
lustrine insulter
lustring rustling
lusts sluts
lute tule
luters luster; lustre; result; rustle;
    sutler; ulster
lutes tules
Luther hurtle
Lutonian Ultonian
Lutonians Ultonians
lyard lardy; Rydal
Lydia daily
lye Ely; ley
lyes leys; lyse; sley
Lyme elmy; ylem
Lyon only
Lyra aryl; ryal
lyrate elytra; realty
lyre rely
lyres slyer
lyric Cyril
Lys sly
lyse leys; lyes; sley
lyses sleys; Yssel
lysing Glynis; singly
lysol Solly
lythe ethyl

M

ma am
ma'am mama
Ma'an Mana
Maasin animas; manias; Manisa;
    Samian
Mab bam
Mabel amble; blame; Melba
mac cam
macaronic carcinoma

mace acme; came
macer Ceram; crame; cream;
    Crema; Merca
macerated camerated; demarcate
maceration cameration
macers crames; creams; scream
maces acmes
mach cham
machairs archaism; charisma

Machen Manche
macks smack
macle camel
Maclean lace-man; manacle
macled calmed
macles camels; mascle; mescal
macs cams
mad dam
madden damned; demand
maddened demanded
maddening demanding
maddens demands
made dame; Edam; mead
Maderno roadmen
madge gamed
Madison daimons; domains
madness desmans
madras dramas
madrasahs madrassah
madrassah madrasahs
madroña mandora
madroñas mandoras
madroño doorman
mads dams
maenad anadem
maenads anadems
Maesteg gametes; metages
maestri Artemis; imarets; maister;
  misrate; semitar; St. Marie
maestro amorets
mag gam
mage game
magenta magnate
Magians siamang
Maginot moating
magister migrates; sterigma
magma gamma
magnate magenta
magnesite geminates; magnetise
magnetise geminates; magnesite
magnetiser germinates
magneto megaton; montage
magnetos megatons;
  montages
mags gams
magus gaums
Mahé ahem; hame
Mahler Harlem; Ramleh
mahmal hammal
mahogany Hogmanay
mahsir marish
maid amid
maided diadem

maiden daimen; Damien; demain;
  median; Medina
maidens demains; medians;
  sideman
maids Midas
Maidstone dominates
maigre gamier; imager; mirage
Maigret migrate; ragtime
maik kaim; kami
maiks kaims; kamis; smaik
mail Liam; lima; mali
mailed medial
mailer Elmira
mailers realism
mails Islam; limas; Milas; salmi;
  Simla
maim imam
maims imams; miasm
main Amin; mina
Maine amine; animé; en ami;
  Menai; minae
mainor Marino; Marion; Mirano
mains Manis; minas
mainyard dairyman
maire Marie; ramie; rimae
maires armies
Mais aims; Amis; Siam; sima
maister Artemis; imarets; maestri;
  misrate; semitar; St. Marie
maisters asterism; misrates;
  semitars
Makarios romaikas
make kame
makes kames
mal lam
malar alarm; ramal
malate tamale
malates tamales
Malay Yamal
male alme; Elam; Elma; lame; leam;
  Lema; meal
maleic malice
males almes; lames; leams; meals;
  Salem; samel; Selma
mali Liam; lima; mali
malic claim
malice maleic
malign laming; lingam
maligner germinal; malinger
maligners malingers
maline Elmina; menial
malines isleman; menials; seminal
malinger germinal; maligner

malingers   maligners
malis   Islam; limas; Milas; salmi;
  Simla
malison   Osmanli; Soliman
malisons   Osmanlis
malls   small
Malone   melano
Malta   tamal
malts   smalt
maltster   martlets
mama   ma'am
Mame   Emma
man   mna; nam
Mana   Ma'an
manacle   lace-man; Maclean
manage   agname
managed   agnamed
managers   Semarang
manages   agnames; Mesagna
manatee   emanate; enemata
manatees   emanates
Manche   Machen
mandatory   damnatory
mandora   madroña
mandoras   madroñas
mane   amen; mean; Mena; name
maned   amend; Medan; menad;
  named
manège   menage
manèged   end-game
manèges   menages
maneh   he-man
maneless   lameness; nameless;
  salesman
manes   amens; manse; means;
  Mensa; names; samen
Manet   meant
manganite   emanating
mange   Megan
mangel   leg-man; mangle
mangels   mangles
manger   engram; german; ragmen
Mangere   germane
mangers   engrams; germans
mangle   leg-man; mangel
mangles   mangels
mango   among
mania   amian; amnia; anima
maniac   caiman
maniacs   caimans
manias   animas; Maasin; Manisa;
  Samian
Manichees   mechanise

manila   animal; lamina
manioc   camion
maniple   impanel
maniples   impanels
Manis   mains; minas
Manisa   animas; Maasin; manias;
  Samian
manlier   marline; mineral; railmen
manliest   ailments; aliments;
  salt-mine
manna   Annam
mannered   Menander
manor   Morna; Norma; Ramon;
  Roman
manors   ramson; ransom; Romans
manred   red-man; remand
manreds   remands
Mansart   artsman; mantras
manse   amens; manes; means;
  Mensa; names; samen
manses   messan
mansion   onanism
mantas   Tasman
mantel   lament; mantle; mental
mantels   laments; mantles
mantes   aments; stamen
manticore   cremation
mantis   matins
mantissa   Satanism
mantle   lament; mantel; mental
mantles   laments; mantels
mantras   artsman; Mansart
manual   alumna
manure   murena
manured   duramen; maunder;
  unarmed
manures   surname
many   myna
Maoist   Taoism
Maori   Mario; Moira; moria
map   amp; pam
maple   ample; pelma
maples   sample
mapper   pamper
mappers   pampers
maps   amps; pams; samp; spam
mar   arm; ram
mara   Aram; Rama
maracas   marasca; mascara
marah   haram
Maranta   amarant
Maras   Samar
marasca   maracas; mascara

maraschino harmonicas
Marat Tamar
marble ambler; blamer; ramble
marbled rambled
marbler rambler
marblers ramblers
marbles amblers; blamers; rambles
marbling rambling
marc cram
marcel calmer; Carmel
march charm
marched charmed
märchen encharm
marcher charmer
marchers charmers
marches mesarch
marchese cashmere
marching charming
marchioness monarchises
Marconi Minorca; Romanic
Marcos caroms
mare ream
mares maser; reams; smear
margarines misarrange
Margate regmata
marge gamer; regma
margent garment; ragment
margents garments, ragments
marges gamers
margin arming; ingram
marginal alarming
marginally alarmingly
margined dreaming; mid-range;
  Niger Dam
Margo groma
Mari amir; Mira; rami; rima
Marian airman; marina
Marianne Armenian
Marie ramie; rimae
Marin inarm; minar
marina airman; Marian
marine airmen; Marnie; remain
mariner rein-arm
mariners rein-arms
marines remains; seminar; sirname
Marinist martinis
Marino mainor; Marion; Mirano
Mario Maori; Moira; moria
Marion mainor; Marino; Mirano
marish mahsir
Marist Ramist
Marists Ramists; tsarism
marital martial

Marken Kerman
marker remark
markers remarks
marled dermal; medlar
marline manlier; mineral; railmen
marlines minerals
Marlon normal
Marne enarm; namer
Marnie airmen; marine; remain
Maronites matronise
maroon Monaro
Maros moras; roams
Marple ampler; palmer
Marples palmers; sampler
Marree reamer
married admirer
marries simarre
mars arms; rams
marsh harms
Marston matrons; transom
mart tram
martel armlet
martels armlets
martens artsmen; sarment;
  smarten
martensite terminates
Martha Matrah
martial marital
martian tamarin
martians tamarins
martin Antrim
martinets stream-tin
martinis Marinist
martlets maltster
Martos Mostar; stroam; stroma
marts smart; trams
Mary army; Myra
mascara maracas; marasca
mascle camels; macles; mescal
mascon socman
mascot comsat
mascots comsats
masculine calumnies
maser mares; reams; smear
masers Ramses; smears
Maseru amuser; mauser
mash hams; sham
mashed shamed
masher harems; shamer
mashers shamers; smasher
mashes shames
mashies Messiah
mashing shaming

mason   moans; monas; Osman
masons   Namsos; Samson
massa   amass; Assam
massé   mesas; seams
Massenet   tameness
masseter   sea-terms; steamers
masseur   amusers; Erasmus;
  mausers
Massine   Messina
mast   mats; tams
master   armets; maters; stream;
  tamers
mastered   streamed
mastering   emigrants; St. Germain;
  streaming
masterless   streamless
masters   streams
master-work   work-master
mastery   streamy
masticot   stomatic
mastics   miscast
mastoid   diatoms
masty   mayst
mat   tam
mate   meat; Meta; tame; team; Tema
mated   tamed
mateless   meatless; tameless
mater   armet; tamer; trema
matériel   eremital; Lemaître;
  real-time
maters   armets; master; stream;
  tamers
mates   meats; Mesta; steam; tames;
  teams
matey   etyma; meaty
matin   tamin
matinees   seminate
mating   taming
matins   mantis
Matisse   asteism; samites; tamises
Matrah   Martha
matrices   ceramist
matricide   diametric
matronise   Maronites
matrons   Marston; transom
matross   stroams
mats   mast; tams
matters   smatter
mattress   smartest; smatters
maturation   natatorium
maturer   erratum
matures   strumae
maud   duma

mauds   adsum; Dumas
maugre   murage
maul   alum; Mula
maund   Munda; undam
maunder   duramen; manured;
  unarmed
maundered   undreamed
maundering   undreaming
maunders   surnamed
maunds   Mundas; undams
mauser   amuser; Maseru
mausers   amusers; Erasmus;
  masseur
mawr   warm
mawrs   swarm; warms
maws   swam
may   Amy; Mya; yam
maybe   beamy; embay
Mayen   meany; yamen
mayest   steamy
mayo   Amoy
mayor   moray
mayors   morays
mays   yams
mayst   masty
mazy   azym
M'Bao   ambo; boma; Moab
me   em
meads   dame; Edam; made
meads   dames
meagre   Graeme
meal   alme; Elam; Elma; lame; leam;
  Lema; male
mealiness   messaline
meals   almes; lames; leams; males;
  Saiem; samel; Selma
mean   amen; mane; Mena; name
meander   amender; enarmed;
  renamed
meanders   amenders
meaner   rename
meaning   amening
meanly   laymen; namely
means   amens; manes; manse;
  Mensa; names; samen
meant   ament; Manet
meany   Mayen; yamen
measly   samely
measures   reassume
meat   mate; Meta; tame; team; Tema
Meath   Thame
meatier   emirate
meatiness   amnesties; seminates

meatless   mateless; tameless
meats   mates; Mesta; steam; tames;
  teams
meaty   etyma; matey
mebos   besom
mechanics   mischance
mechanise   Manichees
medal   lamed
medals   damsel
Medan   amend; maned; menad;
  named
meddle   melded
Mede   deem; deme; meed
Medea   adeem
Medes   deems; demes; meeds
media   aimed; amide
medial   mailed
medials   misdeal; mislead
median   daimen; Damien; demain;
  maiden; Medina
medians   demains; maidens;
  sideman
medical   claimed; decimal; declaim
medically   decimally
medicals   decimals; declaims
medicaster   miscreated
medicate   decimate
medicated   decimated
medicates   decimates
medicating   decimating
medication   decimation
medicinal   adminicle
Medina   daimen; Damien; demain;
  maiden; median
Medise   demise
Medised   demised; misdeed
Medises   demises
Medising   demising
medlar   dermal; marled
Medusa   amused
meed   deem; deme; Mede
meeds   deems; demes; Medes
meer   mere
meercat   ceramet; cremate
meercats   ceramets; cremates
meers   meres; Merse
meet   mete; teem; Teme
meeting   teeming
meets   metes; teems; Temes; temse
Meg   gem
Megan   mange
megasse   message
megaton   magneto; montage

megatons   magnetos; montages
Megiddo   demigod
Meilhac   Michael
mein   mine
meins   mines
Meissen   misseen; nemesis;
  siemens
mélange   gleeman
melano   Malone
Melba   amble; blame; Mabel
melded   meddle
melding   mingled
mêlées   Semele
melic   clime
Melissa   aimless; mesails; samiels;
  seismal
mellay   lamely
mells   smell
melodies   melodise
melodise   melodies
meloid   moiled
melon   lemon
melons   Lemnos; lemons; solemn
Melos   moles
melters   smelter
melton   loment; molten
melts   smelt
Melun   lumen
Memling   lemming
memo   mome
memories   memorise
memorise   memories
memos   momes; Somme
Mena   amen; mane; mean; name
menad   amend; maned; Medan;
  named
Menado   daemon; moaned;
  Modane; Modena; nomade
menads   amends; desman
ménage   manège
ménages   manèges
Menai   amine; animé; en ami;
  Maine; minae
Menander   mannered
men-at-arms   armaments
Mende   emend
mender   red-men
menes   mense; mesne; semen
menial   Elmina; maline
menials   isleman; malines; seminal
meno   nome; omen
Menorca   Cameron; Cremona;
  romance

Mensa amens; manes; manse; means; names; samen
mensal Anselm; lemans
mense menes; mesne; semen
mensurable lebensraum
mensural numerals
mental lament; mantel; mantle
mentally tallymen
mentioners minestrone
mentor Merton; montre
mentors monster; montres; Ore Mtns.
Merano moaner; monera
Merca Ceram; crame; cream; Crema; macer
mercaptide imprecated
Mercator cremator
merceries mercerise
mercerise merceries
Mercia Crimea
Mercian carmine; Crimean
merciful crimeful
merciless crimeless
mere meer
merel Elmer; merle
merels merles
meres meers; Merse
merest Mestre; meters; metres; Termes
meri emir; mire; riem; rime
Mérida admire
Mérignac amercing; creaming; Germanic
meril miler
Merill miller
merils milers; smiler
merinos mersion
merism mimers; simmer
meristem mimester; mismetre
merit mitre; remit; timer
merited demerit; dimeter; Edremit
merits mister; mitres; remits; smiter; timers
merle Elmer; merel
merles merels
merlin limner; Milner
merling gremlin; mingler
merlings gremlins; minglers
merlins limners
meroistic eroticism; isometric
Merops mopers; proems
merriest rimester; triremes
Merse meers; meres

Mersea ameers; seamer
Mersin miners
mersion merinos
mersions minoress
Merton mentor; montre
Meru mure
mesa same; seam
Mesagna agnames; manages
mesail mesial; Salemi; samiel; Sliema
mesails aimless; Melissa; samiels; seismal
mesaraic Americas
mesarch marches
mesas massé; seams
mescal camels; macles; mascle
mese emes; Esme; seem; semé; smee
mesh hems; Shem
mesial mesail; Salemi; samiel; Sliema
mesian Amiens; amines, inseam
mesne menes; mense; semen
mesocarp compares; compears
meson nomes; omens
mesonic Comines; incomes
mesotron Montrose
message megasse
messaline mealiness
messan manses
Messiah mashies
messier remises
Messina Massine
mess-tin missent
Mesta mates; meats; steam; tames; teams
mesto motes; smote; tomes
Mestre merest; meters; metres; Termes
Meta mate; meat; tame; team
metage gamete
metages gametes; Maesteg
metals lamest; samlet
metamer ammeter
metamers ammeters
mete meet; teem; Teme
meteor remote
meter metre
metering regiment
meters merest; Mestre; metres; Termes
metes meets; teems; Temes; temse
metis emits; items; mites; smite; stime; times

Metol motel
metonic entomic
metre meter
metres merest; Mestre; meters;
  Termes
metrician criminate
metricians criminates
metrics cretism
metronome monometer;
  monotreme
metronomes monometers;
  monotremes
Metsu mutes
meu emu
meus emus; muse
mew Wem
mews smew
mho ohm
mhos ohms
Mhow whom
mi I'm
Mia aim
miasm imams; maims
mica amic
micate acmite
Michael Meilhac
miche Chiem; chime
miched chimed
miches chimes
miching chiming
microclimates commercialist
mid dim
Midas maids
midden minded
mid-hour humidor; rhodium
mid-hours humidors
mid-range dreaming; margined;
  Niger Dam
Midrash dirhams
mid-sea amides
mid-term trimmed
mien mine
Mieres misère; remise
migraine imaginer
migraines imaginers
migrants smarting
migrate Maigret; ragtime
migrates magister; sterigma
mihrab Brahmi
mike Kemi
miladies idealism
Milas Islam; limas; malis; salmi;
  Simla

milden limned; Mindel
mildness mindless
mile Emil; lime
miler meril
milers merils; smiler
miles limes; slime; smile
Milesian alienism
milestone limestone
military limitary
milks sklim
miller Merill
millets mistell
millstone stone-mill
Milne Ilmen; limen
Milner limner; merlin
Milo moil
Milos moils
milreis slimier
Milspe impels; simple
mimers merism; simmer
mimester meristem; mismetre
mimesters mismetres
Min nim
mina Amin; main
minae amine; animé; en ami;
  Maine; Menai
minar inarm; Marin
minaret raiment
minars inarms
minas mains; Manis
minded midden
Mindel limned; milden
minder remind
minders reminds
mindless mildness
mine mien
mined denim
miner inerm
mineral manlier; marline; railmen
minerals marlines
miners Mersin
Minerva vermian
mines Nimes
minestrone mentioners
mingled melding
mingler gremlin; merling
minglers gremlins; merlings
minister interims
minks Minsk
Minnesota nominates
Minorca Marconi; Romanic
minoress mersions
Minos Simon

Minot Timon
Minsk minks
minster minters
minsters trimness
mintage teaming; tegmina
mintages steaming
minters minster
mintier interim; termini
minuend unmined
minuet minute; mutine
minuets minutes; mistune;
  mutines
minute minuet; mutine
minute-drop importuned
minutely untimely
minutes minuets; mistune;
  mutines
minxes mixens
mir rim
Mira amir; Mari; rami; rima
Mirabel balmier; mirable; remblai
mirable balmier; Mirabel; remblai
miracle Almeric; Carmiel; claimer;
  reclaim
miracles claimers; reclaims
mirage gamier; imager; maigre
mirages imagers
Mirano mainor; Marino; Marion
mire emir; meri; riem; rime
mired dimer; rimed
mires emirs; miser; Reims; riems;
  rimes
mirier rimier
miriest mistier; rimiest
miring riming
Miro Riom
mirs rims; smir
miry rimy; Ymir
misarrange margarines
misaunter ruminates
miscast mastics
mischance mechanics
miscreant Encratism
miscreated medicaster
miscredit misdirect
miscredited misdirected
miscrediting misdirecting
miscredits misdirects
misdeal medials; mislead
misdealing misleading
misdeals misleads
misdeed demised; Medised
misdirect miscredit

misdirected miscredited
misdirecting miscrediting
misdirects miscredits
misdo odism
misdoer dormies; moiders
mise Seim; semi
misease Siamese
Miseno eonism; monies; Simeon;
  Simone
miser emirs; mires; Reims; riems;
  rimes
misère Mieres; remise
misers remiss
mises seism; semis
misfield misfiled
misfiled misfield
mishap pashim
mislead medials; misdeal
misleader misleared
misleading misdealing
misleads misdeals
misleared misleader
misled slimed; smiled
mismate tammies
mismetre meristem; mimester
mismetres mimesters
misplead impleads
misprint imprints
misprise pismires
misrate Artemis; imarets; maestri;
  maister; semitar; St. Marie
misrates asterism; maisters;
  semitars
misread admires
misreads sidearms
misreport importers
miss isms
missa amiss
missal salmis
misseen Meissen; nemesis;
  siemens
missel slimes; smiles
missend dimness
missent mess-tin
misses seisms
misset smites; stimes; tmesis
misshape emphasis
missile similes
missioner remission
mist smit
misteach tachisme
misted demits; stimed
mistell millets

mister merits; mitres; remits;
 smiter; timers
mistery smytrie
mistier miriest; rimiest
misting smiting; stiming; timings
mistrained administer
mistune minuets; minutes;
 mutines
misuser mussier; surmise
misusers surmises
mite emit; item; time
mites emits; items; metis; smite;
 stime; times
mither hermit
mithers hermits
mitre merit; remit; timer
mitres merits; mister; remits;
 smiter; timers
mittens smitten
mixens minxes
mna man; nam
Moab ambo; boma; M'Bao
moan Amon; mona; Oman
moaned daemon; Menado;
 Modane; Modena; nomade
moaner Merano; monera
moaners Romanes; San Remo
moans mason; monas; Osman
moas Amos; soma
moat atom
moating Maginot
moats atoms; stoma
mobbed bombed
mobbing bombing
mobile bemoil; emboil; emboli
mobiles bemoils; emboils
Mocha Mohác
mocks smock
mod Dom
modal domal
Modane daemon; Menado;
 moaned; Modena; nomade
Modder Modred
mode demo; dome; Edom
models seldom
Modena daemon; Menado;
 moaned; Modane; nomade
modern rodmen
modernise domineers
modernised endodermis
moderns rodsmen
modes demos; domes
Modred Modder

Moers mores; morse; omers; smore
Mohác Mocha
moider dormie
moiders dormies; misdoer
moidore moodier
moil Milo
moiled meloid
moilers Lismore
moils Milos
Moira Maori; Mario; moria
Moissac mosaics
moist omits
moister mortise
moithers isotherm; Stroheim
mokes smoke
molal molla
molar moral
molars morals; morsal
molders smolder
mole Lomé
moles Melos
molest motels; St. Elmo
Molina monial; oil-man
moline oil-men
molla molal
molten loment; melton
mome memo
moment montem
momes memos; Somme
mona Amon; moan; Oman
monacid monadic; nomadic
monad Damon; nomad
monades daemons; nomades
monadic monacid; nomadic
monads damson; nomads
monals salmon
monandry Normandy
monarch nomarch
monarchial harmonical
monarchies monarchise;
 nomarchies
monarchise monarchies;
 nomarchies
monarchises marchioness
monarchs nomarchs
monarchy nomarchy
Monaro maroon
monas mason; moans; Osman
Monastir Romanist
Monday dynamo
Mondays dynamos
moner morne
monera Merano; moaner

Monet monte
monger morgen
mongers morgens
monial Molina; oil man
monies eonism; Miseno; Simeon;
  Simone
monism nomism
monist inmost
monistic nomistic
monists Stimson
mono moon
monodactylous condylomatous
monogram nomogram
monograms nomograms
monograph phonogram
monographs phonograms
monometer metronome;
  monotreme
monometers metronomes;
  monotremes
monopolies monopolise
monopolise monopolies
monosis simoons
monotones moonstone
monotreme metronome;
  monometer
monotremes metronomes;
  monometers
Monroe mooner
monster mentors; montres; Ore
  Mtns.
montage magneto; megaton
montages magnetos; megatons
Montagu Gaumont
Montargis sigmatron; stroaming
monte Monet
montem moment
montre mentor; Merton
montres mentors; monster; Ore
  Mtns.
Montrose mesotron
monture mounter; remount
montures mounters; remounts
moo oom
mood doom
moodier moidore
moods dooms; dsomo; Sodom
mool loom
mools looms; sloom
moon mono
mooner Monroe
moons nomos
moonstone monotones

moor Moro; room
Moore Romeo
moored roomed
moorhen hormone
moorhens hormones
mooring rooming
moorings smooring
moors Moros; Ormos; rooms;
  smoor
moos soom
moot toom
mooted toomed
mooting tooming
moots smoot; tooms
mop pom
mope poem; pome
moper proem; Prome
mopers Merops; proems
mopes Epsom; poems; pomes
mopish Ophism
mops poms
mora Omar; roam; Roma
moraines Romanies; Romanise
moral molar
morals molars; morsal
moras Maros; roams
moray mayor
morays mayors
mordant dormant
more omer; Rome
morel L'Orme
Morelia loamier
morels morsel
morendo doormen
mores Moers; morse; omers; smore
morgen monger
morgens mongers
moria Maori; Mario; Moira
moriche Homeric
Moringa roaming
morn norm
Morna manor; Norma; Ramon;
  Roman
mornay romany
morne moner
mornes sermon
morns norms
Moro moor; room
moronic omicron
Moros moors; Ormos; rooms;
  smoor
morose Romeos
morsal molars; morals

morse   Moers; mores; omers;
  smore
morsel   morels
morses   smores
mortise   moister
morts   storm; Troms
mort-safe   foremast
mort-safes   foremasts
mosaics   Moissac
most   mots; toms
Mostar   Martos; stroam; stroma
mot   tom
mote   tome
motel   Metol
motels   molest; St. Elmo
motes   mesto; smote; tomes
motet   motte; totem
motets   mottes; totems
mothers   smother; thermos
motmot   tomtom
motmots   tomtoms
motors   Tromsö
mots   most; toms
motte   motet; totem
mottes   motets; totems
moues   mouse
moulder   remould
mouldered   remoulded
mouldering   remoulding
moulders   remoulds; smoulder
mount   muton; notum
mountaineer   enumeration
mounted   demount
mounter   monture; remount
mounters   montures; remounts
mounts   mutons
Moura   amour
mourn   Munro; Muron
mourned   Dunmore
mouse   moues
moused   soumed; Usedom
mousers   smouser
mousing   souming
mousse   smouse
mousses   smouses
moutan   amount
moutans   amounts
mover   vomer
movers   vomers
mows   sowm
Mt. Siple   limpest; limpets
much   chum
Mucor   mucro

mucro   Mucor
mud-cones   consumed
muddies   dedimus
mudstone   demounts
mug   gum
muggers   smugger
mugs   gums; smug
Mula   alum; maul
mulga   algum; almug; glaum
mulgas   glaums
mumble   bummle
mumbled   bummled
mumbles   bummles
mumbling   bummling
Munda   maund; undam
mundane   unnamed
Mundas   maunds; undams
Munro   mourn; Muron
Munster   sternum
Mur   rum
murage   maugre
mural   larum; rumal
murals   larums; rumals
murder   Red Rum
murdered   demurred
murderer   demurrer
murderers   demurrers
murdering   demurring
murders   smurred
mure   Meru
mured   demur
murena   manure
mures   muser; Remus; serum;
  Sumer
Murex   Rumex
Murghab   Hamburg
muring   ingrum
Muron   mourn; Munro
Mus   sum
Musca   Camus; caums; sumac
muscadin   scandium
muscatel   calumets
Musci   music
muscone   consume
muse   emus; meus
mused   sedum
muser   mures; Remus; serum;
  Sumer
muses   musse
mush   hums
music   Musci
muss   sums
musse   muses

124

mussels sumless
mussier misuser; surmise
must smut; stum; tums
mustard durmast
muster estrum; stumer
musters stumers
muteness tenesmus
mutes Metsu
mutilate ultimate
mutilates stimulate
mutilators stimulator
mutine minuet; minute

mutines minuets; minutes;
  mistune
muton mount; notum
mutons mounts
mutual umlaut
Mya Amy; may; yam
myelon lemony
mygale gamely; gleamy
myna many
myotic comity
Myra army; Mary
myrtle termly

N

na an
nab ban
Nabeul nebula; unable
nabk bank
nabks banks
nabs bans; snab
nache caneh
naches canehs
nacre crane; crena; rance
nacreous carneous
nacrite Catrine; ceratin; certain;
  crinate
nadir dinar; drain; Drina; Indra
nadirs dinars; drains
nae ane; ean; Ena
nag gan
nagged ganged
nagger ganger; grange
naggers gangers; granges
nagging ganging
Nagina angina
nags sang; snag
naiad Aidan; Diana
naïf fain; Ifan
nail anil; lain
nailed Aldine; alined; Daniel;
  Delian; denial; lead-in
nailer en l'air; larine; linear
nailers Linares
nailery inlayer
nailing alining
nails salin; snail
Nair airn; Iran; rain; rani
Nairn Narni
naker anker; Karen; nerka
nakers ankers; Karens
nala Alan; anal; lana

nalas nasal
nalla Allan
nam man; mna
name amen; mane; mean; Mena
nameable amenable
named amend; maned; Medan;
  menad
nameless lameness; maneless;
  salesmen
namely laymen; meanly
namer enarm; Marne
namers enarms
names amens; manes; manse;
  means; Mensa; samen
Namsos masons; Samson
Namur unarm
Nan Ann
nana anan; anna
nanas annas
Nancy canny
nap pan
nape neap; pane
napes aspen; neaps; panes; peans;
  sneap; spane; spean
Napier rapine
Naples panels; planes
napped append
napper parpen
nappers parpens; parsnep;
  snapper
naps pans; snap; span
Nara Aran; rana
narcotism romantics
nard darn; rand
narded dander; darned
narding darning
Nardo radon

nards   darns; rands
nare   Arne; earn; near; Rena
nares   earns; nears; saner; snare
Narew   awner
narghile   nargileh
nargile   aligner; engrail; learing;
   realign; reginal
nargileh   narghile
nark   knar; kran; rank
narked   danker; darken; ranked
narking   ranking
narks   knars; krans; ranks; skran;
   snark
Narni   Nairn
nary   Ryan; yarn
nasal   nalas
Nash   Hans; shan
Nasik   kinas
Nasser   sarsen; snares
nastier   ratines; resiant; retains;
   retinas; retsina; stainer; starnie;
   stearin
nastiest   instates
nastily   saintly
nasty   tansy
nasute   unseat
nasutes   unseats
Nat   ant; tan
natatorium   maturation
natch   chant
natches   chasten
nates   antes; etnas; Nesta; Senta;
   stane; stean; Teans
nation   anoint
nations   anoints; onanist
natively   venality
nativist   visitant
nativists   visitants
natter   ratten
nattered   rattened
nattering   rattening
natters   rattens
nattier   intreat; iterant; nitrate;
   tartine; tertian
nature   aunter; Neutra; tea-urn
natures   aunters; saunter; tea-urns
nautch   chaunt
nave   Evan; Neva; vane; vena
navel   elvan; levan; venal
naves   avens; Evans; Sevan; vanes
navigate   vaginate
nawab   bwana
nawabs   bwanas

Naxos   axons; Saxon
nay   any
nazes   senza
Nazi   azin
Ndola   nodal; Öland
ne   en
neal   élan; lane; lean; Lena
nealed   aneled; leaden; leaned
nealing   aneling; eanling; leaning
neals   lanes; leans; slane
neap   nape; pane
neaped   peaned
neaping   peaning
neaps   aspen; napes; panes; peans;
   sneap; spane; spean
near   Arne; earn; nare; Rena
neared   deaner; Dearne; earned;
   endear
nearer   earner
nearest   earnest; eastern
nearing   earning; engrain; grannie
nearly   anerly
nearness   ensnares
nears   earns; nares; saner; snare
nearside   arsenide
neat   ante; Aten; etna; Tean
neater   entera; rateen
neath   thane
neatherd   adherent
neatherds   adherents
neb   ben
Nebit-Dag   debating
nebris   brines
nebs   bens; sneb
nebula   Nabeul; unable
nebulose   bluenose
Neckar   canker
necks   sneck
necrose   encores
necrotic   concerti
nectar   canter; carnet; creant;
   Cretan; recant; tanrec; trance
nectared   cantered; crenated;
   decanter; recanted
nectarines   transience
nectarous   courtesan; outrances
Ned   den; end
née   e'en
need   dene; Eden
needers   sneered
needless   lessened
needly   Leyden
needs   denes; dense

nef fen
nefast fasten; Stefan
nefs fens
negation Antigone
negativism time-saving
Negev venge
Negro ergon; Genro; goner
Negroes engores
negroid eroding; Gironde; groined;
   ignored; redoing
negroidal girandole; reloading
Negros goners
neif fine; nife
neifs fines
neighed heeding
Neil lien; line; Nile
Neisse in esse; seines
neist inset; set in; stein; tines
neither therein
Neiva avine
neive nieve
neives envies; nieves
nek ken
neks kens
nelies enisle; ensile; senile; Silene
nelis elsin; lenis; liens; lines; Niles;
   silen
Nelly Lleyn
nematoid dominate
nemesis Meissen; misseen;
   siemens
nemoral almoner
nemorous enormous
Neo eon; Noe; one
neon none
neoteric erection
neotropical percolation
nep pen
Nepal panel; penal; plane; plena
neper preen
nepers preens
nephological phenological
nephologist phenologist
nephologists phenologists
nephology phenology
nephric phrenic; pincher
nephrite trephine
nephritis phrenitis
nepotism pimentos
nereid denier; Edirne; reined
nereids deniers
Nerita ratine; retain; retina; Tiranë
nerka anker; Karen; naker

Nero Nore; oner; Orne; Reno; rone
nerol enrol; loner; Lorne
nerval vernal
nervation veination
nerve erven; never; Vener; Verne
nerved Denver; vender; Verden
nerves Nevers; Severn
nerviest reinvest; servient; sirvente
nesh hens
ness Sens
nest nets; sent; sten; tens
Nesta antes; etnas; nates; Senta;
   stane; stean; Teans
nested sedent; tensed
nester enters; Ernest; rentes;
   resent; Sterne; tenser; ternes
nesters resents
nesting tensing
Neston nonets; sonnet; stonen;
   tenons; tenson; tonnes
Nestos onsets; setons; sets on;
   stones
nests stens
net ten
nete eten; teen; tene
nether threne
nets nest; sent; sten; tens
nett tent
netted detent; tented
netting tenting
netty tenty
Neuquen unqueen
neural ulnare; unreal
neurosis resinous
Neuse ensue
Neustadt unstated; untasted
Neustria urinates
neuter retune; tenure; tureen
neuters retunes; tenures; tureens
Neutra aunter; nature; tea-urn
neutral Renault
Neva Evan; nave; vane; vena
never erven; nerve; Vener; Verne
Nevers nerves; Severn
Neves evens; seven
Nevis veins; vines; visne
new wen
Newark wanker
newish whines
new rich wincher
New Ross worsens
news sewn; wens
newt went

Ney yen
Ngami gamin
Nias anis; Isna; Nisa; sain; Sian
Niassa Asians
nib bin
nibs bins; snib
Nicastro cast-iron
niceness incenses
nicer crine
nicest incest; insect; scient
niche chine
niched chined; inched
niches chines; chinse; inches
niching chining; inching
nickels slicken
nickers snicker
nicks snick
Nicol Colin
Nicole cineol
nicotian inaction
nictate tetanic
nid din; Ind
nide dine; Enid
nidget tinged
nidor Rodin
nidus Indus
niello lionel; O'Neill
niellos lionels
nieve neive
nieves envies; neives
Nièvre envier
nife fine; neif
niffs sniff
Nigde deign
Nigel Elgin; ingle; ligne
Niger reign; renig
Niger Dam dreaming; margined;
   mid-range
niggard grading
nigger ginger
niggers gingers; snigger
niggle gingle
niggled gelding
niggles gingles; sniggle
nigh hing
night thing
nightcap patching
nightless lightness
night-robe bothering
nights things
nigrescent centerings; centreings
Nike kine
nil lin

Nile lien; line; Neil
Niles elsin; lenis; liens; lines; nelis;
   silen
nilgai ailing
nilgais sailing
nim Min
Nimes mines
nines Ennis
ninety-seven seventy-nine
ninety-six sixty-nine
Ningbo boning
niobic bionic
nip pin
Nipa pain; piña
Nipigon opining
nippers snipper
nips pins; snip; spin
nipter Pinter; pterin
nis ins; sin
Nisa anis; Isna; Nias; sain; Sian
nisse sines
nit tin
Nith hint; thin
Nitra intra; riant; train; Trani
nitrate intreat; iterant; nattier;
   tartine; tertian
nitrates intreats; straiten; tartines
nitre inert; inter; Terni; trine
nitric citrin
nits tins
nival Alvin; anvil; Vilna
niveous envious; veinous
nixy iynx
no on
nob bon
Nobel noble
noble Nobel
noblesse boneless
nobs bos'n; snob
nock conk
nocked conked
nocking conking
nocks conks
nod don
nodal Ndola; Öland
nodate atoned; donate
nodder droned
node done
nodes nosed; sonde
no dice codein; coined
nodose noosed
nods dons; snod
nodule louden; Oundle**

nodules loudens
nodus sound
Noe eon; Neo; one
Noel enol; leno; Leon; lone
noes Enos; eons; nose; ones;
    sone
noesis enosis; essoin; noises;
    ossein; sonsie
noetic notice
nogs snog; song
noil lino; lion; loin
noils linos; lions; loins
noise eosin
noised donsie; Edison; onside;
    side-on
noiseless lionesses
noises enosis; essoin; noesis;
    ossein; sonsie
Nola Laon; loan
nomad Damon; monad
nomade daemon; Menado;
    moaned; Modane; Modena
nomades daemons; monades
nomadic monacid; monadic
nomads damson; monads
nomarch monarch
nomarchies monarchies;
    monarchise
nomarchs monarchs
nomarchy monarchy
nome meno; omen
nomes meson; omens
nominates Minnesota
nomism monism
nomistic monistic
nomogram monogram
nomograms monograms
nomos moons
none neon
nonesuch unchosen
nonet tenon; tonne
nonets Neston; sonnet; stonen;
    tenons; tenson; tonnes
non-glare Algernon
Nono noon
non-U noun
nooks snook
noon Nono
noosed nodose
nope open; peon; pone
nor Ron
Nora Arno; Oran; roan; Rona
Norah Rhona

Nore Nero; oner; Orne; Reno; rone
norm morn
Norma manor; Morna; Ramon;
    Roman
normal Marlon
Normandy monandry
norms morns
Norse noser; oners; rones; Ronse;
    Señor; seron; snore
north thorn
northed thorned; throned
norther horrent
northing thorning; throning
norths thorns
North Sea Sheraton
nos. son
nose Enos; eons; noes; ones; sone
nosed nodes; sonde
noseless soleness
noser Norse; oners; rones; Ronse;
    Señor; seron; snore
nosers Señors; sensor; serons;
    snores
noses sones; sonse
nosier senior; soneri
nostalgia analogist
not ton
notal talon; tolan; tonal
notarial rational
notarially rationally
notaries Señorita
notary aroynt
note Eton; tone
Notec cento; conte
noted Donet; toned
noteless toneless
noter tenor; trone
noters Reston; stoner; tenors;
    tensor; Terson; trones
notes Eston; onset; seton; stone;
    Tenos; tones
not-I into
notice noetic
noticer Citroen
notices section
noting toning
Noto onto; oont; toon
Notre Dame emendator
notum mount; muton
noughts gunshot; shotgun
noun non-U
noup Puno; upon
nous onus

nova Avon
Nova Scotia avocations
novel Venlo; Vlonë
novels sloven
now own; won
nowed endow; owned; Woden
nowhere Erewhon; whereon
Nowra rowan
nowt town; wont
noy yon
Nsanje Jansen
nub bun
nubs buns; snub
nuchal launch; unchal
nuclear lucarne; unclear
nuclide include

nuclides includes; unsliced
nude dune; unde
nudes dunes
nudges snudge
nudity untidy
numerals mensural
nuns sunn
nur run; urn
nurled rundle
nurs runs; urns
nurse runes
nursed sunder
nut tun
nuts stun; tuns; Unst
nutters entrust; test run
nuzzles snuzzle

O

oafs sofa
oak koa; oka
oaks koas; okas; soak
oaky kayo; okay
oar ora
oared adore; oread
oaring ignaro; origan
oarless lassoer
oars Oras; osar; Rosa; soar; sora
oast oats; Sato; stoa; Taos
oasts assot; stoas; Tasso
oat Tao
oaten Aneto; atone; Onate
oaths Athos; hoast; hosta; shoat
oats oast; Sato; stoa; Taos
ob bo
obang Gabon
obdurate taboured
Obed bode
obelus blouse; boules
Oberland banderol
Oberon Borneo
obeying biogeny
obeys syboe
obit bito
oblast bloats
oblate lobate
oblation lobation
obligant bloating; bog-Latin
oboes boose
Obok boko; book
observe obverse; verbose
obsess bosses

obsigns bossing
obtainer baritone
obtainers baritones
obtains bastion
obtested besotted
obtesting besotting
obtrude doubter; outbred; redoubt
obtrudes doubters; redoubts
obturate tabouret
obturates tabourets
obverse observe; verbose
ocarina Aaronic
ocean canoe
oceanic cocaine
oceans canoes
ocellated decollate
ocelli collie
ocelots coolest
ochery ochrey
ochre chore
ochrea chorea; Horace; orache
ochres chores; cosher
ochrey ochery
ocrea Corea
Octan acton; canto; cotan
octane at once
octanes costean
Octans actons; cantos
octave avocet
octaves avocets
octillion cotillion
octillions cotillions
octuple couplet

octuples couplets
od do
odal alod; load
odaliques odalisque
odalisque odaliques
odals alods; loads
odd dod
Odda dado
odder roded
odds dods
ode Deo; doe
Odeon Doone
Oder doer; Doré; re-do; rode; roed
odes does; dose
odic Icod
Odin Dino
odism misdo
odorant donator; tornado
Odra Dora; road
odyle yodel; yodle
o'er ore; roe
oestrus estrous; ousters; sourest;
  souters; tousers; trouses; tussore
offset set-off
offsets set-offs
ogle loge
ogled loged
ogles loges; segol
ogre ergo; goer; gore
ogres goers; gores; gorse; Sergo;
  soger
ogress sogers
oh ho
ohm mho
ohmage homage
ohms mhos
oho hoo
Ohre hero; hoer; rheo
oiler Loire; oriel
oilers elisor; lories; oriels; Serlio
oiliness lionises
oil-lamp oil-palm; palm-oil
oil-lamps oil-palms
oilman Molina; monial
oilmen moline
oil-palm oil-lamp; palm-oil
oil-palms oil-lamps
oil-press spoilers
oils Lois; silo; soil; soli
oilstone looniest
oka koa; oak
okas koas; oaks; soak
okay kayo; oaky

okayed kayoed
okaying kayoing
okays kayos
okes Keos; skeo; soke
Olaf foal; loaf
Öland Ndola; nodal
Olav oval; vola
old age age-old; gaoled
older drôle
old man almond; dolman
old men dolmen
Olean alone
oleander reloaned
olent lento; Olten
oleo Looe
oleos loose; soole
Olga gaol; goal
olid idol; lido; Lodi
Olinda Ladino; laid on
olingo looing
olingos loosing; sooling
Oliva viola
olivaceous violaceous
olive voile
olives solive
olivet violet
olivets violets
Olivier rilievo
olpe lope; Opel; pole
olpes elops; lopes; poles; slope
Olt lot
Olten lento; olent
Oman Amon; moan; mona
Omar mora; roam; Roma
ombre brome
ombú umbo
ombús umbos
omen meno; nome
omens meson; nomes
omer more; Rome
omers Moers; mores; morse; smore
omicron moronic
omits moist
omneity omniety
omniety omneity
on no
onager Gerona; orange
onagers oranges
onanism mansion
onanist anoints; nations
Onate Aneto; atone; oaten
once cone
oncer Creon; crone

oncers censor; crones
oncoming gnomonic
ondine done in
ondines Denison
one eon; Neo; Noe
Onega agone; Genoa
O'Neill lionel; niello
on-end Donne; end-on
oner Nero; Nore; Orne; Reno; rone
oners Norse; noser; rones; Ronse;
  Señor; seron; snore
ones Enos; eons; noes; nose; sone
Ongar argon; groan; orang; organ
oniric ironic
only Lyon
onrush Hurons
onset Eston; notes; seton; stone;
  Tenos; tones
onsets Nestos; setons; sets on;
  stones
onside donsie; Edison; noised;
  side-on
onst snot; tons
onstead donates
on tap panto
Ontario oration
on the sly honestly
onto Noto; oont; toon
onus nous
onward draw on
onwards draws on
oodles loosed; sooled
oom moo
oons soon
oont Noto; onto; toon
op Po
opal Pola
opals Palos
op art porta; Prato
ope Poe
oped dope
Opel lope; olpe; pole
open nope; peon; pone
opened depone
opener perone; reopen; repone
openers perones; reopens; repones
opens peons; pones; Posen; snoep
operand padrone; pandore
operands padrones; pandores; San
  Pedro; Sarpedon
operant Paterno; pronate; protean
operants Paterson; pronates
operas Pesaro

operates protease
operating orange-tip
operator poor-rate
operators poor-rates
operettas poetaster
opes epos; peso; pose
Ophism mopish
opining Nipigon
Opole Poole
opposer propose
opposers proposes
oppressor proposers
oppugn pop-gun
oppugns pop-guns
ops pos; sop
opt pot; top
optant Patton
opted depot; poted; toped
optic picot; topic
optical Capitol; coal-pit; pit-coal;
  topical
optically topically
optics picots; topics
opting poting; toping
option potion
options potions
optology topology
opts post; pots; spot; stop; tops
Opuntia Utopian
opus soup
opuscle close-up; couples; upclose
ora oar
orach roach
orache chorea; Horace; ochrea
oraches roaches
orachs Cahors
oracle Carole; coaler
oracles coalers; escolar; solacer
orals soral
Oran Arno; Nora; roan; Rona
orang argon; groan; Ongar; organ
orange Gerona; onager
oranges onagers
orange-tip operating
orangs groans; organs; Sargon;
  sarong
orant toran; trona
Oras oars; osar; Rosa; soar; sora
orate Erato
orating tragion
oration Ontario
oratress assertor; roasters
orb bor; rob

orbed   bored; robed
orbing   boring; robing
orbited   debitor
orbits   bistro
urbs   robs; sorb
orc   cor; roc
Orca   arco; Cora; Roca
orcein   coiner; orcine
orchestra   cart-horse
orchestras   cart-horses
orchis   choirs
orcine   coiner; orcein
orcs   cors; rocs
Orcus   scour
ord   dor; rod
ordain   Dorian; inroad
ordainer   reordain
ordainers   reordains
ordains   inroads
ordeal   Laredo; loader; reload
ordeals   loaders; reloads; sea-lord
orderer   reorder
orderers   reorders
orderless   solderers
orders   dorser
ordinals   Rosalind
ordinate   deration; rationed;
   Rodentia
ordo   door; rood
Ordos   doors; roods; sordo
ords   dors; rods; sord
Ordu   dour; duro
ordure   dourer
ore   o'er; roe
oread   adore; oared
oreads   adores; soared
Oregon   orgone
Orel   eorl; lore; orle; role
Ore Mtns.   mentors; monster;
   montres
ores   Eros; roes; rose; sore
Orestes   osseter
Öresund   resound; sounder;
   undoers
orfe   fore
organ   argon; groan; Ongar; orang
organdies   grandiose; organised
organise   origanes
organised   grandiose; organdies
organist   roasting
organs   groans; orangs; Sargon;
   sarong
orgeat   Tagore

orgone   Oregon
orgue   rogue; rouge
orgues   grouse; rogues; rouges;
   rugose
orgy   gory; Györ
oriel   Loire; oiler
oriels   elisor; lories; oilers; Serlio
oriental   relation
Orientals   Orleanist; relations
orientating   integration
orients   in store; stonier; triones
origan   ignaro; oaring
origane   Iron Age
origanes   organise
Origen   eringo; ignore; region
Orkneys   Yonkers
Orlando   lardoon
orle   eorl; lore; Orel; role
Orleanist   Orientals; relations
orleans   loaners; reloans; Salerno
orles   eorls; Leros; loser; Osler;
   roles; soler; Sorel
Ormos   moors; Moros; rooms;
   smoor
ornate   atoner
Orne   Nero; Nore; oner; Reno; rone
ornis   inros; irons; rosin
orphan   harp on
orphans   harps on
Orpheus   shore up
orpine   Pinero; rope in
orpines   ropes in
orpins   prison
orra   roar
Orrell   roller
orsellic   colliers
Orsha   Horsa
ort   rot; tor
Orta   rota; taro; Tora
Ortegal   gloater; legator
Orton   Troon
orts   rots; sort; tors
os   so
osar   oars; Oras; Rosa; soar; sora
Osbert   sorbet; strobe
Oscars   across
oscillation   colonialist
oscillations   colonialists
oscine   conies; cosine
Oscines   cession; cosines
osculate   lacteous
Ösel   lose; sloe; sole
osier   Rosie; Siero

Osler eorls; Leros; loser; orles;
 roles; soler; Sorel
Oslo loos; solo
Osman mason; moans; monas
Osmanli malison; Soliman
Osmanlis malisons
osmiate atomies; atomise
osmiates atomises
ossein enosis; essoin; noesis;
 noises; sonsie
osseter Orestes
osteal Lao-tse
Ostend doesn't; Donets; stoned
ostent Totnes
ostents stetson; St. Neots
ostler sterol
ostlers sterols
ostracon cartoons; corantos
ostrich chorist
other throe
others Rothes; throes; tosher
otherwise white rose
Otho hoot; toho
Otsu oust; outs
ottar tarot
otters Troste
Otto toot
ouch chou
ouches chouse
Oud duo; udo
ought tough
ounce Cuneo
Oundle louden; nodule
ours sour
ousel louse; Seoul
ousels louses; soleus
oust Otsu; outs
ousted toused
ouster outers; routes; souter;
 touser; trouse
ousters estrous; oestrus; sourest;
 souters; tousers; trouses; tussore
ousting outings; tousing
outbreak break out
outbreaking breaking out
outbreaks breaks out
outbred doubter; obtrude; redoubt
outbroke broke out
outcast cast out
outcasts casts out
outcome come out
outcomes comes out
outcried cried out

outcries citreous; cries out
outcry cry out
outcrying congruity; crying out
outdare read-out
outdares read-outs
outer outré; route; Touré
outers ouster; routes; souter;
 touser; trouse
outfall fallout
outings ousting; tousing
outline elution
outlook lookout
outlooked looked out
outlooking looking out
outlooks lookouts; looks out
outrances courtesan; nectarous
outré outer; route; Touré
outred detour; douter; red out;
 routed; toured
outreds detours; dourest; douters;
 rousted
outride étourdi
outrides outsider
outs Otsu; oust
outsell sell-out
outsells sell-outs
outside tedious
outsider outrides
outspring posturing; sprouting
outstep toupets
outwear outwears
outwears outswear
outwith without
outwork work-out
oval Olav; vola
ovals salvo
ovates avoset
ovenbird bind over
ovenbirds binds over
over rove
overacts overcast
overbusy overbuys
overbuys overbusy
overcast overacts
overdoes overdose
overdose overdoes
overgo groove
overhang hangover
overhangs hangovers
overland rondavel
overlay layover
overlays layovers
overlie relievo

overpass Passover
overpassed eavesdrops; passed
  over
overpost overtops
overrated overtrade
overs roves; Serov; servo; verso
overset estover
overspin provines
overt trove; voter
overtops overpost
overtower overwrote
overtrade overrated
overture trouvère
overtures trouvères
overturn turnover
overturns turnovers
overwrote overtower
Ovid void
owe woe
Owen enow
ower owre; wore
owers serow; sower; swore; worse
owes woes

owl low
owler lower; rowel
owlers lowers; rowels; slower
owlery lowery
owlet towel
owlets Elstow; lowest; towels
owls lows; slow; sowl
own now; won
owned endow; nowed; Woden
owner rowen
owners rowens; worsen
owns snow; sown
owre ower; wore
oxen exon
oxers Sorex
oxhead hoaxed
oyer yore
oyez Yezo
oyster rosety; storey; Troyes;
  tyroes; Yes Tor
oysters storeys
Oz zo

P

pacable capable
pace cape
paced caped
pacer caper; crape; recap
pacers capers; Casper; crapes;
  escarp; parsec; recaps; scrape;
  spacer
paces capes; Caspe; scape; space
pacing caping
packer repack
packers repacks
pack-ice icepack
paction caption; Pontiac
pactioned captioned
pactioning captioning
pactions captions
pad dap
padang pad-nag
padangs pad-nags
padder draped; parded; Praded
pad-nag padang
pad-nags padangs
padre drape; pared; raped; repad
padres drapes; parsed; rasped;
  repads; spared; spread
padrone operand; pandore

padrones operands; pandores; San
  Pedro; Sarpedon
pads daps
Pag gap
pagan panga
pagans pangas
page gape; peag
paged gaped
pages gapes; Gaspé
paging gaping
pah hap
Pai pia
paidle aliped; elapid; Pleiad
paidles alipeds; elapids; lapides;
  palsied; Pleiads
paik pika
paiks pikas
pail Lipa; Pali; pila
paillasse palliasse
paillasses palliasses
pails lapis; spial
pain Nipa; piña
painless spaniels
pains piñas; Spain; spina
paint inapt; patin; pinta
painted patined

painter Patenir; pertain; pine-tar;
  repaint
painters pantries; Parentis;
  pertains; pinaster; repaints
paintress pinasters
paints patins; pintas; ptisan
paired diaper; pardie; repaid
pairs Ispra; Paris; Parsi
pais Apis; Pias; Pisa
pal alp; lap
pale leap; peal; pela; plea
paled pedal; plead
paler lepra; parle; pearl; repla
pales Elaps; lapse; leaps; peals;
  pleas; salep; sepal; spale; speal
palest palets; pastel; petals; plates;
  pleats; septal; staple
Palestine penalties
palet leapt; lepta; pelta; petal; plate;
  pleat
palets palest; pastel; petals; plates;
  pleats; septal; staple
palette peltate
Pali Lipa; pail; pila
palings lapsing; sapling
palliasse paillasse
palliasses paillasses
palls spall
palm lamp
palmary palmyra
palmated date-palm
palmed lamped
palmer ampler; Marple
palmers Marples; sampler
Palmerston emplastron
palmette template
palmettes templates
palmier impearl; lempira
palmiest implates; palmiets;
  petalism; septimal
palmiet implate
palmiets implates; palmiest;
  petalism; septimal
palming lamping
palmists psalmist
palm-oil oil-lamp; oil-palm
palms lamps; plasm; psalm
palm-tree Lampeter
palm-trees emplaster
palmy amply
palmyra palmary
Palos opals
palp Lapp; plap

palped dapple; lapped
palping lapping
palps Lapps; plaps
palpus slap-up
pals Alps; laps; salp; slap
palsied alipeds; elapids; lapides;
  paidles; Pleiads
palsy plays; splay
palsying splaying
palter plater
palterers plasterer
palters per-salt; plaster; platers;
  psalter; Spartel; stapler
paltry partly
paly play
pam amp; map
pamper mapper
pampers mappers
pams amps; maps; samp; spam
pan nap
pance pecan
pances pecans
pander repand
pandoors spadroon
pandore operand; padrone
pandores operands; padrones; San
  Pedro; Sarpedon
pandy Pydna
pane nape; neap; pean
panel Nepal; penal; plane; plena
panels Naples; planes
panes aspen; napes; neaps; peans;
  sneap; spane; spean
panga pagan
pangas pagans
pangs spang
panicle capelin; pelican
panicles capelins; pelicans
panics panisc
panisc panics
pans naps; snap; span
panted pedant; pentad
panter arpent; enrapt; entrap;
  parent; trepan
panters arpents; entraps; parents;
  pastern; trepans
panther Penarth
panties patines; sapient; spinate
pantiles plainest
pantine pinnate
pantler planter; replant
pantlers planters; replants
panto on tap

pantries painters; Parentis; pertains; pinaster; repaints
papal appal
papers sapper
papery prepay
par Arp; rap
parables sparable
parades aspread
paradise Sparidae
parasite aspirate; septaria
parasites aspirates; satrapies
parcel carpel; placer
parcels carpels; clasper; placers; scalper
parcheesi eparchies
parchesi seraphic
pard drap; prad
parded draped; padder; Praded
pardie diaper; paired; repaid
pards draps; prads
pare pear; Pera; rape; reap
pared drape; padre; raped; repad
parent arpent; enrapt; entrap; panter; trepan
parental paternal; prenatal
Parentis painters; pantries; pertains; pinaster; repaints
parents arpents; entraps; panters; pastern; trepans
parers parser; rasper; sparer
pares asper; parse; pears; prase; presa; rapes; reaps; spaer; spare; spear
paresis aspires; praises; Serapis
parge gaper; grape
parges gapers; gasper; grapes; sparge
paries aspire; Persia; praise
paring raping
parings parsing; rasping; sparing
Paris Ispra; pairs; Parsi
parish Hispar; raphis; Shairp
parkas Kaspar
parks spark
parle lepra; paler; pearl; repla
parled pedlar
parles pearls
parley pearly; player; replay
parleyed replayed
parleying replaying
parleys parsley; players; replays; sparely
Parmesan spearman

parodic picador
parol polar
paroled leopard
paroles reposal
Paros proas; psora; sapor; sopra
parpen napper
parpens nappers; parsnep; snapper
parried drapier
parries praiser; rapiers; raspier; repairs
parrot raptor
parroted predator; prorated; tear-drop
parroting prorating
parrots raptors
parse asper; pares; pears; prase; presa; rapes; reaps; spaer; spare; spear
parsec capers; Casper; crapes; escarp; pacers; recaps; scrape; spacer
parsecs escarps; scrapes; spacers
parsed drapes; padres; rasped; repads; spared; spread
Parsees asperse
parser parers; rasper; sparer
parsers raspers; sparers; sparser
parses aspers; passer; repass; spaers; spares; sparse; spears
Parsi Ispra; pairs; Paris
parsing parings; rasping; sparing
parsley parleys; players; replays; sparely
parsnep nappers; parpens; snapper
parsneps snappers
parson aprons; Prosna
part prat; rapt; trap
parted depart; petard; prated; traped
parter prater
parters praters
parti atrip; tapir
partial patrial
partialism patrialism
parties piastre; pirates; praties; traipse
parting gin trap; prating; traping
partisan aspirant
partisans aspirants
partite tear-pit
partitioned trepidation

partlet platter; prattle
partlets platters; prattles; splatter; sprattle
partly paltry
parts prats; spart; sprat; strap; traps
party praty
parure uprear
parures uprears
parvis Privas
pas asp; sap; spa
Pasch chaps
pash haps; hasp; Shap
pashed hasped; phased; shaped
pashes phases; shapes
pashim mishap
pashing hasping; phasing; shaping
Pashto pathos; potash
paspy sappy
pass asps; saps; spas
passé apses; spaes
passed sepads; spades
passed over eavesdrops; overpassed
passer aspers; parses; repass; spaers; spares; sparse; spears
Passeres asperses; repasses
passive pavises
passman sampans
Passover overpass
past pats; spat; stap; taps
paste pates; septa; spate; speat; tapes
pasted adepts
pastel palest; palets; petals; plates; pleats; septal; staple
pastels staples
paster paters; Praest; prates; repast; tapers; trapes
pastern arpents; entraps; panters; parents; trepans
pasters repasts
pastes spates; speats; stapes
Pasteur pasture
pastime impaste
pastimes impastes
pastor asport; portas; sap-rot
pastors asports
pastries piastres; raspiest; Tarsipes; traipses
pasts spats; staps
pasture Pasteur
pasty patsy; pyats

pat apt; tap
Patarine Tarpeian
patcher chapter
patchers chapters
patches hep-cats
patchier chapiter; phreatic
patching nightcap
pate peat; tape
pated adept; taped
paten tapen
Patenir painter; pertain; pine-tar; repaint
patent patten
patented pattened
patents pattens
pater apert; peart; Petra; prate; taper; trape
paternal parental; prenatal
Paterno operant; pronate; protean
paternoster penetrators
paters paster; Praest; prates; repast; tapers; trapes
Paterson operants; pronates
pates paste; septa; spate; speat; tapes
path Ptah
pathos Pashto; potash
patin inapt; paint; pinta
patined painted
patines panties; sapient; spinate
patins paints; pintas; ptisan
patly aptly
patness aptness
Patras satrap; Sparta
patrial partial
patrialism partialism
patrol portal
patrols portals
patron tarpon
patroness transpose
pats past; spat; stap; taps
patsy pasty; pyats
patten patent
pattened patented
pattens patents
patterns transept
patters spatter; tapster
Patti Pitta
pattles peltast
Patton optant
Paul Pula
paves Vespa
pavid vapid

138

pavise spavie
pavises passive
paw wap
pawls spawl
pawner enwrap
pawners enwraps; spawner
pawns spawn
paws spaw; swap; waps; wasp
pay pya; yap
payer apery; Peary; repay
payers repays; speary
pays spay; yaps
pea ape
peach chape; cheap
peachers preaches; sea-perch
peag gape; page
peaks spake; speak
peal leap; pale; pela; plea
pealed leaped
pealing leaping
peals Elaps; lapse; leaps; pales;
    pleas; salep; sepal; spale; speal
pean nape; neap; pane
peaned neaped
peaning neaping
peans aspen; napes; neaps; panes;
    sneap; spane; spean
pear pare; Pera; rape; reap
pearl lepra; paler; parle; repla
pearled pleader
pearlers relapser
pearlies espalier
pearlin plainer; praline
pearls parles
pearly parley; player; replay
pears asper; pares; parse; prase;
    presa; rapes; reaps; spaer; spare;
    spear
peart apert; pater; Petra; prate;
    taper; trape
pear-tree repartee; repeater
pear-trees repeaters
Peary apery; payer; repay
peas apes; apse; spae
peasant anapest
peasants anapests
peat pate; tape
pecan pance
pecans pances
peches cheeps; speech
Pechora poacher
pecks speck
Pecos copes; copse; scope

pecs spec
pectin incept
pectins incepts; inspect
peculator opcculate
peculation unpoetical
peculations speculation
peculators speculator
pedal paled; plead
pedals lapsed; pleads
pedant panted; pentad
pedantries pedestrian
pedants pentads
pederast predates; trapesed
pedesis despise
pedestrian pedantries
pedicel pedicle
pedicels pedicles
pedicle pedicel
pedicles pedicels
pedlar parled
pedro doper; pored; roped
pedros dopers; prosed
peds sped
peed deep
peek keep; peke
peeking keeping
peeks keeps; pekes; Speke
peel Pele
peelers sleeper; speeler
peelings sleeping; speeling
peels sleep; speel
peened deepen
peer pree
peered deeper; De Pere
peering preeing
peerless sleepers; speelers
peers perse; prees; prese; speer;
    spree
pees seep
peke keep; peek
pekes keeps; peeks; Speke
Pekin Penki
pela leap; pale; peal; plea
Pelagians Pelasgian
Pelasgian Pelagians
Pele peel
pelican capelin; panicle
pelicans capelins; panicles
Pella lapel
pells spell
pelma ample; maple
pelmet temple
pelmets stempel; stemple; temples

peloids despoil; diploes; dipoles; soliped; spoiled
Pelops peplos
pelorism implores; sperm-oil
pelta leapt; lepta; palet; petal; plate; pleat
peltast pattles
peltate palette
pelter petrel
pelters petrels; spelter
peltries epistler; reptiles
peltry pertly
pelts slept; spelt
pen nep
penal Nepal; panel; plane; plena
penalties Palestine
Penarth panther
penates pesante
pencils splenic
pended depend
pends spend
pendular uplander
penetrant repentant
penetrators paternoster
penial alpine; Epinal; pineal
penis pines; snipe; spine
Penistone stone-pine
Penki Pekin
pensil Pilsen; spinel; spline
pensils spinels; splines
pentad panted; pedant
pentads pedants
peon nope; open; pone
peonism impones
peons opens; pones; Posen; snoep
peopling popeling
pepla appel; apple
peplos Pelops
peplus supple
pepo pope
pepos popes
Pepsi-Cola episcopal
per rep
Pera pare; pear; rape; reap
percale replace
percase Caprese; escaper
percept precept
perceptive preceptive
percepts precepts
percolation neotropical
percuss spruces
percussion supersonic

perdu drupe; duper; Dupré; prude; pured
perdues perused
perdus drupes; dupers; prudes; pursed
perfect prefect
perfects prefects
perform preform
performed preformed
performing preforming
performs preforms
peri pier; ripe
pericopes periscope
peril piler; plier
perils lisper; Perlis; pilers; pliers
Perim prime
period dopier
peripatetic precipitate
periplus supplier
perique re-equip; repique
peris épris; piers; pries; prise; ripes; speir; spire
periscope pericopes
perish reship; seriph
perished hesperid; shred-pie
peristome temporise
peristomes temporises
Perlis lisper; perils; pilers; pliers
perlite reptile
permeating impregnate
permissibility impressibility
permissible impressible
permission impression
permissive impressive
permissively impressively
permissiveness impressiveness
permits imprest
permitter pretermit
permitters pretermits
perms sperm
Pernod ponder
Peron prone
perone opener; reopen; repone
perones openers; reopens; repones
per pro proper
perries reprise; respire
perry pryer; ryper
per-salt palters; plaster; platers; psalter; Spartel; stapler
per-salts plasters; psalters; staplers
perse peers; prees; prese; speer; spree
Perseid predies; preside; speired

Perseids despiser; disperse; presides
Perseus peruses
Persia aspire; paries; praise
Persic cripes; precis; prices; spicer
persico copiers
Persism impress; premiss; simpers
persist priests; sprites; stirpes; stripes
persistent prettiness
persisting springiest
person prones
personate Esperanto
perstringe estreping; pestering; Presteign
pertain painter; Patenir; pine-tar; repaint
pertains painters; pantries; Parentis; pinaster; repaints
pertinacity antipyretic
pertly peltry
pertness presents; serpents
pertuse reputes
pertusion eruptions
Peru puer; pure
perusal serpula
peruse purées; rupees
perused perdues
perusers pressure
peruses Perseus
pervade deprave
pervaded depraved
pervades depraves
pervading depraving
perverse preserve
pervert Prévert
pervious previous; viperous
Pesah heaps; phase; shape
pesante penates
Pesaro operas
peso epos; opes; pose
pesos poses; posse; speos
pest pets; sept; step
pester peters; preset
pestered estreped
pestering estreping; perstinge; Presteign
pesters presets
pests septs; steps
Pétain pineta
petal leapt; lepta; palet; pelta; plate; pleat
petaline tapeline

petalism implates; palmiest; palmiets; septimal
petals palest; palets; pastel; plates; pleats; septal; staple
petard depart; parted; prated; traped
petards departs
peter petre
peters pester; preset
petitioner repetition
Petra apert; pater; peart; prate; taper; trape
petre peter
petrel pelter
petrels pelters; spelter
petri piert; tripe
petrochemical cephalometric
petrography typographer
petrosal prolates
petrous posture; pouters; Proteus; septuor; spouter; troupes
pets pest; sept; step
pews spew
phaetons Stanhope; Stephano
phanerogam anemograph
phare hepar; raphe
phares phrase; raphes; seraph; shaper; Sherpa; sphaer
Pharisees apheresis
phase heaps; Pesah; shape
phased hasped; pashed; shaped
phases pashes; shapes
phasing hasping; pashing; shaping
phasmid dampish
pheers herpes; Hesper; sphere
phenological nephological
phenologist nephologist
phenologists nephologists
phenology nephology
pheon phone
pheons phones
phese sheep
phi hip
philter philtre
philters philtres
philtre philter
philtres philters
phoca poach
pholades asphodel
phonautographs anthropophagus
phone pheon
phones pheons
phonetics Ctesiphon

phonic chopin
phonics chopins
phonogram monograph
phonograms monographs
phrase phares; raphes; seraph;
   shaper; Sherpa; sphaer
phrased sharped
phraser harpers; sharper
phrasers sharpers
phrases seraphs; shapers; Sherpas;
   sphaers
phrasing sharping
phreatic chapiter; patchier
phrenic nephric; pincher
phrenitis nephritis
physic scyphi
pia Pai
Pias Apis; pais; Pisa
piastre parties; pirates; praties;
   traipse
piastres pastries; raspiest; Tarsipes;
   traipses
picador parodic
picadors sporadic
picas aspic; Capis; spica
pice epic
picker ripeck
pickers ripecks
pickets skeptic
pickler prickle
picklers prickles
picks spick
picot optic; topic
picoté poetic
picots optics; topics
picrates crispate; practise
Picton Pontic
picture cuprite
piecer pierce; recipe
piecers pierces; precise; recipes
pieces specie
piece-work workpiece
piend pined
piends sniped; spined
pier peri; ripe
pierce piecer; recipe
pierces piecers; precise; recipes
piers épris; peris; pries; prise; ripes;
   speir; spire
piert petri; tripe
pies pisé; sipe
piets piste; spite; stipe
pig gip

pigeon epigon
pigeons epigons
pigs gips
pigskin spiking
pigsny spying
pika paik
pikas paiks
pike kepi; kipe
pikelets spikelet
pikes kepis; kipes; Pisek; spike
pila Lipa; pail; Pali
Pilar April; prial
pilaster plaister; plaiters
pilastered plaistered
pilasters plaisters
Pilate aplite
pileate epilate
pileated depilate; epilated
piled lepid; plied
piler peril; plier
pilers lisper; perils; Perlis; pliers
piles plies; slipe; spiel; spile
pillagers aspergill
pillages spillage
pills spill
pilots pistol; postil; spoilt
Pilsen pensil; spinel; spline
pilules pullies
piment pitmen
pimento emption
pimentos nepotism
pin nip
piña Nipa; pain
piñas pains; Spain; spina
pinaster painters; pantries;
   Parentis; pertains; repaints
pinasters paintress
pincase icepans; inscape
pincer prince
pincers Crespin; princes
pincher nephric; phrenic
pinchers pinscher
pinches sphenic
pineal alpine; Epinal; penial
pined piend
Pinero orpine; rope in
pines penis; snipe; spine
pineta Pétain
pine-tar painter; Patenir; pertain;
   repaint
pingers springe
pingle pin-leg
pingles pin-legs; spignel

pink gin kingpin; pinking
pink gins kingpins
pinking kingpin; pink gin
pinks Pinsk; spink
pin-leg pingle
pin legs pingles; spignel
pinnate pantine
pinners spinner
pins nips; snip; spin
Pinsk pinks; spink
pinscher pinchers
pinta inapt; paint; patin
pintails alpinist
pintas paints; patins; ptisan
Pinter nipter; pterin
pintles plenist
pinto piton; point; Ponti; potin
pintos piston; pitons; points
piny pyin
piolets pistole; Ploesti
pipers sipper
pique equip
piques equips
Piraeus spuriae; upraise
Piran Pirna
pirate pratie; pteria
pirated diptera
pirates parties; piastre; praties; traipse
piratically capillarity
Pirna Piran
pirnies inspire; spinier
pirogue groupie
pirogues groupies
Pisa Apis; pais; Pias
piscator apricots
pisces spices
pisé pies; sipe
Pisek kepis; kipes; pikes; spike
pish hips; ship
pismires misprise
piss sips
pisses sepsis; speiss
piste piets; spite; stipe
pistes spites; stipes
pistol pilots; postil; spoilt
pistole piolets; Ploesti
pistols postils
piston pintos; pitons; points
pit tip
pitchers spitcher
pit-coal Capitol; coal-pit; optical; topical

pith hipt
pitmen piment
piton pinto; point; Ponti; potin
pitons pintos; piston; points
pits spit; tips
pit-saw sawpit
pit-saws sawpits
Pitta Patti
pitters spitter; tipster
placatory play-actor
place caple
placer carpel; parcel
placers carpels; clasper; parcels; scalper
places caples
plaice epical; plicae
plainer pearlin; praline
plainest pantiles
plains spinal
plaint pliant
plaister pilaster; plaiters
plaistered pilastered
plaisters pilasters
plaiters pilaster; plaister
plaits spital
plane Nepal; panel; penal; plena
planes Naples; panels
planet platen
planets platens
planta platan
planter pantler; replant
planters pantlers; replants
plap Lapp; palp
plaps Lapps; palps
plashes hapless
plasm lamps; palms; psalm
plasma lampas
plasms psalms
plaster palters; per-salt; platers; psalter; Spartel; stapler
plasterer palterers
plasters per-salts; psalters; staplers
plastery psaltery
platan planta
platanes pleasant
platans saltpan
plate leapt; lepta; palet; pelta; petal; pleat
platen planet
platens planets
plater palter
platers palters; per-salt; plaster; psalter; Spartel; stapler

plates palest; palets; pastel; petals; pleats; septal; staple
platinous pulsation
plats spalt; splat
platter partlet; prattle
platters partlets; prattles; splatter; sprattle
play paly
play-actor placatory
player parley; pearly; replay
players parleys; parsley; replays; sparely
plays palsy; splay
plea leap; pale; peal; pela
pleach chapel
plead paled; pedal
pleader pearled
pleaders relapsed
pleads lapsed; pedals
pleas Elaps; lapse; leaps; pales; peals; salep; sepal; spale; speal
pleasant platanes
please asleep; elapse; sapele
pleased delapse; elapsed
pleaser leapers; relapse; repeals
pleasers relapses
pleases elapses
pleasing elapsing
pleat leapt; lepta; palet; pelta; petal; plate
pleats palest; palets; pastel; petals; plates; septal; staple
Pleiad aliped; elapid; paidle
Pleiads alipeds; elapids; lapides; paidles; palsied
plena Nepal; panel; penal; plane
plenist pintles
plenum lumpen
pliant plaint
plicae epical; plaice
plied lepid; piled
plier peril; piler
pliers lisper; perils; Perlis; pilers
plies piles; slipe; spiel; spile
plim limp
plims limps
plissé slipes; spiels; spiles
Ploesti piolets; pistole
plot polt
Plotinus unspoilt
plots polts; Stolp
ploys slopy; Pylos
plug gulp

plug-in puling
plugs gulps
plum lump
plumed dumple; lumped
pluming lumping
plums lumps; slump
plumy lumpy
pluteus pustule
Po op
poach phoca
poacher Pechora
poachy pochay
pochay poachy
pocks Spock
poco coop
podex poxed
Poe ope
poem mope; pome
poems Epsom; mopes; pomes
poesy sepoy
poet pote; tope
poetaster operettas
poetic picoté
poets estop; potes; stoep; stope; topes
pogo goop
poh hop
point pinto; piton; Ponti; potin
pointe pontie
pointel pontile; top-line
pointer protein; pterion; tropine
pointers proteins
points pintos; piston; pitons
poises posies
poisons poisson
poisson poisons
pokal polka
pokals polkas
poker Koper; proke
pokers prokes
pokes spoke
Pola opal
polar parol
pole lope; olpe; Opel
poled loped
polemic compile
polemics compiles; complies
poler prole
polers proles; splore
poles elops; lopes; olpes; slope
poling loping
polka pokal
polkas pokals

polo   loop; pool
polt   plot
polts   plots; Stolp
polyps   sloppy
polyester   proselyte
polyesters   proselytes
polythene   telephony
pom   mop
pome   mope; poem
pomes   Epsom; mopes; poems
poms   mops
ponder   Pernod
ponders   respond
pone   nope; open; peon
pones   opens; peons; Posen; snoep
pongid   doping
Ponti   pinto; piton; point; potin
Pontiac   caption; paction
Pontic   Picton
pontie   pointe
pontile   pointel; top-line
pontoons   spontoon
poodle   looped; pooled
poodles   spooled
poofs   spoof
pooh   hoop
pool   loop; polo
Poole   Opole
pooled   looped; poodle
pooling   looping
pools   loops; sloop; spool
poor   proo; roop
poorest   Pooters
poor-rate   operator
poor-rates   operators
poort   Porto; troop
poorts   troops
Pooters   poorest
pope   pepo
popeling   peopling
poperin   propine
poperins   propines
popery   pyrope
popes   pepos
pop-gun   oppugn
pop-guns   oppugns
popish   hippos; shippo
popsy   soppy
porches   Porsche
pore   rope
pored   doper; pedro; roped
porer   prore; roper
porers   prores; proser; ropers

pores   poser; prose; ropes; Soper; spore
porgies   serpigo
poring   roping
Porsche   porches
porta   op art; Prato
portal   patrol
portals   patrols
portas   asport; pastor; sap-rot
Porte   repot; toper; trope
ported   deport; de trop
portend   protend
portends   protends
porter   pretor; report
porterage   reportage
porters   pretors; reports; sporter
portions   positron
Porto   poort; troop
portrayed   predatory
portress   sporters
ports   sport; strop
Portslade   Adlestrop
pos   ops; sop
pose   epos; opes; peso
posed   dopes; spode
Posen   opens; peons; pones; snoep
poser   pores; prose; ropes; Soper; spore
posers   proses; spores
poses   pesos; posse; speos
posh   hops; shop; soph
posher   ephors; hopers
posies   poises
posit   topis
posited   deposit; dopiest; topside
positional   spoliation
positron   portions
poss   sops
posse   pesos; poses; speos
posset   estops; stoeps; stopes
post   opts; pots; spot; stop; tops
postage   Gestapo
postboy   pot-boys
posted   depots; despot; stoped
poster   presto; repost; repots; topers; tropes
postern   Preston
posters   reposts
postil   pilots; pistol; spoilt
postils   pistols
posting   stoping
postings   signpost; stopings
postman   tampons

posts   spots; stops
posture   petrous; pouters; Proteus;
  septuor; spouter; troupes
postured   proudest; sprouted
postures   spouters
posturing   outspring; sprouting
pot   opt; top
potamic   Tampico
potash   Pashto; pathos
pot-boys   postboy
pote   poet; tope
poted   depot; opted; toped
potes   estop; poets; stoep; stope;
  topes
pother   thorpe
pothers   strophe; thorpes
potin   pinto; piton; point; Ponti
poting   opting; toping
potion   option
potions   options
potman   tampon
pots   opts; post; spot; stop;
  tops
pottered   repotted
pottering   pottinger; repotting
potters   protest; spotter
potties   tiptoes
pottiness   stone-pits
pottinger   pottering; repotting
pottingers   protesting
potty   typto
poules   souple
poultice   epulotic
pounce   uncope
pounced   uncoped
pounces   uncopes
pouncing   uncoping
pour   roup
poured   rouped
pouring   ingroup; rouping
pours   roups
pouter   troupe
pouters   petrous; posture; Proteus;
  septuor; spouter; troupes
pouts   spout; stoup
pow   wop
pows   sowp; swop; wops
poxed   podex
practise   crispate; picrates
practised   crispated
prad   drap; pard
Praded   draped; padder; parded
prads   draps; pards

Praest   paster; paters; prates; repast;
  tapers; trapes
praetors   Raptores
praise   aspire; paries; Persia
praised   aspired; despair; diapers
praiser   parries; rapiers; raspier;
  repairs
praises   aspires; paresis; Serapis
praising   aspiring
praline   pearlin; plainer
pram   ramp
prams   ramps
prangs   sprang
prase   asper; pares; parse; pears;
  presa; rapes; reaps; spaer; spare;
  spear
prat   part; rapt; trap
prate   apert; pater; peart; Petra;
  taper; trape
prated   depart; parted; petard;
  traped
prater   parter
praters   parters
prates   paster; paters; Praest; repast;
  tapers; trapes
pratie   pirate; pteria
praties   parties; piastre; pirates;
  traipse
prating   gin trap; parting; traping
Prato   op art; porta
prats   parts; spart; sprat; strap; traps
prattle   partlet; platter
prattles   partlets; platters; splatter;
  sprattle
praty   party
prayers   respray; sprayer
prays   raspy; spray
preach   eparch
preaches   peachers; sea-perch
preachy   eparchy
precast   carpets; spectra
precept   percept
preceptive   perceptive
precepts   percepts
precipitate   peripatetic
precis   cripes; Persic; prices; spicer
precise   piecers; pierces; recipes
precursor   procurers
predate   red tape; tapered
predates   pederast; trapesed
predator   parroted; prorated;
  tear-drop
predators   tear-drops

predatory portrayed
predial lip-read
predicants discrepant
predictions description
predictiveness vice-presidents
predicts scripted
predies Perseid; preside; speired
pree peer
preeing peering
preen neper
preens nepers
prees peers; perse; prese; speer;
 spree
prefect perfect
prefects perfects
preform perform
preformed performed
preforming performing
preforms performs
prelim limper
prelims limpers; simpler
preludes repulsed
prelusive pulverise; repulsive
premiers simperer
premise empires; emprise;
 epimers; imprese; spireme
premised demireps; simpered
premises emprises; impreses;
 spiremes
premising simpering
premiss impress; Persism; simpers
premisses impresses
premorse emperors
prenatal parental; paternal
prentices prescient; reinspect
prep repp
prepare repaper
prepares repapers
prepay papery
Prerov prover
presa asper; pares; parse; pears;
 prase; rapes; reaps; spaer; spare;
 spear
presage asperge
presaged asperged
presager asperger
presagers aspergers
presages asperges
presaging asperging
prescient prentices; reinspect
prese peers; perse; prees; speer;
 spree
present repents; serpent

presented serpented
presenter repenters; represent
presenters represents
presenting serpenting
presentive vespertine
presents pertness; serpents
preserve perverse
preses speers; sperse; sprees
preset pester; peters
presets pesters
preside Perseid; predies; speired
presides despiser; disperse;
 Perseids
pressed depress; spersed
presser repress
pressing spersing; springes
pression ropiness
pressure perusers
Prestea repeats
Presteign estreping; perstinge;
 pestering
presto poster; repost; repots;
 topers; tropes
Preston postern
presume supreme
presuming impugners
pretense terpenes
preterist preterits
preterit prettier
preterits preterist
pretermit permitter
pretermits permitters
pretor porter; report
Pretoria priorate
pretors porters; reports; sporter
prettier preterit
prettiness persistent
Prévert pervert
previous pervious; viperous
prewar warper
prexies expires
prexy Pyrex
prey pyre; rype
preys pyres; Ypres
prial April; Pilar
prials spiral
Priam prima
prices cripes; Persic; precis; spicer
prickle pickler
prickles picklers
pride pried; redip; riped
prides prised; redips; risped;
 spider; spired

pried   pride; redip; riped
prier   riper
pries   épris; peris; piers; prise; ripes;
  speir; spire
priest   esprit; ripest; Pteris; sprite;
  stripe; tripes
priestly   spritely
priests   persist; sprites; stirpes;
  stripes
prig   grip
prigs   grips; sprig
prima   Priam
primage   epigram
primal   imparl
primaries   impresari
primatial   impartial
prime   Perim
primes   simper
primrose   promiser
primroses   promisers
prims   prism
primus   purism
prince   pincer
princes   Crespin; pincers
printer   reprint
printers   reprints
printless   splinters
prints   sprint
priorate   Pretoria
Pripet   tipper
prise   épris; peris; piers; pries; ripes;
  speir; spire
prised   prides; redips; risped;
  spider; spired
prises   speirs; spires
prising   risping; spiring
prism   prims
prison   orpins
Privas   parvis
proas   Paros; psora; sapor; sopra
probationer   reprobation
probe   rebop
probed   bedrop
procedure   reproduce
procedures   reproduces
process   corpses
procreant   copartner
procreation   incorporate
procure   crouper
procured   producer
procurers   precursor
procures   croupers
prod   dorp; drop

prods   dorps; drops; sprod
produce   crouped
producer   procured
proem   moper; Prome
proems   Merops; mopers
proke   Koper; poker
prokes   pokers
prolate   La Porte
prolates   petrosal
prole   poler
proles   polers; splore
prom   romp
Prome   moper; proem
promise   imposer; semi-pro
promiser   primrose
promisers   primroses
promises   imposers; semi-pros
proms   romps
pronate   operant; Paterno; protean
pronates   operants; Paterson
prone   Peron
prones   person
pronto   proton
proo   poor; roop
propel   lopper
propels   loppers
proper   per pro
propine   poperin
propines   poperins
propose   opposer
proposers   oppressor
proposes   opposers
prorated   parroted; predator;
  tear-drop
prorating   parroting
prore   porer; roper
prores   porers; proser; ropers
prose   pores; poser; ropes; Soper;
  spore
prosed   dopers; pedros
proselyte   polyester
proselytes   polyesters
proser   porers; prores; ropers
proses   posers; spores
prosit   tripos
Prosna   aprons; parson
protean   operant; Paterno; pronate
proteas   seaport
protease   operates
proteids   diopters; dioptres;
  dipteros; riposted
protein   pointer; pterion; tropine
proteins   pointers

protend portend
protends portends
protest potters; spotter
protesting pottingers
protests spotters
Proteus petrous; posture; pouters; septuor; spouter; troupes
prothesis sophister; store-ship
protist tropist
protists tropists
proton pronto
proud pudor
proudest postured
Proust sprout; stroup; stupor
prover Prerov
provides disprove
provines overspin
proxies Siporex
prude drupe; duper; Dupré; perdu; pured
prudent uptrend
prudes drupes; dupers; perdus; pursed
pruners spurner
prussic Scirpus
pryer perry; ryper
psalm lamps; palms; plasm
psalmist palmists
psalms plasms
psalter palters; per-salt; plaster; platers; Spartel; stapler
psalters per-salts; plasters; staplers
psaltery plastery
psaltress strapless
pseud dupes; spued
psi sip
psittacine antiseptic
psoas apsos; soaps
psora Paros; proas; sapor; sopra
Ptah path
ptarmic crampit
ptarmics crampits
pteria pirate; pratie
pterin nipter; Pinter
pterion pointer; protein; tropine
Pteris esprit; priest; ripest; sprite; stripe; tripes
pteryla apertly
ptisan paints; patins; pintas
ptomain tampion
ptyalin inaptly
publisher republish
pudent punted

pudic cupid
pudicity cupidity
pudor proud
puds spud
puer Peru; pure
puers pures; purse; sprue; super
pug gup
puisne supine
Pula Paul
puled duple; upled
pules pulse; spule
puling plug-in
pullies pilules
pulper purple; repulp
pulpers purples; repulps
pulsation platinous
pulse pules; spule
pulverise prelusive; repulsive
puncher unperch
punier purine; unripe
puniest punties
punish unship
punks spunk
punnet unpent
punnets unspent
Puno noup; upon
puns spun
punster punters
punted pudent
punters punster
punties puniest
puntos unstop
pupils slip up
purdah hard up
pure Peru; puer
pured drupe; duper; Dupré; perdu; prude
purée rupee
purées peruse; rupees
purely Purley
pures puers; purse; sprue; super
purest erupts
purine punier; unripe
purism primus
purist spruit; stir up; uprist
purists spruits; stirs up
puritan uptrain
puritans Rasputin; uptrains
purled drupel
Purley purely
purple pulper; repulp
purples pulpers; repulps
purposes supposer

purs spur
purse puers; pures; sprue; super
pursed drupes; dupers; perdus;
  prudes
purses sprues; supers
purslane supernal
pursued usurped
pursuer usurper
pursuers usurpers
pursuing usurping
pursy Pyrus; syrup
pus sup; ups
push hups
Pushtu shut up
puss sups
pustule pluteus
put tup

puts tups
putters sputter
putti titup
pya pay; yap
pyats pasty; patsy
Pydna pandy
Pye yep
pyin piny
Pylos ploys; slopy
pyre prey; rype
pyres preys; Ypres
Pyrex prexy
pyrogenic recopying
pyrope popery
Pyrus pursy; syrup
pythonic hypnotic

Q

quads squad
quaestor equators
quails squail
quakes squeak
quantise antiques
quartets squatter
quartile requital
quartiles requitals
queries esquire
querist requits
quester request
questers requests
questor quoters; roquets; torques
quickest quickset

quickset quickest
quids squid
quiet quite
quieter requite
quills squill
quinate antique
quince cinque
quires Quseir; risqué; squire
quite quiet
quits squit
quoter roquet; torque
quoters questor; roquets; torques
Quseir quires; risqué; squire

R

Ra ar
Raab Arab; arba
Rab bar; bra
rabbet barbet
rabbets barbets; stabber
rabble barbel
rabbled dabbler
rabbles barbels; slabber
rabi Bari
rabic baric; Carib
rabid Baird; braid
rabies braise; Serbia

Rabot abort; boart; tabor
race acer; acre; care
raced acred; arced; cadre; cared;
  cedar
raceme amerce
racemed amerced; creamed
racemes amerces
racer crare
racers crares
races acers; acres; cares; carse;
  scare; scrae; sérac
rach arch; char

rache   Caher; chare; reach
raches   arches; chares; chaser;
   eschar; search
rachis   chairs; Charis
racial   Alaric
racialist   satirical
Racine   in care
racing   arcing; caring
racists   sacrist
rack   cark
racked   arcked; carked; dacker
racket   tacker
rackets   stacker; tackers
racking   arcking; carking
racks   carks
racoon   corona
racoons   coronas
racy   Cary
raddle   Aldred; ladder; larded
raddles   ladders; saddler
rade   ared; dare; dear; eard; read
radian   Adrian; Andria
radians   Sindara
radiate   tiaraed
radicel   decrial; radicle
radicels   radicles
radices   sidecar
radicle   decrial; radicel
radicles   radicels
radicule   auricled
radio   aroid
radios   aroids
radius   Darius
radome   roamed
radon   Nardo
Raf   far; fra
raffia   affair
raffle   farfel
raft   fart
rafted   dafter; farted
rafter   farter
rafters   farters
rafting   farting
rafts   farts
rag   gar
raga   agar; Agra
ragas   Sagar
rage   gare; gear; Gera
raged   Edgar; Gerda; grade
rager   regar
rages   gears; sager; sarge
ragged   dagger
raggle   gargle; lagger

raggled   draggle; gargled
raggles   gargles; laggers
raggling   gargling
ragi   gair
ragingly   grayling
ragmen   engram; german; manger
ragment   garment; margent
ragments   garments; margents
rags   gars; Gras
rag-tag   tagrag
ragtime   Maigret; migrate
ragweed   Edgware; wagered
raid   arid; dari
raider   arride
raiders   arrides
raids   Sidra
raik   raki
raiked   daiker
Raikes   Kaiser
rail   aril; lair; liar; lira; rial
railed   derail; laired; Lérida; relaid
railer   rerai!
railers   rerails
railing   glairin; lairing
railman   laminar
railmen   manlier; marline; mineral
rails   lairs; liars; liras; rials
raiment   minaret
rain   airn; Iran; Nair; rani
rained   Dairen; Darien; randie
raininess   sirenians
raining   ingrain
rains   ranis
rain-tree   Eritrean; retainer
rain-trees   Eritreans; retainers;
   ternaries
raise   aesir; Aries; arise; Riesa; serai;
   Seria
raised   aiders; irades
raiser   airers; Sérrai; sierra
raisers   sierras
raises   arises; serais
raising   arising
rait   airt
raited   airted; tirade
raits   airts; astir; sitar; Sitra; stair;
   stria; tarsi; Trias
raj   jar
raja   ajar
rake   reak
raked   arked; daker; drake
rakes   asker; kesar; reaks; saker;
   skear

raki   raik
raking   arking
rakish   shikar
râle   earl; lare; lear; real
rallied   dallier; dialler
ram   arm; mar
Rama   Aram; mara
ramal   alarm; malar
ramble   ambler; blamer; marble
rambled   marbled
rambler   marbler
ramblers   marblers
rambling   marbling
Rameses   seamers
rami   amir; Mari; Mira; rima
ramie   maire; Marie; rimae
ramis   simar
Ramist   Marist
Ramists   Marists; tsarism
Ramle   lamer
Ramleh   Harlem; Mahler
Ramon   manor; Morna; Norma;
   Roman
ramp   pram
ramped   damper
ramps   prams
rams   arms; mars
Ramses   masers; smears
ramson   manors; ransom; Romans
ramsons   ransoms
ramus   arums; rusma; Sarum
rana   Aran; Nara
rance   crane; crena; nacre
ranced   cedarn; craned; dancer
rancel   lancer
rancels   lancers
rances   casern; cranes
ranched   endarch
ranches   chenars
rancho   anchor; archon; Charon
ranchos   anchors; archons
rancing   craning
rand   darn; nard
Randers   darners; errands
randie   Dairen; Darien; rained
random   rodman
rands   darns; nards
rang   gnar; gran
range   anger; Regan; renga
ranged   danger; gander; garden
ranger   garner
rangers   garners
ranges   angers; Sanger; serang

ranginess   angriness
rangy   angry
rani   airn; Iran; Nair; rain
ranis   rains
rank   knar; kran; nark
ranked   danker; darken; narked
ranking   narking
rankle   lanker
ranks   knars; krans; narks; skran;
   snark
ransel   learns
ransom   manors; ramson; Romans
ransoms   ramsons
rant   tarn
ranted   ardent; endart; red ant
ranter   errant
rants   starn; tarns
rap   Arp; par
rape   pare; pear; Pera; reap
raped   drape; padre; pared; repad
rapes   asper; pares; parse; pears;
   prase; presa; reaps; spaer; spare;
   spear
raphe   hepar; phare
raphes   phares; phrase; seraph;
   shaper; Sherpa; sphaer
raphis   Hispar; parish; Shairp
rapids   spraid
rapier   repair
rapiers   parries; praiser; raspier;
   repairs
rapine   Napier
raping   paring
rapist   tapirs
rapparee   reappear
rapparees   reappears
rapped   dapper
rappel   lapper
rappels   lappers; slapper
raps   rasp; spar
rapt   part; prat; trap
raptor   parrot
Raptores   praetors
raptors   parrots
rare   rear
rarebit   arbiter
rarebits   arbiters
ras   sar
rascal   lascar; sacral; scalar
rascals   lascars; scalars
rase   Ares; arse; ears; eras; sear; sera
rased   dares; dears; reads
rases   arses; rasse; sears

rasher sharer

rashers sharers

rashes shares; shears

rasing grains; Sangir

rasp raps; spar

rasped drapes; padres; parsed; repads; spared; spread

rasper parers; parser; sparer

raspers parsers; sparers; sparser

raspier parries; praiser; rapiers; repairs

raspiest pastries; piastres; Tarsipes; traipses

rasping parings; parsing; sparing

raspingly sparingly

rasps spars

Rasputin puritans; uptrains

raspy prays; spray

rasse arses; rases; sears

raster arrest; arrêts; raters; Sartre; starer; terras

rasters arrests; starers

Rastus Straus; sutras; Tarsus

rat art; tar

rata tara

ratable Alberta

ratal altar; talar

ratan antra

ratas tasar

ratbite battier; biretta

ratbites birettas

ratch chart

ratchet chatter

ratchets chatters

rate aret; tare; tear

rated adret; dater; tared; trade; tread

rateen entera; neater

ratel alert; alter; artel; later; taler

ratels alerts; alters; artels; laster; salter; slater; staler; stelar; tarsel

rater arrêt; terra

raters arrest; arrêts; raster; Sartre; starer; terras

rates arets; aster; astre; earst; reast; resat; stare; strae; tares; tears; teras

rath hart; tahr; thar

rathe earth; Harte; hater; heart; Herat; Thera; thrae

rathest hatters; shatter; threats

rat-hole loather

rat-holes loathers

raths harts; tahrs; thars; trash

ratine Nerita; retain; retina; Tiranë

ratines nastier; resiant; retains; retinas; retsina; stainer; starnie; stearin

rating taring

ratings staring

ratio ariot

ration aroint

rational notarial

rationale alienator

rationalise realisation

rationally notarially

rationed deration; ordinate; Rodentia

rations aroints

ratios Artois

ratite attire; Tiaret

ratlin trinal

ratline entrail; Latiner; latrine; reliant; retinal; trenail

ratlines entrails; Latiners; latrines; trenails

ratlings starling

rats arts; star; tars; tsar

ratsbane ant-bears

rattan Tantra; tartan

rattans Tantras; tartans

ratted tarted; tetrad

ratteen entreat; ternate

ratteens entreats

ratten natter

rattened nattered

rattening nattering

rattens natters

ratters restart; starter

rattle latter; tatler

rattlers startler

rattles slatter; starlet; startle; tatlers; Telstar

rattlings startling

ratton rottan

rattons rottans

ratty tarty

raun Arun

rave Arve; aver; vare; Vera

raved drave; Revda; Varde

ravel laver; Reval; velar

ravels lavers; salver; serval; slaver; versal

raves avers; saver; vares

Ravi riva; vair

ravin Invar

ravine Erivan; vainer; Vanier

ravined invader
ravines Servian
raving Girvan
raw war
rawing waring
rawn warn
rawness answers
rawns warns
ray ary; Ayr
rayed deary; deray; ready; yeard
raying grainy
rayless slayers
rays Syra
raze Ezra
razed zerda
re er
reabsorb absorber
reabsorbs absorbers
reach Caher; chare; rache
reached Ardèche
reachers research; searcher
react caret; carte; cater; crate; recta;
  trace
reacted catered; cedrate; created
reacting argentic; catering;
  citrange; creating
reaction creation
reactions creations
reactive creative
reactively creatively
reactivity creativity
reactor acroter; creator
reactors acroters; creators
reacts carets; cartes; caster; caters;
  crates; Cresta; recast; traces
read ared; dare; dear; eard; rade
readdress addresser
Reade arede; deare; eared
reader dearer; reared; reread
readers redsear; rereads
readies dearies
readiest steadier
reading areding; dearing; deraign;
  gradine; grained
readings deraigns; gradines
readjust adjuster
readjusts adjusters
read-out outdare
read-outs outdares
reads dares; dears; rased
ready deary; deray; rayed; yeard
readying deraying; yearding
reaffirm affirmer

reaffirms affirmers
Reagan Grenaa
reagent grantee; greaten
reagents estrange; grantees;
  greatens; segreant; sergeant
reak rake
reaks asker; kesar; rakes; saker;
  skear
real earl; lare; lear; râle
realign aligner; engrail; learing;
  nargile; reginal
realigned engrailed; Geraldine
realigning engrailing
realignment engrailment
realignments engrailments
realigns aligners; engrails;
  Salinger; sanglier; seal-ring
realisation rationalise
realised sidereal
realism mailers
realist Alister; retails; saltier;
  saltire; slatier
realistic eristical
realists saltiers; saltires; slaister
realities Israelite
reals Arles; earls; lares; laser; lears;
  seral
re-alter relater
re-alters relaters
real-time eremital; Lemaître;
  matériel
realtor relator
realtors relators
realty elytra; lyrate
ream mare
reamed remade
reamer Marree
reaming Germain
reams mares; maser; smear
reap pare; pear; Pera; rape
reappear rapparee
reappears rapparees
reaps asper; pares; parse; pears;
  prase; presa; rapes; spaer; spare;
  spear
rear rare
reared dearer; reader; reread
rearing angrier; earring; grainer
rearmed dreamer
rearrest arrester
rearrests arresters
rears Sarre; serra
reascend ascender

reascends   ascenders
reascent   sarcenet
reason   Señora
reasons   Señoras
reassert   asserter; serrates
reasserts   asserters
reassume   measures
reassure   erasures
reast   arets; aster; astre; earst; rates;
   resat; stare; strae; tares; tears; teras
reasted   dearest; derates; estrade
reasting   angriest; astringe;
   ganister; gantries; granites; inert
   gas; ingrates
reasts   assert; asters; astres; stares;
   Stresa
reasty   estray; stayer; yarest
reate   arête; eater; Taree
reates   arêtes; easter; eaters; reseat;
   saeter; teaser; Teresa
reaves   averse; Varese
reaving   vinegar
reback   backer
rebacks   backers
rebate   beater; berate
rebated   berated; betread; debater
rebates   beaters; berates
rebating   berating
rebid   bride; Diber
rebids   brides
rebind   binder; brined; inbred
rebinds   binders
rebit   biter; Tiber; tribe
rebloom   bloomer
reblooms   bloomers
reboil   boiler
reboils   boilers
rebop   probe
rebound   bounder; unrobed
rebounds   bounders; suborned
rebroadcast   broadcaster
rebroadcasts   broadcasters
rebuff   buffer
rebuffed   buffered
rebuffing   buffering
rebuffs   buffers
rebuild   builder
rebuilds   builders
rebus   burse; suber
rebut   brute; tuber
rebuts   brutes; buster; tubers
rebuttal   burletta
rebutted   buttered

rebutting   buttering
recall   caller; cellar
recalled   cellared
recalling   cellaring
recalls   callers; cellars; scleral
recant   canter; carnet; creant;
   Cretan; nectar; tanrec; trance
recanted   cantered; crenated;
   decanter; nectared
recanter   recreant
recanters   recreants
recanting   cantering
recants   canters; carnets; Cretans;
   tanrecs; trances
recap   caper; crape; pacer
recaps   capers; Casper; crapes;
   escarp; pacers; parsec; scrape;
   spacer
recast   carets; cartes; caster; caters;
   crates; Cresta; reacts; traces
recasting   citranges
recasts   actress; casters; Castres
recede   decree
receded   decreed
recedes   decrees; seceder
received   deceiver
recent   center; centre; tenrec
recentness   sentencers
recepts   respect; sceptre; spectre
recessed   seceders
Rechab   Béchar; breach
Recife   fierce
recipe   piecer; pierce
recipes   piecers; pierces; precise
recital   article
recitals   articles; sterical
recite   cerite; tierce
recites   tierces
recked   decker
reckon   conker
reckons   conkers
reclaim   Almeric; claimer; miracle
reclaimed   declaimer
reclaims   claimers; miracles
reclinate   interlace; lacertine
reclines   licenser; silencer
recloses   coreless; sclerose
recluses   cureless
reclusion   Cornelius
recognise   congeries
recomfort   comforter
recomforts   comforters
recondition   conditioner

reconditions conditioners
reconvert converter
reconverts converters
reconvey conveyer
reconveys conveyers
recopying pyrogenic
recount cornute; counter; trounce
recounted countered
recounting countering
recounts construe; cornutes;
  counters; trounces
recoup couper; croupe; cuerpo
recoups coupers; croupes
recourse resource
recreant recanter
recreants recanters
recross crosser
recruits crustier
recta caret; carte; cater; crate; react;
  trace
rectal cartel; claret; tarcel
recti trice
rectifiable certifiable
rectification certification
rectified certified
rectifier certifier
rectifiers certifiers
rectifies certifies
rectify certify
rectifying certifying
rectitude certitude
rectus cruets; cruset; Custer; eructs;
  truces
recur curer
recures rescuer; securer
recurs curers; curser
recusant centaurs; Etruscan;
  untraces
recusants Etruscans
recuse Cereus; ceruse; Creuse;
  rescue; secure
recused reduces; rescued; secured;
  seducer
recuses rescues; secures
recusing rescuing; securing
redact carted; crated; Dectra; traced
redactions draconites
redans sander; snared
red ant ardent; endart; ranted
red ants endarts; stander
Red Bay brayed
red-book brooked
redbreast bestarred

rebud budder
redbuds budders
redcap carped; craped
redcaps scarped; scraped
Redcar carder
red cent centred; credent
Red China inarched
redcoat cordate
reddens Dresden
reddle Eldred
red-dog dodger
reddy ydred
rede deer; dere; dree; reed
redeems demerse; emersed
redeliver deliverer
redelivers deliverers
redes deres; drees; reeds; Seder
red giant derating; gradient;
  treading
red giants gradients
red-hat dearth; hatred; thread
red-hats dearths; hardest; hatreds;
  threads; trashed
redhead adhered
red-heat earthed; hearted
red-hot dehort
redia aider; aired; irade
redip pride; pried; riped
redips prides; prised; risped;
  spider; spired
rediscover discoverer
rediscovers discoverers
red-man manred; remand
red-men mender
redness senders
Red Nile relined
re-do doer; Doré; Oder; rode; roed
redoubt doubter; obtrude; outbred
redoubts doubters; obtrudes
redound rounded; underdo
redounding underdoing
red out detour; douter; outred;
  routed; toured
redraft drafter
redrafts drafters
redraw drawer; reward; warder;
  warred
redraws drawers; rewards;
  warders
redress dresser
Red Rum murder
Red Sea aredes; deares; erased;
  reseda; seared

redsear readers; rereads
red tape predate; tapered
reduces recused; rescued; secured; seducer
reduction introduce
reductions discounter; introduces
redwing wringed
reech cheer
re-echo cheero; choree; cohere; echoer
reechy cheery
reed deer; dere; dree; rede
reedily yielder
reeding dreeing; energid; reigned
re-edit retied
re-editing reignited
re-edits reisted; re-sited
reeds deres; drees; redes; Seder
reedstop reposted
reef feer; fere; free
reefed feeder; feered
reefing feering; feigner; freeing
reefs feers; feres; frees
reeks esker; skeer
reel leer; lere
reeled leered
reeling leering
reels leers; leres
re-endow endower
re-endows endowers
re-enlist enlister; Leinster; listener
re-enlists enlisters; listeners
re-enter enterer; terrene
re-enters enterers; resenter; terrenes
re-equip perique; repique
re-equips repiques
reest ester; reset; retes; steer; stere; teers; terse; trees
reested steered
reesting integers; steering; streigne
reests esters; resets; steers; steres
reeved veered
reeves severe
reeving veering
re-export exporter
re-exports exporters
ref erf
refel fleer
refels fleers
refer freer
refill filler

refills fillers
refine enfire; ferine; Fernie; fineer; infere
refined enfired
refines enfires; fineers
refining enfiring; infringe
refits sifter; strife
reflated faltered
reflating faltering
refloat floater; floreat
refloats floaters; forestal
reflow flower; fowler; wolfer
reflowed deflower; flowered
reflowing flowering
reflows flowers; fowlers; wolfers
refoot foetor; footer; tofore
reform former
reformed deformer
reforms formers
refound founder
refounds founders
refresh fresher
reft fret
refuel ferule
refuels ferules
refunded underfed
refurbish furbisher
refurnish furnisher
refusal earfuls
refute feutre
refutes feutres
Reg erg
regain earing; gainer; graine; regina
regains earings; erasing; gainers; searing; Seraing; seringa
regal Elgar; glare; lager; large; Regla
regalia Algeria
regalian Algerian
regally allergy; gallery; largely
regals glares; lagers
Regan anger; range; renga
regar rager
regard Gerard; grader
regards graders
regelate relegate
regelated relegated
regelates relegates
regelating relegating
regelation relegation
regent gerent
regents gerents

Reggie Geiger
regime émigré
regiment metering
regimes émigrés
regina earing; gainer; graine; regain
reginal aligner; engrail; learing; nargile; realign
region eringo; ignore; Origen
regions ignores; Signore
regius guiser
Regla Elgar; glare; lager; large; regal
regma gamer; marge
regmata Margate
regnal angler
regrant granter
regrants granters; stranger
regrate greater
regrated gartered; garreted; Tredegar
regrating gartering
regrind grinder
regrinds grinders
regroup grouper
regroups groupers
reh her
rehear hearer
reheard adherer
rehears hearers; shearer
reheat aether; heater; hereat
reheats heaters; Theresa
reheel heeler
reheels heelers
rehoused rose-hued
Reid dire; ride
reif fire; Frei; rife
reify fiery
reign Niger; renig
reigned dreeing; energid; reeding
reignited re-editing
reigns Ingres; renigs; resign; signer; singer
Reims emirs; mires; miser; riems; rimes
rein Erin; in re; Reni
rein-arm mariner
rein-arms mariners
reined denier; Edirne; nereid
reinfect frenetic
reinforce confrérie
reinforces confréries
reinform informer; reniform

reinforms informers
reins resin; rinse; risen; serin; siren
reinsert reinters; rentiers; terrines
reinspect prentices; prescient
reinsured surreined
reinter rentier; terrine
reinterpret interpreter
reinterprets interpreters
reinters reinsert; rentiers; terrines
reinvest nerviest; servient; sirvente
reird direr; drier; rider
reirds derris; driers; riders; sirred
reis Eris; rise; sire
reist resit; rites; Siret; tiers; tires; tries
reisted re-edits; re-sited
reists resist; resits; sister
reiter étrier; retire
reiters étriers; retires; retries; terries
reive revie; rieve
reived derive; revied; rieved
reiver riever
reivers rievers
reives revies; revise; rieves
reiving rieving
rejoin joiner
rejoins joiners
relaid derail; laired; Lérida; railed
relapse leapers; pleaser; repeals
relapsed pleaders
relapser pearlers
relapses pleasers
relate elater; Tralee
related alerted; altered; treadle
relater re-alter
relaters re-alters
relates elàters; Laertes; stealer
relating alerting; altering; integral; triangle
relation oriental
relations Orientals; Orleanist
relative levirate
relatives versatile
relator realtor
relators realtors
relax laxer
relay early; layer
relayed delayer; layered
relaying layering; yearling
relays layers; slayer
releasing Algerines
relegate regelate**

relegated regelated
relegates regelates
relegating regelating
relegation regelation
relets Lester; streel
relevant levanter
reliably Bareilly
reliance cinereal
reliant entrail; Latiner; latrine;
   ratline; retinal; trenail
relic Creil
relics slicer
relict Tricel
relied lieder
relief liefer
relies resile
relieves Elsevier
relieving inveigler
relievo overlie
relight lighter
relights lighters; slighter
reline lierne
relined Red Nile
relines liernes
relish hirsel; hirsle
relishes heirless
relit litre; tiler
relive liever; revile
relived deliver; livered; reviled
relives Liévres; reviles; servile
reliving reviling
reload Laredo; loader; ordeal
reloading girandole; negroidal
reloads loaders; ordeals; sea-lord
reloan loaner; Lorena
reloaned oleander
relocation iconolater
reluct culter; cutler
relucts cluster; culters; cutlers;
   custrel
rely lyre
remade reamed
remain airmen; marine; Marnie
remains marines; seminar; sirname
remand manred; red-man
remanded demander
remands manreds
remark marker
remarks markers
remblai balmier; Mirabel; mirable
remigate emigrate
remigated emigrated
remigates emigrates

remigating emigrating
remigation emigration
remind minder
reminds minders
remise Mieres; misère
remises messier
remising Isengrim
remiss misers
remission missioner
remit merit; mitre; timer
remits merits; mister; mitres;
   smiter; timers
remitter trimeter
remitters trimester; trimeters
remodel Delorme
remora roamer
remoras roamers
remote meteor
remould moulder
remoulded mouldered
remoulding mouldering
remoulds moulders; smoulder
remount monture; mounter
remounts montures; mounters
Remus mures; muser; serum;
   Sumer
Rena Arne; earn; nare;
   near
renal Larne; learn
rename meaner
renamed amender; enarmed;
   meander
renaming enarming
Renard darner; errand
renascent entrances
Renault neutral
renay yearn
renayed deanery; yearned
renaying yearning
renays senary; yearns
rend dern
rending grinned
rends derns
Rene erne
renegate generate; green tea;
   teenager
renegates generates; teenagers
renege Greene
reneged greened
reneging greening
renga anger; range; Regan
Reni Erin; in re; rein
reniform informer; reinform

renig Niger; reign
renigs Ingres; reigns; resign; signer; singer
rennet tenner
rennets tenners
Reno Nero; Nore; oner; Orne; rone
Renoir ironer
rent tern
rental altern; antler; learnt; ternal
rentals antlers; saltern; sternal
rente enter; terne; treen
rented tender; terned
rentes enters; Ernest; nester; resent; Sterne; tenser; ternes
rentier reinter; terrine
rentiers reinsert; reinters; terrines
renting ringent; terning
rents Ernst; stern; terns
renvois version
reopen opener; perone; repone
reopens openers; perones; repones
reordain ordainer
reordains ordainers
reorder orderer
reorders orderers
rep per
repack packer
repacks packers
repad drape; padre; pared; raped
repads drapes; padres; parsed; rasped; spared; spread
repaid diaper; paired; pardie
repaint painter; Patenir; pertain; pine-tar
repaints painters; pantries; Parentis; pertains; pinaster
repair rapier
repairs parries; praiser; rapiers; raspier
repand pander
repaper prepare
repapers prepares
repartee pear-tree; repeater
repass aspers; parses; passer; spaers; spares; sparse; spears
repassed aspersed
repasses asperses; Passeres
repassing aspersing
repast paster; paters; Praest; prates; tapers; trapes
repasts pasters
repasture apertures

repay apery; payer; Peary
repays payers; speary
repeal Lapeer; leaper
repeals leapers; pleaser; relapse
repeater pear-tree; repartee
repeaters pear-trees
repeating interpage
repeats Prestea
repel leper
repels lepers
repentant penetrant
repenters presenter; represent
repents present; serpent
repetition petitioner
repined Dnieper
repines en prise; erepsin
repique perique; re-equip
repiques re-equips
repla lepra; paler; parle; pearl
replace percale
replant pantler; planter
replants pantlers; planters
replay parley; pearly; player
replayed parleyed
replaying parleying
replays parleys; parsley; players; sparely
repletion interlope
replica caliper
replicas calipers; spiracle
replies spieler
replum lumper; rumple
repone opener; perone; reopen
repones openers; perones; reopens
report porter; pretor
reportage porterage
reports porters; pretors; sporter
reposal paroles
reposing spongier
reposit riposte
reposits ripostes
repost poster; presto; repots; topers; tropes
reposted reedstop
reposts posters
repot Porte; toper; trope
repots poster; presto; repost; topers; tropes
repotted pottered
repotting pottering; pottinger
repoussé espouser
repp prep
represent presenter; repenters

represents presenters
repress presser
reprint printer
reprints printers; sprinter
reprise perries; respire
reprised respired
reprises respires
reprising respiring; springier
reprobation probationer
reproduce procedure
reproduces procedures
reptile perlite
reptiles epistler; peltries
Reptilia liparite
republish publisher
repulp pulper; purple
repulps pulpers; purples
repulsed preludes
repulsive prelusive; pulverise
reputed erupted
reputes pertuse
reputing erupting
request quester
requests questers
requital quartile
requitals quartiles
requite quieter
requits querist
rerail railer
rerails railers
re-rate tearer
re-rates serrate; tearers
reread dearer; reader; reared
rereading grenadier
rereads readers; redsear
resale leaser; sealer; Searle
resat arets; aster; astre; earst; rates;
    reast; stare; strae; tares; tears; teras
rescale cereals
rescaled declares
rescind cinders; discern
rescinded discerned
rescinding discerning
rescinds discerns
rescuable securable
rescue Cereus; ceruse; Creuse;
    recuse; secure
rescued recused; reduces; secured;
    seducer
rescuer recures; securer
rescuers securers
rescues recuses; secures
rescuing recusing; securing

research reachers; searcher
reseat arêtes; easter; eaters; reates;
    saeter; teaser; Teresa
reseating stingaree
reseats easters; saeters; teasers;
    tessera
resect certes; erects; secret
resected secreted
resecting secreting
resection erections; secretion
resections secretions
resects cresset; secrets
reseda aredes; deares; erased; Red
    Sea; seared
reseeding energised
resell seller
resells sellers
resent enters; Ernest; nester;
    rentes; Sterne; tenser; ternes
resenter enterers; re-enters; terrenes
resents nesters
reserve reveres; reverse
reserved reversed
reserves reverses
reserving reversing
reset ester; reest; retes; steer; stere;
    teers; terse; trees
resets esters; reests; steers; steres
reshape sphaere
reshapes sphaeres
reship perish; seriph
reships seriphs
Resht Herts.; tehrs
resiance increase
resiant nastier; ratines; retains;
    retinas; retsina; stainer; starnie;
    stearin
reside desire; eiders
resided derides; desired
resident Dniester; inserted;
    sintered
residents dissenter; tiredness
resides desires
residing desiring; ringside
resign Ingres; reigns; renigs;
    signer; singer
resigned designer; energids
resigns ingress; signers; singers
resile relies
resiling Riesling
resin reins; rinse; risen; serin; siren
Resina arisen; arsine
resinata artesian; Erastian

resinous neurosis
resins rinses; serins; sirens
resist reists; resits; sister
resistant straitens
resisted editress
resistent interests; triteness
resistor roisters; sorriest
resists sisters
resit reist; rites; Siret; tiers; tires; tries
re-site reties
re-sited re-edits; reisted
re-siting igniters; strigine
resits reists; resist; sister
resold dorsel; drôles; solder
resort roster; sorter; storer
resorted Desterro; restored; rostered
resorter restorer; retrorse
resorting restoring; rostering
resorts rosters; sorters; storers
resound Öresund; sounder; undoers
resounds dourness; sounders
resource recourse
respect recepts; sceptre; spectre
respects sceptres; spectres
respell speller
respells spellers
respire perries; reprise
respired reprised
respires reprises
respiring reprising; springier
respond ponders
respray prayers; sprayer
resprays sprayers
rest erst; rets
restart ratters; starter
restarts starters
restate estreat
restates estreats
rest-day strayed
rested desert; deters
restful fluster; fluters
restiff stiffer
resting stinger
restive veriest
restless tressels
restocking stockinger
Reston noters; stoner; tenors; tensor; Terson; trones
restored Desterro; resorted; rostered

restorer resorter; retrorse
restoring resorting; rostering
restrain strainer; terrains; trainers; transire
restrains strainers; transires
restrict critters; stricter
rests tress
resty Steyr; treys; tyres
restyle tersely
result luster; lustre; luters; rustle; sutler; ulster
resulted ulstered
results lusters; lustres; rustles; sutlers; ulsters
retail retial
retailed elaterid
retails Alister; realist; saltier; saltire; slatier
retain Nerita; ratine; retina; Tiranë
retained detainer
retainer Eritrean; rain-tree
retainers Eritreans; rain-trees; ternaries
retains nastier; ratines; resiant; retinas; retsina; stainer; starnie; stearin
retakes sakeret
retard darter; dartre; tarred; trader
retards darters; starred; traders
retches Chester; etchers
rete teer; tree
retell teller
retells tellers
retes ester; reest; reset; steer; stere; teers; terse; trees
rethink thinker
rethinks thinkers
retial retail
retied re-edit
reties re-site
retina Nerita; ratine; retain; Tiranë
retinae Aintree; trainee
retinal entrail; Latiner; latrine; ratline; reliant; trenail
retinas nastier; resiant; ratines; retains; retsina; stainer; starnie; stearin
retinue reunite; uterine
retinues esurient; reunites
retiral retrial; trailer
retire étrier; reiter
retired retried

retires étriers; reiters; retries; terries
retort rotter; torret
retorts rotters; torrets
retotal Loretta
retouch toucher
retour router; tourer
retours routers; tourers; trouser
retrace caterer; terrace
retraced terraced
retraces caterers; terraces
retracing terracing
retread treader
retreading intergrade
retreads serrated; treaders
retreat treater
retreats treaters
retrench trencher
retrial retiral; trailer
retrials trailers
retried retired
retries étriers; reiters; retires; terries
retrieves River Tees
retrorse resorter; restorer
retrospection interoceptors
retry terry; tryer
rets erst; rest
retsina nastier; resiant; ratines; retains; retinas; stainer; starnie; stearin
retting gittern
retund turned
retune neuter; tenure; tureen
retunes neuters; tenures; tureens
returf Erfurt
return turner
returns turners
reunite retinue; uterine
reunites esurient; retinues
Reus rues; ruse; sure; ures; user
reusing Giresun
Reuss ruses; users
reutter utterer
reutters utterers
Reval laver; ravel; velar
revamp vamper
revamps vampers
Revda drave; raved; Varde
reveal laveer; leaver
revealing inveagler
reveals laveers; leavers; several
revel elver; lever

revels elvers; levers
reveres reserve; reverse
revers server; verser
reversal slaveror
reversals slaverers
reverse reserve; reveres
reversed reserved
reverses reserves
reversi reviser
reversing reserving
revest everts; revets
revet evert
revets everts; revest
revie reive; rieve
revied derive; reived; rieved
revies reives; revise; rieves
review viewer
reviews viewers
revile liever; relive
reviled deliver; livered; relived
reviles Liévres; relives; servile
reviling reliving
revise reives; revies; rieves
revised derives; deviser; De Vries; diverse
reviser reversi
revises ivresse
revolute true-love
Rewa ware; wear
reward drawer; redraw; warder; warred
rewards drawers; redraws; warders
Rewari warier
rewind winder
rewinds winders
rewords sworder
rework worker
reworks workers
rewound wounder
rhaetic rich tea
rhe her; reh
rhea hare; hear; Hera
rheas hares; hears; share; shear
Rhein Henri; rhine
Rheine herein; inhere
rheo hero; hoer; Ohre
rhes hers
rhesus rushes; ushers
rhine Henri; Rhein
rhines shiner; shrine
Rhoda hoard

Rhodes hordes; horsed; shoder; shored
rhodium humidor; mid-hour
Rhona Norah
rhone heron; Horne
rhones herons; Senhor
Rhus rush
rhyton thorny
ria air; Ira
rial aril; lair; liar; lira; rail
rials lairs; liars; liras; rails
Rialto tailor
riant intra; Nitra; train; Trani
rias airs; Asir; Isar; sair; sari
ribald bridal; labrid
ribbed bribed; dibber
ribbing bribing
Ribe bier; Brie
Ribera Barrie
Ribes biers; birse
ribless birsles
rice ciré; eric; icer
riced cider; cried; dicer
richen enrich
richened enriched
richening enriching
richer chirre
richest estrich
rich tea rhaetic
ricked dicker
rickets Sickert; sticker; tickers
rickle licker
rickles lickers; slicker
ridable bedrail
riddance cider-and
ridded didder
ridden rinded
riddle dirled
riddled diddler
riddles slidder
ride dire; Reid
rident tinder; trined
rider direr; drier; reird
ridered Deirdre; derider
riders derris; driers; reirds; sirred
rides dries; sider; sired
ridge dirge; gride
ridged grided
ridgel gilder; girdle; glider; lidger
ridgels gilders; girdles; gliders; grisled; lidgers
ridges dirges; grides; grised
ridging griding

riding Ingrid
riel leir; lier; lire; rile
riels leirs; liers; riles; siler
riem emir; meri; mire; rime
riems emirs; mires; miser; Reims; rimes
Riesa aesir; Aries; arise; raise; serai; Seria
Riesling resiling
Riet rite; tier; tire
rieve reive; revie
rieved derive; reived; revied
riever reiver
rievers reivers
rieves reives; revies; revise
rieving reiving
Rif fir
rife fire; Frei; reif
riffed differ
rifle filer; flier; lifer
rifleman inflamer
rifles filers; fliers; lifers
rift frit
rifts first; frist; frits
Rigel liger
rigged digger
right girth; grith
rigs gris
rile leir; lier; lire; riel
riled idler
riles leirs; liers; riels; siler
rilievo Olivier
Rilke liker
rillet tiller
rillets stiller; tillers; trellis
rim mir
rima amir; Mari; Mira; rami
rimae maire; Marie; ramie
rime emir; meri; mire; riem
rimed dimer; mired
rimes emirs; mires; miser; Reims; riems
rimester merriest; triremes
rimier mirier
rimiest miriest; mistier
riming miring
rimless smilers
rimmed dimmer
rims mirs; smir
rimy miry; Ymir
rind Drin
rinded ridden
ring girn; grin

ringed dering; dinger; engird; girned

ringent renting; terning

ringer erring

ringing girning

ringless slingers

ringlet tingler; tringle

ringlets sterling; tinglers; tringles

ring out routing; touring

rings girns; grins

ringside desiring; residing

ringtail trailing

rink kirn

rinks kirns

rinse reins; resin; risen; serin; siren

rinsed diners

rinses resins; serins; sirens

Riom Miro

Rion inro; iron

riot tiro; tori; trio

rioted editor; tie-rod; triode

rioters roister

riots roist; rosit; tiros; trios

ripe peri; pier

ripeck picker

ripecks pickers

riped pride; pried; redip

ripens sniper

riper prier

ripes épris; peris; piers; pries; prise; speir; spire

ripest esprit; priest; Pteris; sprite; stripe; tripes

riposted diopters; dioptres; dipteros; proteids

ripostes triposes

ripped dipper

ripples slipper

ripplet tippler; tripple

ripplets stippler; tipplers; tripples

rips risp

ript trip

rise Eris; reis; sire

risen reins; resin; rinse; serin; siren

rises sires

rising siring

risk irks; kris

risked dikers

risking girkins; griskin

risp rips

risped prides; prised; redips; spider; spired

risping prising; spiring

risque quires; Quseir; squire

Riss sirs

rite Riet; tier; tire

rites reist; resit; Siret; tiers; tires; tries

rits stir

ritter territ; triter

ritters territs

riva Ravi; vair

rivage Argive; garvie

rivages Argives; garvies

rival viral

rived diver; drive; Verdi

rivel liver; livre

rivels livers; livres; silver; sliver

riven viner

Rivera arrive; varier

riveret riveter

riverets riveters

River Tees retrieves

rives siver

riveter riveret

riveters riverets

rivets stiver; strive; trevis

riving Irving; virgin

roach orach

roaches oraches

road Dora; Odra

road-end adorned

roading adoring; Gordian; gradino

roadmen Maderno

roads Doras; dorsa; Rodas; sorda

roam mora; Omar; Roma

roamed radome

roamer remora

roamers remoras

roaming Moringa

roams Maros; moras

roan Arno; Nora; Oran; Rona

roans arson; sonar

roar orra

roared adorer

roast Astor; rotas; Sarto; taros; Troas

roasted torsade

roasters assertor; oratress

roasting organist

roasts assort

rob bor; orb

robe Boer; bore; Ebro

robed bored; orbed

robes Boers; bores; brose; sober

robin inorb

robing   boring; orbing
robins   inorbs
robs   orbs; sorb
roc   cor; orc
Roca   arco; Cora; Orca
rochet   hector; tocher; troche
rochets   hectors; tochers; torches;
   troches
rock   cork
rocked   corked; docker
rocker   corker
rockers   corkers
rocketer   cork-tree
rocketers   cork-trees
rockier   corkier
rockiest   corkiest; stockier
rocking   corking
rocks   corks
rocky   corky
rocquet   croquet
rocs . cors; orcs
rod   dor; ord
Rodas   Doras; dorsa; roads; sorda
rode   doer; Doré; Oder; re-do; roed
roded   odder
Rodentia   deration; ordinate;
   rationed
rodents   Dorsten; snorted
rodes   doers; dorse; rosed
Rodin   nidor
rodless   dorsels; solders
rodman   random
rodmen   modern
Rodney   yonder
rods   dors; ords; sord
rodsmen   moderns
roe   o'er; ore
roed   doer; Doré; Oder; re-do; rode
roes   Eros; ores; rose; sore
rogers   groser
Roget   ergot
rogue   orgue; rouge
rogued   drogue; gourde; rouged
rogues   grouse; orgues; rouges;
   rugose
roguing   rouging
roiled   Del Rio
roiling   ligroin
roils   loris
roist   riots; rosit; tiros; trios
roisted   editors; rosited; sortied;
   steroid; storied; tie-rods; triodes
roister   rioters

roisterer   terrorise
roisterers   terrorises
roisters   resistor; sorriest
roists   rosits
Roland   Arnold; Landor; lardon;
   Ronald
role   eorl; lore; Orel; orle
roles   eorls; Leros; loser; orles;
   Osler; soler; Sorel
roller   Orrell
Roma   mora; Omar; roam
romaikas   Makarios
Roman   manor; Morna; Norma;
   Ramon
romance   Cameron; Cremona;
   Menorca
Romanes   moaners; San Remo
Romanians   San Marino
Romanic   Marconi; Minorca
Romanies   moraines; Romanise
Romanise   moraines; Romanies
Romanist   Monastir
Romans   manors; ramson; ransom
romantics   narcotism
Romany   mornay
Rome   more; omer
Romeo   Moore
Romeos   morose
romp   prom
romps   proms
Ron   nor
Rona   Arno; Nora; Oran; roan
Ronald   Arnold; Landor; lardon;
   Roland
rondache   anchored
rondavel   overland
ronde   drone
rondes   drones; snored; sorned
rondo   donor; doorn
rondos   donors; doorns
rondure   rounder; unorder
rondures   rounders; unorders
rone   Nero; Nore; oner; Orne; Reno
roneos   seroon; sooner
rones   Norse; noser; oners; Ronse;
   Señor; seron; snore
Ronse   Norse; noser; oners; rones;
   Señor; seron; snore
rood   door; ordo
roods   doors; Ordos; sordo
roofed   foredo
rook   Kroo
rooks   Kroos

room moor; Moro
roomed moored
rooming mooring
rooms moors; Moros; Ormoc; smoor
roop poor; proo
roops sopor; spoor
roost roots; stoor; torso
rooster rooters; toreros
roosts stoors; torsos
rooter torero
rooters rooster; toreros
rootiest tortoise
rootle looter; Loreto; tooler
rootles looters; toolers
roots roost; stoor; torso
rope pore
roped doper; pedro; pored
rope in orpine; Pinero
roper porer; prore
ropers porers
ropes pores; poser; prose; Soper; spore
ropes in orpines
ropiness pression
roping poring
roquet quoter; torque
roquets questor; quoters; torques
Rosa oars; Oras; osar; soar; sora
Rosalind ordinals
Rosaline ailerons; alerions; alienors
Rosas saros; soars
rose Eros; ores; roes; sore
roseate tea-rose
rose-cut scouter
rosed doers; dorse; rodes
rose-hips Seriphos
rose-hued rehoused
roses sores
roset estro; rotes; store; tores; torse
rosets sortes; stores; torses; tosser
Rosetta rotates; toaster; to-tears
rosety oyster; storey; Troyes; tyroes; Yes Tor
Rosie osier; Siero
rosiest sorites; sorties; stories
rosin inros; irons; ornis
rosined indorse; sordine
rosing girons; grison; groins; Signor
rosit riots; roist; tiros; trios

rosited editors; roisted; sortied; steroid; storied; tie-rods; triodes
rositing roisting
rosits roists
roster resort; sorter; storer
rostered Desterro; resorted; restored
rostering resorting; restoring
rosters resorts; sorters; storers
Rosyth shorty
rot ort; tor
rota Orta; taro; Tora
rotas Astor; roast; Sarto; taros; Troas
rotate to-tear
rotates Rosetta; toaster; to-tears
rote tore
rotes estro; roset; store; tores; torse
Rothes others; throes; tosher
roting Girton; trigon
rots orts; sort; tors
rottan ratton
rottans rattons
rotted detort
rotten Trento
rotter retort; torret
rotters retorts; torrets
rotund untrod
roué euro
roués euros; rouse
rouge orgue; rogue
rouged drogue; gourde; rogued
rouges grouse; orgues; rogues; rugose
rouging roguing
roulade Urodela
rounded redound; underdo
roundel lounder; roundle
roundels lounders; roundles
rounder rondure; unorder
rounders rondures; unorders
roundest tonsured; unsorted
roundle lounder; roundel
roundles lounders; roundels
roup pour
rouped poured
rouping ingroup; pouring
roups pours
rouse euros; roués
roused douser; soured
rouses serous
rousing souring

roust routs; stour; sutor; torus; tours
rousted detours; dourest; douters
rousts stours; sutors
rout tour
route outer; outré; Touré
routed detour; douter; outred; red out; toured
router retour; tourer
routers retours; tourers; trouser
routes ouster; outers; souter; touser; trouse
routing ring out; touring
routs roust; stour; sutor; torus; tours
rove over
roved Dover; drove
roves overs; Serov; servo; verso
rowan Nowra
rowdily wordily
rowdiness windroses; wordiness
rowdy dowry; wordy
rowed dower
rowel lower; owler
rowelled well-doer
rowels lowers; owlers; slower
rowen owner
rowens owners; worsen
rowers worser
rowt trow; wort
rowted trowed
rowth throw; worth; wroth
royalist solitary
rub bur
rubato tabour
rubble burble; lubber
rubella rulable
rubied burdie; buried
rubies bruise; buries; busier
rubine Brunei
ruble bluer
rubles Elbrus
rubs burs
ruby bury
ruc cru; cur
rucked ducker
ruckles suckler
rucs crus; curs; scur
rude dure; rued; urdé
ruder Dürer
rue Ure
rued dure; rude; urdé
rues Reus; ruse; sure; ures; user

ruffed duffer
ruffes suffer
ruffian funfair
ruffians funfairs
rugged grudge
rugose grouse; orgues; rogues; rouges
ruin Irun
ruinate taurine; uranite; urinate
ruinated daturine; indurate; urinated
ruined inured
ruiners insurer
ruining inuring
rulable rubella
rule lure
ruled lured
rules lures
ruling luring
rum Mur
rumal larum; mural
rumals larums; murals
rumba Burma; umbra
rumbas sambur
rumble lumber
rumbled drumble
rumbles Burslem; lumbers; slumber
Rumex Murex
ruminates misaunter
rumple lumper; replum
rumples lumpers
rums smur
run nur; urn
runch churn
runcinate encurtain; uncertain
rund durn
rundale Arundel; launder; lurdane
rundle nurled
rundlet trundle
rundlets trundles
runds durns
runed Düren; under; urned
runes nurse
runic incur
runnet unrent
runs nurs; urns
runt turn
runts turns
rupee purée
rupees peruse; purées
rusa sura; Ursa
ruse Reus; rues; sure; ures; user

ruses   Reuss; users
rush   Rhus
rushes   rhesus; ushers
rushier   hurries
rusine   insure; inures; urcine
rusk   Krus
rusma   arums; ramus; Sarum
russet   estrus; tusser
russets   trusses
rust   ruts
rustable   baluster
rusted   duster
rustic   citrus
rusticate   urticates
rustle   luster; lustre; luters; result;
   sutler; ulster
rustled   lustred; strudel
rustles   lusters; lustres; results;
   sutlers; ulsters
rustling   lustring
rusts   truss
Rute   true
ruth   hurt; thru; Thur

ruthful   hurtful
ruthfully   hurtfully
ruthless   hurtless; hustlers
ruthlessly   hurtlessly
ruthlessness   hurtlessness
rutin   Turin
ruts   rust
rutter   turret
rutters   turrets
ryal   aryl; Lyra
ryals   aryls
Ryan   nary; yarn
Rydal   lardy; lyard
Ryde   drey; dyer; yerd
Ryder   Derry; dryer
rye-wolf   flowery
ryot   tory; troy; tyro
ryots   story; tyros
rype   prey; pyre
ryper   perry; pryer
Ryton   try on
ryve   very

S

Saab   abas; baas; Saba
Saadi   Saida
Saar   Aras; Sara
Saba   abas; baas; Saab
Sabah   abash
Sabal   balas; balsa; basal
saber   bares; baser; bears; braes;
   sabre
sabers   sabres
sabin   basin
Sabines   Bassein
sabins   basins
sable   ables; bales; Basel; Basle;
   blaes; blasé
sabot   basto; boast; boats; Sobat
sabots   boasts
sabra   Arabs; arbas; Basra
sabre   bares; baser; bears; braes;
   saber
sabred   ardebs; beards; breads;
   debars; serdab
sabres   sabers
saccharine   cane-chairs
sachem   schema
sachet   chaste; cheats; scathe;
   taches

sachets   scathes
sack   cask
sacked   casked
sacker   crakes; creaks; screak
sackers   screaks
sacking   casking
sacks   casks
sacque   casque
sacques   casques
sacral   lascar; rascal; scalar
sacred   cadres; cedars; scared
sacrify   scarify
sacring   scaring
sacrist   racists
sad   ads; das
sadden   dedans; sanded
sadder   adders; dreads
saddle   addles
saddled   daddles
saddler   ladders; raddles
Sadi   aids; dais; Dias; said; Sida
Sadie   aides; aside; ideas
Sado   soda
sae   eas; sea
saeter   arêtes; easter; eaters; reates;
   reseat; teaser; Teresa

saeters   easters; reseats; teasers;
  tessera
safer   fares; farse; fears
safest   feasts
sag   gas
Sagar   ragas
sage   ages; gaes
sagene   senega
sager   gears; rages; sarge
sages   gases
sagest   stages
sagger   aggers; eggars; seggar
saggers   aggress; seggars
said   aids; dais; Dias; Sadi; Sida
Saida   Saadi
sail   ails; Isla; Lias; Lisa; sial
sailed   aisled; deasil; ideals; ladies
sailer   Israel; serail; serial
sailers   airless; serails; serials
sailing   nilgais
sails   Lissa; Silas; sisal
sain   anis; Isna; Nias; Nisa; Sian
sains   sasin
saint   satin; stain; Tanis
sainted   Danites; detains; instead;
  stained
Saintes   entasis; sestina; Staines;
  tansies; tisanes
saintly   nastily
saints   Säntis; satins; Sistan; stains
sair   airs; Asir; Isar; rias; sari
saith   taish; Thais
Sakai   sakia
sake   Aske; kaes; keas
saker   asker; kesar; rakes; reaks;
  skear
sakeret   retakes
sakers   askers; kesars; skears
saki   sika
sakia   Sakai
sakis   sikas
sal   als
Sala   alas
salable   Las Bela
sale   ales; Elsa; leas; seal; slae
Salem   almes; lames; leams; males;
  meals; samel; Selma
Salemi   mesail; mesial; samiel;
  Sliema
salep   Elaps; lapse; leaps; pales;
  peals; pleas; sepal; spale; speal
Salerno   loaners; orleans; reloans
salerooms   salesroom

sales   salse; seals; slaes
salesmen   lameness; maneless;
  nameless
salesroom   salerooms
Salian   lianas; salina
Salians   salinas
salient   eastlin; elastin; entails;
  slàinte; staniel
salients   eastlins; staniels
salina   lianas; Salian
salinas   Salians
saline   aliens; alines; lianes; Selina;
  silane
Salinger   aligners; engrails;
  realigns; sanglier; seal-ring
saliva   avails; salvia; Valais
salivate   aestival
sallad   Dallas
sallee   allées
sallet   Stella
sallied   dallies
sallow   allows
sallying   signally
salmi   Islam; limas; mails; malis;
  Milas; Simla
salmis   missal
salmo   loams
salmon   monals
salon   loans; sloan; solan; Solna
salons   sloans; solans
saloon   solano
salp   Alps; laps; pals; slap
salps   slaps
sals   lass
salse   sales; seals; slaes
salses   lasses
salt   last; lats; slat
Salta   atlas
saltation   stational
salted   deltas; desalt; lasted; slated;
  staled
salter   alerts; alters; artels; laster;
  ratels; slater; staler; stelar; tarsel
saltern   antlers; rentals; sternal
salters   artless; lasters; slaters;
  tarsels
saltier   Alister; realist; retails;
  saltire; slatier
saltiers   realists; saltires;
  slaister
saltiness   slatiness; stainless
salting   anglist; lasting; slating;
  staling

saltire   Alister; realist; retails;
  saltier; slatier
saltires   realists; saltiers; slaister
saltly   lastly
salt-mine   allments; aliments;
  manliest
Salto   altos; Talos; tolas
saltpan   platans
salts   lasts; slats
saltus   saults; tussal
salty   slaty
salvage   lavages
salvages   Las Vegas
salve   Elvas; laves; selva; slave;
  vales; valse
salved   slaved; valsed
salver   lavers; ravels; serval; slaver;
  versal
salvers   servals; slavers; versals
salves   selvas; slaves; valses
Salvi   Alvis; silva; vails; valis; vials
salvia   avails; saliva; Valais
salving   slaving; valsing
salvo   ovals
Salwin   in-laws
Samar   Maras
Sambo   ambos; bomas
Sambres   ambers; breams; embars
sambur   rumbas
same   mesa; seam
samel   almes; lames; leams; males;
  meals; Salem; Selma
samely   measly
samen   amens; manes; manse;
  means; Mensa; names
Samian   animas; Maasin; manias;
  Manisa
samiel   mesail; mesial; Salemi;
  Sliema
samiels   aimless; Melissa; mesails;
  seismal
samisen   inseams
samite   tamise
samites   asteism; Matisse; tamises
samlet   lamest; metals
Samnite   inmates
Samos   Samsö
samoyed   someday
samp   amps; maps; pams; spam
sampans   passman
samphire   seraphim
sample   maples
sampler   Marples; palmers

Samsö   Samos
Samson   masons; Namsos
sanction   canonist; contains
sanctions   canonists
Sanctus   Tuscans
sand   dans
sanded   dedans; sadden
sander   redans; snared
sanders   sarsden
sandhi   Danish
San Diego   agonised; diagnose
sandier   sardine
sandiver   invaders
sane   eans; sean; Sena
saner   earns; nares; nears; snare
sanest   assent; snaste; stanes; steans
sang   nags; snag
Sanger   angers; ranges; serang
Sangir   grains; rasing
sanglier   aligners; engrails; realigns;
  Salinger; seal-ring
sangliers   seal-rings
Sangrado   Granados
sangs   snags
sanicles   laciness
sanies   sasine
sanity   satiny
sank   kans
San Marino   Romanians
San Pedro   operands; padrones;
  pandores; Sarpedon
San Remo   moaners; Romanes
sansculotterie   interosculates
sanserif   fairness
Santa   Satan; tsana
santalin   annalist
santir   instar; Sintra; strain; trains
santirs   instars; strains
Säntis   saints; satins; Sistan; stains
santon   sonant
santons   sonants
santur   Saturn
sap   asp; pas; spa
sapele   asleep; elapse; please
sapient   panties; patines; spinate
sapling   lapsing; palings
sapor   Paros; proas; psora; sopra
sapper   papers
sappers   appress
sappy   paspy
sap-rot   asport; pastor; portas
saps   asps; pass; spas
sar   ras

Sara Aras; Saar
Sarawak Arawaks
sarcenet reascent
sardel alders
sardine sandier
sardines aridness
sardonic Draconis
sarge gears; rages; sager
Sargent garnets; Stanger; strange
sargo Argos
sargus sugars
sari airs; Asir; Isar; rias; sair
saris arsis
sark arks; Kars
sarment artsmen; martens; smarten
sarments smartens
sarong groans; orangs; organs; Sargon
saros Rosas; soars
Sarpedon operands; padrones; pandores; San Pedro
Sarre rears; serra
sarsden sanders
sarsen Nasser; snares
sarsenet assenter; earnests
Sarthe earths; haters; hearts; 'sheart
Sarto Astor; roast; rotas; taros; Troas
Sartre arrest; arrèts; raster; raters; starer; terras
Sarum arums; ramus; rusma
sarus suras
sashed dashes; shades
sashes she-ass
sasin sains
sasine sanies
sasse asses
sat Ats
Satan Santa; Tsana
satanical Castalian
Satanism mantissa
Satanists assistant
satchel chalets; latches
sate east; eats; seat; seta; taes; teas
sated dates; stade; stead
sateen ensate; senate; steane
sates asset; seats; tasse; Tessa
sati aits; Asti; itas; Sita
satiable Baalites; labiates
satin saint; stain; Tanis
satinet instate

sating gainst; giants
satin-paper appertains
satins saints; Säntis; Sistan; stains
satiny sanity
satire striae
satires tirasse
satirical racialist
Sato oast; oats; stoa; Taos
satori aorist
satrap Patras; Sparta
satrapies aspirates; parasites
Satu-Mare amateurs
sat up sputa
Saturn santur
Saturnalia Australian
Saturnian Turanians
satyr stray; trays
satyra astray; tayras
satyrs strays
sauce cause
sauced caused
saucer causer; cesura; Creüsa
saucers causers; cesuras; sucrase
sauces causes
sauciest suitcase
saucing causing
sauger argues; augers; Segura; usager
sault talus; Tulsa
saults saltus; tussal
saunter aunters; natures; tea-urns
sauntered denatures
saury Surya
sausage assuage
sausages assuages
saut utas
Sava vasa
save Aves; vaes; vase
saved devas; vades; Vedas
saver avers; raves; vares
saves vases
savin vains
saviour various
savourily variously
saw was
sawder Seward; waders
sawed wades
sawer sware; swear; wares; wears
sawers swears; wrasse
sawing aswing
sawn awns; swan
sawpit pit-saw
sawpits pit-saws**

sawset   sweats; tawses; wastes
sawyer   swayer
sawyers   swayers
Saxe   axes
Saxon   axonoj Naxos
sayer   eyras; years
sayest   yeasts
sayst   stays
S-bend   bends
'sblood   bloods
scab   cabs
scad   cads
scalar   lascar; rascal; sacral
scalars   lascars; rascals
scale   claes; laces
scaled   decals
scalene   cleanse; elances; enlaces
scaler   Clares; clears; sclera
scales   Cassel
scall   calls
scalloped   collapsed
scalloping   collapsing
scalp   claps; clasp
scalped   clasped
scalper   carpels; clasper; parcels;
  placers
scalpers   claspers
scalping   clasping
scalps   clasps
scaly   clays
scamble   becalms
scamp   camps
scamped   decamps
scamper   campers
scan   cans
scandia   Dacians
scandium   muscadin
scanner   canners
scant   canst; cants
scanted   decants; descant
scantier   canister
scape   capes; Caspe; paces; space
scaped   spaced
scapes   spaces
scaping   spacing
scapular   capsular
scapulary   capsulary
scar   arcs; cars
scarab   barsac; Scarba
scarabs   barsacs
Scarba   barsac; scarab
scare   acers; acres; cares; carse;
  races; scrae; sérac

scared   cadres; cedars; sacred
scares   caress; carses; crases; scraes;
  séracs
scarier   carries
scarify   sacrify
scaring   sacring
scarlet   cartels; clarets; tarcels
scarp   carps; craps; scrap
scarped   redcaps; scraped
scarper   scraper
scarpers   scrapers
scarping   scraping
scarps   scraps
scarred   carders
scars   crass
scart   carts; scrat
scarth   charts; starch
scarts   scrats
Scarus   scaurs
scary   scray
scat   acts; cast; cats
scathe   chaste; cheats; sachet; taches
scathes   sachets
scatole   alecost; lactose; locates;
  talcose
scats   casts
scattier   citrates; cristate
scaurs   Scarus
scaw   caws
sceat   caste; cates
scena   canes
scenarise   increases
scenarist   canisters
scended   descend
scene   cense
scened   censed
scenes   censes
scenical   calcines
scening   censing
scent   cents
scented   descent
sceptral   spectral
sceptre   receipts; respect; spectre
sceptres   respects; spectres
Scheele   leeches
schema   sachem
schematic   catechism
schiavone   anchovies
Schlei   chesil; chiels; chiles; chisel;
  elchis
scholar   lorchas
Schubert   butchers
schwa   chaws

173

Schwerin winchers
scient incest; insect; nicest
sciential Catilines; inelastic
Scilla lilacs
sciolist solicits
scion coins; icons; sonic
Scirpus prussic
sciurine incisure
sclate castle; cleats
sclates castles
sclave calves; cavels; claves
sclera Clares; clears; scaler
scleral callers; cellars; recalls
sclerite tiercels
sclerose coreless; recloses
scoff coffs
scoffer coffers
scog cogs
scold clods; colds
scolding codlings
scollop collops
scolloped clodpoles
Scomber combers
scone cones; Cosne; sonce
scontion Coniston
scoop coops
scooper coopers
scoot coost; coots
scope copes; copse; Pecos
Scopelus close-ups; upcloses
scopes copses
score ceros; cores; corse
scored Cedros; coders; credos
scorer corers; crores
scores corses; scorse
scorn corns
scorned conders; corsned
scorner corners
scorse corses; scores
scorsed crossed
scorses crosses
scorsing crossing
scot cost; cots
scoter corset; Cortes; coster; escort; sector; Tresco
scoters corsets; costers; escorts; sectors
scot-free cost-free
Scotian actions; cations
Scotland cotlands
scots costs
scour Orcus
scoured coursed

scourer courser
scourers coursers; cursores
scourge scrouge
scourged scrouged
scourges scrouges
scourging scrouging
scouring coursing
scouter rose-cut
scouts custos
scow cows
scowl clows; cowls
scowrie cowries
scrab crabs
scrae acers; acres; cares; carse; races; scare; sérac
scraes caress; carses; crases; scares; séracs
scrag crags
scram crams
scramble cambrels; clambers
scran crans
Scranton Cranston
scrap carps; craps; scarp
scrape capers; Casper; crapes; escarp; pacers; parsec; recaps; spacer
scraped redcaps; scarped
scraper scarper
scrapers scarpers
scrapes escarps; parsecs; spacers
scraping scarping
scraps scarps
scrat carts; scart
scrats scarts
scrattle clatters
scraw craws
scrawl crawls
scrawler crawlers
scray scary
screak crakes; creaks; sacker
screaks sackers
scream crames; creams; macers
screamer creamers
scree ceres; crees
screech creches
screed creeds
screen censer; secern
screened secerned
screening secerning
screens censers; secerns
screich scriech
screiched scrieched
screiches scrieches

screiching screiching
screw crews
scribble cribbles
scriech screich
scrieched screiched
scrieches screiches
screiching screiching
scried ciders; dicers
scries crises
scrieve service
scrieved serviced
scrieves services
scrieving servicing
scrike ickers; sicker
scrimp crimps
scrip crisp
scrips crisps
scripted predicts
scrod cords
scrota actors; castor; Castro; Croats; tarocs
scrotal crotals
scrouge scourge
scrouged scourged
scrouges scourges
scrouging scourging
scrow crows
scrub curbs
scruto courts; Turcos
scrutoire courtiers
scud cuds
scuddle cuddles
scudler curdles
scuff cuffs
scull culls
sculler cruells; cullers
sculling cullings
scullion cullions
sculpin insculp; unclips
sculpins insculps
scumber cumbers
scup cups; cusp
scupper cuppers
scur crus; curs; rucs
scurries cruisers
scut cuts
scutcher crutches
scutter cutters
scuttle cutlets; cuttles
scye syce
scyes syces
scyphi physic
scythe chesty

'sdeath deaths; hasted; tashed
sdeign deigns; design; signed; singed
sdeigned designed
sdeigning designing
sdeigns designs
sea eas; sae
sea-bat abates
sea-bed debase
seabird air-beds; braised; darbies
sea-cat acates
sea-dog dagoes; dosage; sea-god
sea-dogs dosages; sea-gods
sea-fir fraise
sea-fire arefies; faeries; freesia
sea-firs fraises
sea-fret afreets; feaster
sea-girt agister; gaiters; stagier; strigae; triages
sea-god dagoes; dosage; sea-dog
sea-gods dosages; sea-dogs
seagull ullages
seahorse seashore
seahorses seashores
seal ales; Elsa; leas; sale; slae
sealed leased
sea-legs ageless
sealer leaser; resale; Searle
sealers earless; leasers
sealing leasing; linages
sea-lord loaders; ordeals; reloads
seal-ring aligners; engrails; realigns; Salinger; sanglier
seal-rings sangliers
seals sales; salse; slaes
seam mesa; same
seamed adeems
seamen enemas; enseam
seamer ameers; Mersea
seamers Rameses
seaming enigmas; gamines
seams massé; mesas
Seamus amuses; assume
sean eans; sane; Sena
seance Cesena; encase; Seneca
seances encases
sea-perch peachers; preaches
seaport proteas
sear Ares; arse; ears; eras; rase; sera
searce crease
searced creased
searces creases

search   arches; chares; chaser;
   eschar; raches
searcher   reachers; research
searchers   archeress
searcing   creasing; Grecians
seared   aredes; deares; erased; Red
   Sea; reseda
searing   earings; erasing; gainers;
   regains; seraing; seringa
Searle   leaser; resale; sealer
sears   arses; rases; rasse
seashore   seahorse
seashores   seahorses
seaside   disease
seat   east; eats; sate; seta; taes;
   teas
sea-term   steamer
sea-terms   masseter; steamers
seating   easting; Gastein; genista;
   ingates; ingesta; tangies; teasing;
   tsigane
Seaton   atones; Easton
seats   asset; sates: tasse; Tessa
Sebat   abets; baste; bates; beast;
   beats; besat; tabes
secant   ascent; enacts; stance
secants   ascents; stances
secco   cosec
seceder   decrees; recedes
seceders   recessed
secern   censer; screen
secerned   screened
secernent   sentencer
secerning   screening
secerns   censers; screens
seckel   cleeks
seclude   Culdees
seconde   encodes
seconder   seed-corn
seconding   consigned
secondly   condyles
secret   certes; erects; resect
secreta   cerates; creates
secreted   resected
secretes   sesterce
secreting   resecting
secretion   erections; resection
secretions   resections
secrets   cresset; resects
sectarian   ascertain; Cartesian
sectarians   ascertains; Cartesians
section   notices
sectional   coastline

sector   corset; Cortes; coster; escort;
   scoter; Tresco
sectorial   loricates
sectors   corsets; costers; escorts;
   scoters
secund   dunces
securable   rescuable
secure   Cereus; ceruse; Creuse;
   recuse; rescue
secured   recused; reduces; rescued;
   seducer
securer   recures; rescuer
securers   rescuers
secures   recuses; rescues
securing   recusing; rescuing
sedan   Andes; Danes; deans;
   Desna; snead
sedans   sneads
sedate   easted; seated; teased
sedated   dead-set; steaded
sedating   d'Estaing; steading
sedative   deviates
sedent   nested; tensed
Seder   deres; drees; redes; reeds
sederunt   dentures; underset;
   undesert
sederunts   undersets
sedes   seeds
sedge   edges
sedile   diesel; elides; seiled
sedilia   dailies
sedition   editions
seduce   deuces; educes
seduced   deduces
seducer   recused; reduces; rescued;
   secured
seduction   eductions
seductor   eductors
sedum   mused
seed-corn   seconder
seedily   eyelids
seedings   edginess
seeds   sedes
seedsmen   demesnes
seeing   eignes; genies
seek   ekes; skee
seeker   kreese
seekers   kreeses
seeking   skeeing
seeks   skees
seel   eels; else; lees; sele;
   slee
seels   seles

seem   emes; Esme; mese; semé;
  smee
seen   esne
seep   pees
seer   Erse; sere
seers   seres
sees   esse
seethed   sheeted
seething   sheeting
Sefton   soften
seggar   aggers; eggars; sagger
seggars   aggress; saggers
segni   singe
segno   Sogne
sego   goes
segol   loges; ogles
Segre   egers; grees; grese; serge
segreant   estrange; grantees;
  greatens; reagents; sergeant
segregate   Easter egg
segregates   Easter eggs
Segura   argues; augers; sauger;
  usager
seil   Elis; isle; leis; lies; sile
seiled   diesel; elides; sedile
seils   isles; siles
Seim   mise; semi
seined   denies
seiner   serein; serine
seines   in esse; Neisse
seining   insigne
seism   mises; semis
seismal   aimless; Melissa; mesails;
  samiels
seisms   misses
seizable   sizeable
sekos   skeos; sokes
selah   hales; halse; heals; leash;
  shale; sheal
seld   sled
seldom   models
sele   eels; else; lees; seel; slee
select   elects
selection   elections
selector   corselet; electors
selectors   corselets
seled   deles; Edsel; Leeds
Selenga   Senegal
selenic   license; silence
seles   seels
self-same   fameless
Selina   aliens; alines; lianes; saline;
  silane

seling   ingles; lignes; single
Selk   elks; leks
sell   ells
seller   recoll
sellers   resells
sell-out   outsell
sell-outs   outsells
Selma   almes; lames; leams; males;
  meals; Salem; samel
selva   Elvas; laves; salve; slave;
  vales; valse
selvas   salves; slaves; valses
selves   vessel
Semarang   managers
semé   emes; Esme; mese; seem;
  smee
Semele   mêlées
semen   menes; mense; mesne
semi   mise; Seim
seminal   isleman; malines; menials
seminar   marines; remains; sirname
seminars   sirnames
seminate   matinées
seminates   amnesties; meatiness
semiotic   comities
semi-pro   imposer; promise
semi-pros   imposers; promises
semis   mises; seism
semitar   Artemis; imarets; maestri;
  maister; misrate; St. Marie
semitars   asterism; maisters;
  misrates
Semlin   limens; simnel
sen   ens
Sena   eans; sane; sean
senary   renays; yearns
senate   ensate; sateen; steane
senates   steanes
senator   treason
senatorial   alienators
senators   assentor; star-nose;
  treasons
send   dens; ends; sned
Sendai   Adenis
sendal   Landes
sender   denser
senders   redness
sends   sneds
send-up   up-ends; upsend
send-ups   upsends
Seneca   Cesena; encase; seance
senega   sagene
Senegal   Selenga

senescent sentences
senga Agnes; geans; genas
Senhor herons; rhones
Senhora Hornsea
Senhorita Hortensia
senile enisle; ensile; nelies; Silene
senior nosier; soneri
Senlac cleans; lances
sennit sinnet; tennis
sennits sinnets
Señor Norse; noser; oners; rones;
  Ronse; seron; snore
Señora reason
Señoras reasons
Señorita notaries
Señoritas assertion
Señors nosers; sensor; serons;
  snores
Sens ness
sense esnes; Essen
sensing ensigns
sensor nosers; Señors; serons;
  snores
sensual unseals
sent nest; nets; sten; tens
Senta antes; etnas; nates; Nesta;
  stane; stean; Teans
sentencer secernent
sentencers recentness
sentences senescent
sentries trenises
Senusis Senussi
Senussi Senusis
senza nazes
Seoul louse; ousel
sepad spade; spaed
sepads passed; spades
sepal Elaps; lapse; leaps; pales;
  peals; pleas; salep; spale; speal
sepalous espousal
sepals lapses; spales;
  speals
sepoy poesy
sepsis pisses; speiss
sept pest; pets; step
septa paste; pates; spate; speat;
  tapes
septal palest; palets; pastel; petals;
  plates; pleats; staple
septaria aspirate; parasite
septimal implates; palmiest;
  palmiets; petalism
septs pests; steps

septuor petrous; posture; pouters;
  Proteus; spouter; troupes
sera Ares; arse; ears; eras; rase; sear
sérac acers; acres; cares; carse;
  races; scare; scrae
séracs caress; carses; crases; scares;
  scraes
seraglio girasole
serai aesir; Aries; arise; raise; Riesa;
  Seria
serail Israel; sailer; serial
serails airless; sailers; serials
Seraing earings; erasing; gainers;
  regains; searing; seringa
serais arises; raises
serang angers; ranges; Sanger
seraph phares; phrase; raphes;
  shaper; Sherpa; sphaer
seraphic parchesi
seraphim samphire
seraphs phrases; shapers; Sherpas;
  sphaers
Serapic Epacris
Serapis aspires; paresis; praises
Serbia braise; rabies
serdab ardebs; beards; breads;
  debars; sabred
sere Erse; seer
serein seiner; serine
serenata arsenate
seres seers
Sereth Esther; Hester; threes
serfish fishers; sherifs
serge egers; grees; grese; Segre
sergeant estrange; grantees;
  greatens; reagents; segreant
sergeants estranges; greatness
Sergo goers; gores; gorse; ogres;
  soger
Seria aesir; Aries; arise; raise; Riesa;
  serai
serial Israel; sailer; serail
serialised idealisers
serialized idealizers
serials airless; sailers; serails
seric cries; erics; icers
sericon coiners; crinose; cronies
serif fires; fries
serin reins; resin; rinse; risen; siren
serine seiner; serein
seringa earings; erasing; gainers;
  regains; searing; Seraing
serins resins; rinses; sirens

seriph   perish; reship
Seriphos   rose-hips
seriphs   reships
serk   erks; sker
serks   skers
Serlio   elisor; lories; oilers; oriels
sermon   mornes
sermonic   incomers
seron   Norse; noser; oners; rones;
   Ronse; Señor; snore
serons   nosers; Señors; sensor;
   snores
seroon   roneos; sooner
serous   rouses
Serov   overs; roves; servo; verso
serow   owers; sower; swore; worse
serows   sowers
serpent   present; repents
serpented   presented
serpenting   presenting
serpents   pertness; presents
serpigo   porgies
serpula   perusal
serr   errs
serra   rears; Sarre
Sérrai   airers; raiser; sierra
serranid   drainers
serrate   re-rates; tearers
serrated   retreads; treaders
serrates   asserter; reassert
serrature   treasurer
serried   desirer; Dreiser
serum   mures; muser; Remus;
   Sumer
serval   lavers; ravels; salver; slaver;
   versal
servals   salvers; slavers; versals
servant   taverns; versant
servants   St. Servan
serve   sever; veers; verse
served   versed
server   revers; verser
servers   versers
serves   severs; Sèvres, verses
Servia   varies
Servian   ravines
service   scrieve
serviced   scrieved
services   scrieves
servicing   scrieving
servient   nerviest; reinvest; sirvente
servile   Liévres; relives; reviles
serving   versing

Servite   restive
servo   overs; roves; Serov; verso
session   essoins
sesterce   secretes
sestet   testes; tsetse
sestets   tsetses
sestina   entasis; Saintes; Staines;
   tansies; tisanes
Sestos   tosses
seta   east; eats; sate; seat; taes; teas
setae   tease
setback   backets; backset
setbacks   backsets
Sète   Este; tees
Seth   Esth; hest; shet
Sethon   honest; Stheno
set in   inset; neist; stein; tines
set-off   offset
set-offs   offsets
seton   Eston; notes; onset; stone;
   Tenos; tones
setons   Nestos; onsets; sets on;
   stones
sets   Tess
sets in   insets; steins; Tessin
sets on   Nestos; onsets; setons;
   stones
sett   stet; test
setter   street; tester
setters   streets; tersest; testers
setting   testing
settle   ettles
settler   letters; sterlet; trestle
settlers   sterlets; trestles
set-to   totes
setts   tests
set-up   stupe; upset
setwall   wallets
Seurat   Atreus; Auster
Sevan   avens; Evans; naves; vanes
seven   evens; Neves
seventy-nine   ninety-seven
seventy-six   sixty-seven
sever   serve; veers; verse
several   laveers; leavers; reveals
severe   reeves
severed   deserve
Severn   nerves; Nevers
severs   serves; Sèvres; verses
Sèvres   serves; severs; verses
sewan   wanes; weans
Seward   sawder; waders
sewed   swede; sweed; weeds

sewel   Lewes; sweel; weels; Wesel
sewels   sweels
sewen   enews; weens
sewer   ewers; sweer; Weser
sewers   sweers
sewin   sinew; swine; wines
sewing   swinge; winges
sewn   news; wens
sexes   Essex
sexist   exists
sexpartite   extirpates
sextan   Texans
sey   sye; yes
shack   hacks
shackle   hackles
Shackleton   shecklaton
shad   dahs; dash
shaddock   haddocks
shade   Hades; heads
shaded   dashed
shades   dashes; sashed
shading   dashing
shady   Hyads
shaft   hafts
shafter   fathers
shag   gash; hags
shah   hash
Shairp   Hispar; parish; raphis
shaker   kasher
shaking   Kashing
Shakti   skaith
shale   hales; halse; heals; leash;
  selah; sheal
shales   halses; hassle; lashes; sheals
shall   halls
shallow   hallows
shalt   halts; laths; Stahl
sham   hams; mash
shamble   hambles
shame   hames; Shema
shamed   mashed
shamer   harems; masher
shamers   mashers; smasher
shames   mashes
shaming   mashing
shammer   hammers
shams   smash
shan   Hans; Nash
shand   hands
Shane   ashen; Hanse
shank   ankhs; hanks; khans
shans   snash
shan't   Hants.; snath

shanties   anthesis
Shap   haps; hasp; pash
shape   heaps; Pesah; phase
shaped   hasped; pashed; phased
shaper   phares; phrase; raphes;
  seraph; Sherpa; sphaer
shapers   phrases; seraphs; Sherpas;
  sphaers
shapes   pashes; phases
shaping   hasping; pashing; phasing
shard   hards
share   hares; hears; rheas; shear
shared   dasher
share-outs   authoress
sharer   rasher
sharers   rashers
shares   rashes; shears
Shari   arish; hairs
sharing   garnish
shark   harks
sharp   harps
sharped   phrased
sharper   harpers; phraser
sharpers   phrasers
sharpest   sharp-set
sharping   phrasing
sharp-set   sharpest
shatter   hatters; rathest; threats
shattering   straighten
shave   haves; sheva
shaven   havens; Hesvan
shaver   havers
shaw   haws; wash
shawling   whalings
shawm   hawms
shaws   swash
shay   ashy; hays
sheading   headings
sheal   hales; halse; heals; leash;
  selah; shale
shealing   leashing
sheals   halses; hassle; lashes; shales
shear   hares; hears; rheas; share
sheared   adheres; headers
shearer   hearers; rehears
shearing   hearings
shears   rashes; shares
'sheart   earths; haters; hearts;
  Sarthe
she-ass   sashes
sheath   heaths
sheave   heaves
Shebat   bathes

shecklaton Shackleton
she-devil dishevel
she-devils dishevels
sheel heels; heles
sheen Esneh
sheens Hessen; sneesh
sheep phese
sheer Esher; herse
sheering greenish
sheers herses
sheet thees; these
sheeted seethed
sheeting seething
sheets theses
sheik hikes
Sheila Ilesha
sheiling shieling
shelf flesh
shelfy fleshy
shell hells
sheller hellers
Shelta haslet; lathes; Thales
shelve helves
Shem hems; mesh
Shema hames; shame
Shensi shines
She'ol holes
Sheraton North Sea
sherd herds; shred
sherds shreds
sheriat hastier
sherif fisher
sherifs fishers; serfish
Sherpa phares; phrase; raphes;
  seraph; shaper; sphaer
Sherpas phrases; seraphs; shapers;
  sphaers
shes Hess
shet Esth; hest; Seth
Shetland Stendhal
shets hests
sheugh Hughes
sheva haves; shave
shew hews
shewel wheels
shewing hewings; whinges
shicker skriech
shied hides
shieling sheiling
shier heirs; hires; shire
shiers shires
shiest heists; shites; sithes; Theiss;
  thesis

shikar rakish
shill hills
shin hisn; sinh
shindig dishing; hidings
shiner rhines; shrine
shiners shrines
shines Shensi
shingle English
shingled hind legs
ship hips; pish
shipmates steamship
shippo hippos; popish
shir Shri
shire heirs; hires; shier
shires shiers
shirra arrish; Harris; sirrah
shirty Irtysh; thyrsi
shit hist; hits; sith; this; Tshi
shite heist; sithe; Thiès
shites heists; shiest; sithes; Theiss;
  thesis
shiting insight
shits hists
shive hives
shiver hivers; shrive
shivered shrieved
shivering shrieving
shivers shrives
shoal halos; shola; solah
shoals sholas; solahs
shoat Athos; hoast; hosta; oaths
shoats hoasts; hostas; Thasos
shock hocks
shocker chokers; hockers
shod hods
shoder hordes; horsed; Rhodes;
  shored
shoe hoes; hose
shoed doseh; hosed
shoer hoers; horse; shore
shoers horses; shores
shoes hoses
shog gosh; hogs
shola halos; shoal; solah
sholas shoals; solahs
shone hones; hosen
shoo Soho
shook hooks
shoot hoots; sooth; Sotho
shooter hooters; soother
shooters soothers
shooting soothing
shoots Sothos

shop hops; posh; soph
shopper hoppers
shopping hoppings
shops sophs; sposh
shore hoers; horse; shoer
shore-crab broachers
shored hordes; horsed; Rhodes; shoder
shores horses; shoers
shore up Orpheus
shoring horsing
shorn horns
short horst
shorted dehorts
shorten hornets; thrones
shortened dethrones
shortie hoister
shorts horsts
shorty Rosyth
shot host; hots; tosh
shote ethos; those
shotgun gunshot; noughts
shotguns gunshots
shout south; thous
shouted southed
shouter souther
shouters southers
shouting southing
shouts souths
shove hoves
shovel hovels
shover hovers; shrove
shovers shroves
show band bow-hands
shower whores
shred herds; sherd
shred-pie hesperid; perished
shred-pies hesperids
shreds sherds
shrew wersh
Shri shir
shriek hikers; shrike
shrieks shrikes
shrieval lavisher
shrieved shivered
shrieving shivering
shrift firths; friths
shrike hikers; shriek
shrikes shrieks
shrine rhines; shiner
shrined hinders
shrines shiners
shrive hivers; shiver

shrived dervish
shrives shivers
shroudy hydrous
shrove hovers; shover
shroves shovers
shrub brush
shul lush; Suhl
shun Huns
shuns snush
shunt hunts
shunter hunters
shunters huntress
shut huts; thus; tush
shut up Pushtu
si is
sial ails; Isla; Lias; Lisa; sail
Siam aims; Amis; Mais; sima
siamang Magians
siamangs amassing
Siamese misease
Sian anis; Isna; Nias; Nisa; sain
sib bis
Siberian Iberians
Sican Canis; Incas
sice ices
Sicel ceils; ciels; Leics.; slice
Sicels slices
sicker ickers; scrike
Sickert rickets; sticker; tickers
sickled slicked
Sid Dis
Sida aids; dais; Dias; Sadi; said
Sidcup cupids; cuspid
side dies; Ides
sidearms misreads
sideboard broadside
sideboards broadsides
sidecar radices
sidecars Cressida
sideman demains; maidens; medians
side-on donsie; Edison; noised; onside
side-post deposits; topsides
sider dries; rides; sired
sideral derails
sidereal realised
side-step despites
sidle deils; idles; slide
sidles slides
sidling sliding
Sidney Disney
Sidra raids

siemens   Meissen; misseen; nemesis
Siena   Aisne; anise
sienna   insane
Siero   osier; Rosie
sierra   airers; raiser; Sérrai
sierras   raisers
siesta   tassie
siestas   tassies
sieved   devise; viséed
sieves   essive
sift   fist; fits
sifted   fisted
sifter   refits; strife
sifting   fisting
sifts   fists
sight   thigs
sigmatron   Montargis; stroaming
sign   gins; sing; snig
Signac   casing
signal   aligns
signally   sallying
signatory   gyrations
signature   gauntries
signboard   boardings
signed   deigns; design; sdeign; singed
signer   Ingres; reigns; renigs; resign; singer
signers   ingress; resigns; singers
signet   ingest; tinges
signets   ingests
Signor   girons; grison; groins; rosing
Signora   ignaros; soaring
Signoras   assignor
Signore   ignores; regions
signpost   postings; stopings
signs   sings; snigs
sika   saki
sikas   sakis
sike   Eisk
Sikel   likes
sikes   skies
silane   aliens; alines; lianes; saline; Selina
Silas   Lissa; sails; sisal
sild   lids; slid
sile   Elis; isle; leis; lies; seil
silen   elsin; lenis; liens; lines; nelis; Niles
silence   license; selenic
silenced   declines; licensed

silencer   licenser; reclines
silencers   licensers
silences   licenses
silencing   licensing
Silene   enisle; ensile; nelies; senile
silens   elsins
silent   enlist; inlets; listen; tinsel
siler   leirs; liers; riels; riles
siles   isles; seils
silhouette   hotel suite
silhouettes   hotel suites
silken   inkles; likens
sill   ills
silly   slily
silo   Lois; oils; soil; soli
silo'd   idols; Isold; lidos; sloid; soldi; solid
siloed   Isolde; soiled
siloing   soiling
Silone   eloins; esloin; insole; lesion
silos   soils
silt   list; slit
silted   idlest; listed; tildes
silting   listing
silts   lists; slits
silva   Alvis; Salvi; vails; valis; vials
silvan   anvils
silver   livers; livres; rivels; sliver
silvered   delivers; desilver; slivered
silvering   slivering
silvers   slivers
sima   aims; Amis; Mais; Siam
simar   ramis
simarre   marries
Simeon   eonism; Miseno; monies; Simone
similes   missile
Simla   Islam; limas; mails; malis; Milas; salmi
simmer   merism; mimers
simmered   immersed
simmering   immersing
simnel   limens; Semlin
Simon   Minos
Simone   eonism; Miseno; monies; Simeon
simoons   monosis
simp   imps
simper   primes
simpered   demireps; premised
simperer   premiers
simpering   premising
simpers   impress; Persism; premiss

simple   impels; Milspe
simpler   limpers; prelims
sin   ins; nis
since   Cenis
sincere   ceresin
sind   dins
Sindara   radians
sine   Ines
sinecure   insecure
sines   nisse
sinew   sewin; swine; wines
sinewed   endwise
sinews   swines
sinewy   winsey
sing   gins; sign; snig
singable   Belgians; Bengalis
singe   segni
singed   deigns; design; sdeign;
   signed
singer   Ingres; reigns; renigs;
   resign; signer
singers   ingress; resigns; signers
singes   gneiss
single   ingles; lignes; seling
singled   dingles; engilds
singles   Lessing
singlet   glisten; tingles
singlets   glistens
singling   gin-sling; slinging
singly   Glynis; lysing
sings   signs; snigs
singult   lusting
sinh   hisn; shin
sink   inks; kins; skin
sinker   inkers
sinks   skins
sinned   Dennis
sinner   inners
sinnet   sennit; tennis
sinnets   sennits
sinning   innings; inn-sign
sinter   insert; inters; Strine; trines
sintered   Dneister; inserted;
   resident
sintering   inserting
sinters   inserts
Sintra   instar; santir; strain; trains
sinuate   aunties
Sion   ions
sip   psi
sipe   pies; pisé
siped   spied
sipes   spies

siphons   sonship
Siporex   proxies
sipper   pipers
sippled   slipped
sippling   slipping
sips   piss
sir   Sri
sire   Eris; reis; rise
sired   dries; rides; sider
siren   reins; resin; rinse; risen; serin
sirenians   raininess
sirens   resins; rinses; serins
sires   rises
Siret   reist; resit; rites; tiers; tires;
   tries
siring   rising
sirname   marines; remains; seminar
sirnames   seminars
sirrah   arrish; Harris; shirra
sirred   derris; driers; reirds; riders
sirs   Riss
sirvente   nerviest; reinvest; servient
sirventes   reinvests
sisal   Lissa; sails; Silas
Sistan   saints; Säntis; satins; stains
sisted   deists; desist
sister   reists; resist; resits
sisters   resists
sistra   sitars; stairs
sistrum   trismus; truisms
sit   its; tis
Sita   aits; Asti; itas; sati
sitar   airts; astir; raits; Sitra; stair;
   stria; tarsi; Trias
sitars   sistra; stairs
site   stie; ties
sited   deist; diets; dites; edits; id est;
   St. Dié; stied; tides
sites   sties
sith   hist; hits; shit; this; Tshi
sithe   heist; shite; Thiès
Sithes   heists; shiest; shites; Theiss;
   thesis
Sitra   airts; astir; raits; sitar; stair;
   stria; tarsi; Trias
Sittang   stating; tasting
sittar   artist; strait; strati; traits
sittars   artists; straits; tsarist
sitter   titres; trites
situs   suits
Siva   Avis; visa
Sivan   vinas
Sivas   visas

siver rives
sixte exist; exits
sixty xysti
sixty-nine ninety-six
sixty-seven seventy-six
sizeable seizable
skail kails; kalis; laiks; Laski
skaith Shakti
Skåne skean; snake; sneak
skart karst; karts; stark; strak
skat kats; taks; task
skate Keats; Skeat; stake; steak;
  takes; teaks
skated staked; tasked
skater strake; streak; takers; tasker
skaters strakes; streaks; taskers
skates stakes; steaks
skating staking; takings; tasking
skean Skåne; snake; sneak
skeans snakes; sneaks
skear asker; kesar; rakes; reaks
  saker
skears askers; kesars; sakers
Skeat Keats; skate; stake; steak;
  takes; teaks
skee ekes; seek
skeeing seeking
skeer esker; reeks
skeers eskers
skees seeks
skeet skete
skeg kegs
skein Skien
skeletal lakelets
skene keens; knees
skeo Keos; okes; soke
skeos sekos; sokes
skep keps
skeptic pickets
sker erks; serk
skerry skryer
skers serks
skete skeet
skewer Wesker
skid disk; kids
skids disks
skied dikes
Skien skein
skier keirs; kiers
skiers kisser
skies sikes
skiey Yeisk
skill kills

skin inks; kins; sink
skink kinks
skins sinks
skint knits; stink; tinks
skip kips
skipper kippers
skirret striker
skirrets strikers
skirt stirk
skirting striking
skirts stirks
skis kiss
skit kist; kits
skite kites; tikes
skittle kittles
skiving Vikings
sklim milks
skran knars; krans; narks; ranks;
  snark
skreigh skriegh
skreighed skrieghed
skreighing skrieghing
skreighs skrieghs
skriech shicker
skriegh skreigh
skrieghed skreighed
skrieghing skreighing
skrieghs skreighs
skryer skerry
skua auks
Skye keys; syke; yesk
skyey Yeysk
skyte kytes; tykes
slab albs; labs
slabbed dabbles
slabber barbels; rabbles
slack calks; lacks
slacker calkers; lackers
slade dales; deals; lades; leads
slae ales; Elsa; leas; sale; seal
slaes sales; salse; seals
slag gals; lags
slagged daggles
slaid Aldis; dalis; dials
slain nails; snail
slàinte eastlin; elastin; entails;
  salient; staniel
slaister realists; saltiers; saltires
slake kales; lakes; leaks
slakes Kassel
slam alms; lams
slander enlards; landers; snarled
slane lanes; leans

slang glans
slanged dangles
slangish slashing
slap Alps; laps; pals; salp
slapped dapples
slapper lappers; rapples
slaps salps
slap-up palpus
slashed hassled
slasher ashlers; lashers
slashes hassles
slashing hassling; lashings;
  slangish
slat last; lats; salt
slate least; leats; Stael; stale; steal;
  stela; taels; tales; teals; tesla
slated deltas; desalt; lasted; salted;
  staled
slater alerts; alters; artels; laster;
  ratels; salter; staler; stelar; tarsel
slaters artless; lasters; salters;
  tarsels
slates stales; steals; tassel; teslas
slather halters; harslet; Herstal;
  lathers
slatier Alister; realist; retails;
  saltier; saltire
slatiness saltiness; stainless
slating anglist; lasting; salting;
  staling
slats lasts; salts
slatter rattles; starlet; startle;
  tatlers; Telstar
slattern trentals
slatters starlets; startles
slaty salty
slave Elvas; laves; salve; selva;
  vales; valse
slaved salved; valsed
slaver lavers; ravels; salver; serval;
  versal
slaverer reversal
slaverers reversals
slavers salvers; servals; versals
slaves salves; selvas; valses
Slavic cavils; clavis
slaving salving; valsing
slaw awls; laws
slay lays
slayer layers; relays
slayers rayless
sleave leaves
sled seld

sledge gledes; gleeds; ledges
sledger gelders; ledgers
slee eels; else; lees; seel; sele
sleek keels; leeks
sleeker keelers
sleep peels; speel
sleeper peelers; speeler
sleepers peerless; speelers
sleeping peelings; speeling
sleeps speels
sleet leets; steel; stele
sleeted deletes; steeled
sleeting gentiles; steeling
sleets steels; steles
sleety steely
sleeve levees
slender lenders
slept pelts; spelt
sleuth hustle
sleuths hustles
slew Wels
slewing swingle
sley leys; lyes; lyse
sleys lyses; Yssel
slice ceils; ciels; Leics.; Sicel
slicer relics
slices Sicels
slick licks
slicked sickled
slicken nickels
slicker lickers; rickles
slid lids; sild
slidden dindles
slidder riddles
slide deils; idles; sidle
slider idlers
slides sidles
sliding sidling
Sliema mesail; mesial; Salemi;
  samiel
'slife Felis; files; flies
slight lights
slighted delights
slighter lighters; relights
slily silly
slime limes; miles; smile
slimed misled; smiled
slimes missel; smiles
slimier milreis
sliming smiling
sling lings
slinger lingers
slingers ringless

slinging gin-sling; singling
sling ink inklings; slinking
slink kilns; links
slinking inklings; sling ink
slip lips; lisp
slipe piles; plies; spiel; spile
slipes plissé; spiels; spiles
slipped sippled
slipper ripples
slipping sippling
slips lisps
slipt spilt; split
slip up pupils
slit list; silt
slits lists; silts
slitter litters; stilter; testril; tilters; titlers
slitting stilting; Tlingits
slive Elvis; evils; levis; lives; veils; vleis
slived devils
Sliven livens; snivel
sliver livers; livres; rivels; silver
slivered delivers; desilver; silvered
slivering silvering
slivers silvers
sloan loans; salon; solan; Solna
sloans salons; solans
slob Bols; lobs
sloe lose; Ösel; sole
sloes loess; loses; soles
slog Glos.; logs
slogged dog-legs
slogger loggers
slogs gloss
sloid idols; Isold; lidos; silo'd; soldi; solid
sloom looms; mools
sloop loops; pools; spool
sloops spools
slop lops
slope elops; lopes; olpes; poles
sloppy polyps
slopy ploys; Pylos
slot lost; lots; St. Lô
sloth Holst; holts
slotted dottles
slough ghouls; loughs
slove loves; solve; voles
sloven novels
slow lows; owls; sowl
slowed dowels; sowled
slower lowers; owlers; rowels

slowing sowling
slowness snowless
slows sowls
slubber burbles; lubbers
slued duels; dulse
slug lugs
slugger gurgles; luggers
sluices Celsius
slum lums
slumber Burslem; lumbers; rumbles
slump lumps; plums
slumped dumples
slung lungs
slurb blurs; burls
slut lust
sluts lusts
sly Lys
slyer lyres
slyest styles
smack macks
smaik kaims; kamis; maiks
small malls
smalt malts
smart marts; trams
smarten artsmen; martens; sarment
smartened tradesmen
smartens sarments
smarter armrest
smartest mattress; smatters
smarting migrants
smash shams
smasher mashers; shamers
smatter matters
smatters mattress; smartest
smear mares; maser; reams
smears masers; Ramses
smeath Thames
smee emes; Esme; mese; seem; semé
smeeth themes
smell mells
smelt melts
smelter melters
smelters termless
smew mews
smile limes; miles; slime
smiled misled; slimed
smiler merils; milers
smilers rimless
smiles missel; slimes
smiling sliming

smir   mirs; rims
smirch   chrism
smit   mist
smite   emits; items; metis; mites;
   stime; times
smiter   merits; mister; mitres;
   remits; timers
smites   misset; stimes; tmesis
smiting   misting; stiming; timings
smitten   mittens
smock   mocks
smoke   mokes
smolder   molders
smoor   moors; Moros; Ormos;
   rooms
smooring   moorings
smoot   moots; tooms
smore   Moers; mores; morse; omers
smored   dromes
smores   morses
smote   mesto; motes; tomes
smother   mothers; thermos
smoulder   moulders; remoulds
smouse   mousse
smouser   mousers
smouses   mousses
smug   gums; mugs
smugger   muggers
smur   rums
smurred   murders
smut   must; stum; tums
smuts   stums
smytrie   mistery
snab   bans; nabs
snafu   fauns; Fusan
snag   nags; sang
snags   sangs
snail   nails; slain
snailed   denails; lead-ins
snake   Skåne; skean; sneak
snakes   skeans; sneaks
snap   naps; pans; span
snapped   appends
snapper   nappers; parpens;
   parsnep
snappered   end-papers
snappers   parsneps
snaps   spans
snare   earns; nares; nears; saner
snared   redans; sander
snares   Nasser; sarsen
snark   knars; krans; narks; ranks;
   skran

snarled   enlards; landers; slander
snary   yarns
snash   shans
snaste   assent; sanest; stanes; steans
snastes   assents
snatch   chants; stanch
snatched   stanched
snatcher   chanters; stancher;
   tranches
snatchers   stanchers
snatches   stanches
snatching   stanching
snath   Hants.; shan't
snathe   Athens; hasten; sneath;
   thanes
snathes   hastens; sneaths
snead   Andes; Danes; deans;
   Desna; sedan
sneads   sedans
sneak   Skåne; skean; snake
sneaks   skeans; snakes
sneap   aspen; napes; neaps; panes;
   peans; spane; spean
sneaped   speaned
sneaping   speaning
sneaps   aspens; spanes; speans
sneath   Athens; hasten; snathe;
   thanes
sneaths   hastens; snathes
sneb   bens; nebs
sneck   necks
sned   dens; ends; send
sneds   sends
Sneek   knees
sneer   ernes
sneered   needers
sneesh   Hessen; sheens
snib   bins; nibs
snick   nicks
snicked   dickens
snicker   nickers
snide   Denis; dines
sniff   niffs
snig   gins; sign; sing
snigger   gingers; niggers
sniggle   gingles; niggles
sniggled   geldings
snigs   signs; sings
snip   nips; pins; spin
snipe   penis; pines; spine
sniped   piends; spined
sniper   ripens
snipes   spines

snipper nippers
snips spins
snivel livens; Sliven
snob bos'n; nobs
snobs bos'ns
snod dons; nods
snoep opens; peons; pones; Posen
snog nogs; song
snogs songs
snook nooks
snool loons; Solon
snoop spoon
snooped spooned
snooper Spooner
snooping spooning
snoops spoons
snore Norse; noser; oners; rones;
  Ronse; Señor; seron
snored drones; rondes; sorned
snorer sorner
snorers sorners
snores nosers; Señors; sensor;
  serons
snoring sorning
snorted Dorsten; rodents
snot onst; tons
snotter stentor
snotters stentors
snow owns; sown
snowed endows
snowk knows
snowless slowness
snub buns; nubs
snudge nudges
snug gnus; guns; sung
snush shuns
snuzzle nuzzles
so os
soak koas; oaks; okas
soaker arkose
soap apso
soaped apodes
soaps apsos; psoas
soar oars; Oras; osar; Rosa; sora
soare arose
soared adores; oreads
soaring ignaros; Signora
soars Rosas; saros
Sobat basto; boast; boats; sabot
sobbing gibbons
sober boers; bores; broes; robes
sobered bedsore
sobole lobose

sobs boss
soc cos
socager cargoes; corsage
socagers corsages
soccer escroc
Soche chose
social Licosa
societal aloetics
Socinus cousins
socle close; coles
socles closes
socman mascon
Socrates coarsest; coasters
Socratic acrostic
sod dso
soda Sado
Sodom dooms; dsomo; moods
sods doss; dsos
sofa oafs
softa fatso
soften Sefton
softener enforest
softeners enforests
soger goers; gores; gorse; ogres;
  Sergo
sogers ogress
Sogne segno
Soho shoo
soil Lois; oils; silo; soli
soiled Isolde; siloed
soiling siloing
soils silos
soke Keos; okes; skeo
sokes sekos; skeos
Sokol kolos; looks
sola also; Laos
solacer escolar; oracles
solacers escolars; lacrosse
solah halos; shoal; shola
solahs shoals; sholas
solan loans; salon; sloan; Solna
solano saloon
solans salons; sloans
solas lasso
solder dorsel; drôles; resold
solderers orderless
solders dorsels; rodless
soldi idols; Isold; lidos; silo'd; sloid;
  solid
sole lose; Ösel; sloe
solecises isosceles
solecist solstice
solecists solstices

soled Delos; doles; lodes
solemn Lemnos; lemons; melons
soleness noseless
Solent stolen; telson
soler eorls; Leros; loser; orles; Osler; roles; Sorel
solers lessor; losers
soles loess; loses; sloes
soleus louses; ousels
sol-fa foals; loafs
soli Lois; oils; silo; soil
solicit colitis
solicitation coalitionist
solicitations coalitionists
solicits sciolist
solid idols; Isold; lidos; silo'd; sloid; soldi
solids dossil
Soliman malison; Osmanli
soling losing
soliped despoil; diploes; dipoles; peloids; spoiled
solipeds despoils
solitary royalist
solitudes dissolute
solive olives
Solly lysol
Solna loans; salon; sloan; solan
solo loos; Oslo
Solon loons; snool
sols loss
solstice solecist
solstices solecists
Solti Isolt; toils
soluble lobules
solus souls
solve loves; slove; voles
solver lovers
solves Lesvos
soma Amos; moas
somatist atomists
Sombor brooms
someday samoyed
Somme memos; momes
son nos.
sonance ancones
sonances canoness
sonant santon
sonants santons
sonar arson; roans
sonce cones; Cosne; scone
sonde nodes; nosed
sondeli dolines; Leonids

Sondrio indoors; sordino
sone Enos; eons; noes; nose; ones
soneri nosier; senior
sones noses; sonse
song nogs; snog
songs snogs
sonic coins; icons; scion
sonless lessons
sonnet Neston; nonets; stonen; tenons; tenson; tonnes
sonnets Stenson; tensons
Sonnite intones; tension
sonse noses; sones
sonship siphons
sonsie enosis; essoin; noesis; noises; ossein
sontag Gaston; tangos; tongas
soole loose; oleos
sooled loosed; oodles
sooles looses
sooling loosing; olingos
soom moos
soon oons
sooner roneos; seroon
sooth hoots; shoot; Sotho
soother hooters; shooter
soothers shooters
soothing shooting
sootiest tootsies
sop ops; pos
Soper pores; poser; prose; ropes; spore
soph hops; posh; shop
sophister prothesis; store-ship
sophisters store-ships
sophs shops; sposh
sopor roops; spoor
Sopot stoop
soppy popsy
sopra Paros; proas; psora; sapor
sops poss
sora oars; Oras; osar; Rosa; soar
soral orals
sorb orbs; robs
sorbet Osbert; strobe
sord dors; ords; rods
sorda Doras; dorsa; roads; Rodas
sordes dorses; dosser
sordine indorse; rosined
sordino indoors; Sondrio
sordo doors; Ordos; roods
sords dross
sore Eros; ores; roes; rose

soredium dimerous
Sorel eorls; Leros; loser; orles;
  Osler; roles; soler
sores roses
Sorex oxers
sorites rosiest; sorties, stories
sorned drones; rondes; snored
sorner snorer
sorners snorers
sorning snoring
soroche chooser
sorriest resistor; roisters
sort orts; rots; tors
sortable bloaters; storable
sorted Dorset; stored; strode
sorter resort; roster; storer
sorters resorts; rosters; storers
sortes rosets; stores; torses;
  tosser
sortie tiroes; tories
sortied editors; roisted; rosited;
  steroid; storied; tie-rods; triodes
sorties rosiest; sorites; stories
sorting storing; trigons
sortment torments
sortments sternmost
sorus sours
Sotho hoots; shoot; sooth
Sothos shoots
sots toss
sought toughs
souled loused
souls solus
Soult lotus; louts
soumed moused; Usedom
souming mousing
sound nodus
sounder Öresund; resound;
  undoers
sounders dourness; resounds
soup opus
souple poules
sour ours
source cerous; course; crouse;
  Crusoe
sources courses; Croesus; sucrose
soured douser; roused
sourest estrous; oestrus; ousters;
  souters; tousers; trouses; tussore
souring rousing
sours sorus
souses Sousse
Sousse souses

souter ouster; outers; routes;
  touser; trouse
souters estrous; oestrus; ousters;
  sourest; tousers; trouses; tussore
south shout; thous
southed shouted
souther shouter
southers shouters
southing shouting
souths shouts
soviets stovies
sowed dowse
sower owers; serow; swore; worse
sowers serows
sowl lows; owls; slow
sowled dowels; slowed
sowling slowing
sowls slows
sowm mows
sown owns; snow
sowp pows; swop; wops
sowps swops
sowter stower; stowre; towers;
  towser; twoers
sowters stowers; stowres; towsers
spa asp; pas; sap
space capes; Caspe; paces; scape
spaced scaped
spacer capers; Casper; crapes;
  escarp; pacers; parsec; recaps;
  scrape
spacers escarps; parsecs; scrapes
spaces scapes
spacing scaping
spade sepad; spaed
spades sepads; passed
spadroon pandoors
spae apes; apse; peas
spaed sepad; spade
spaer asper; pares; parse; pears;
  prase; presa; rapes; reaps; spare;
  spear
spaers aspers; parses; passer;
  repass; spares; sparse; spears
spaes apses; passé
spahi aphis; apish
Spain pains; piñas; spina
spake peaks; speak
spale Elaps; lapse; leaps; pales;
  peals; pleas; salep; sepal; speal
spales lapses; sepals; speals
spall palls
spalt plats; splat

spalts splats
spam amps; maps; pams; samp
span naps; pans; snap
spancel enclasp
spancels enclasps
spane aspen; napes; neaps; panes; peans; sneap; spean
spanes aspens; sneaps; speans
spang pangs
spangler sprangle
spanglers sprangles
spaniel alpines
spaniels painless
spank knaps
spans snaps
spar raps; rasp
sparable parables
spare asper; pares; parse; pears; prase; presa; rapes; reaps; spaer; spear
spared drapes; padres; parsed; rasped; repads; spread
sparely parleys; parsley; players; replays
sparer parers; parser; rasper
sparers parsers; raspers; sparser
spares aspers; parses; passer; repass; spaers; sparse; spears
sparge gapers; gasper; grapes; parges
sparged grasped
sparger grasper
spargers graspers
sparges gaspers
sparging grasping
Sparidae paradise
sparing parings; parsing; rasping
sparingly raspingly
spark parks
sparred drapers
spars rasps
sparse aspers; parses; passer; repass; spaers; spares; spears
sparser parsers; raspers; sparers
sparsest trespass
spart parts; prats; sprat; strap; traps
Sparta Patras; satrap
Spartan tarpans; trapans
Spartel palters; per-salt; plaster; platers; psalter; stapler
spas asps; pass; saps
spat past; pats; stap; taps

spate paste; pates; septa; speat; tapes
spates pastes; speats; stapes
spathed heptads
spats pasts; staps
spatter patters; tapster
spatters tapsters
spavie pavise
spaw paws; swap; waps; wasp
spawl pawls
spawling lapwings
spawn pawns
spawner enwraps; pawners
spaws swaps; wasps
spay pays; yaps
speak peaks; spake
speal Elaps; lapse; leaps; pales; peals; pleas; salep; sepal; spale
speals lapses; sepals; spales
spean aspen; napes; neaps; panes; peans; sneap; spane
speaned sneaped
speaning sneaping
speans aspens; sneaps; spanes
spear asper; pares; parse; pears; prase; presa; rapes; reaps; spaer; spare
spearman Parmesan
spears aspers; parses; passer; repass; spaers; spares; sparse
speary payers; repays
speat paste; pates; septa; spate; tapes
speats pastes; spates; stapes
spec pecs
specie pieces
speck pecks
spectra carpets; precast
spectral sceptral
spectre recepts; respect; sceptre
spectres respects; sceptres
spectrum crumpets
specula capsule
speculate peculates
speculation peculations
speculator peculators
sped peds
speech cheeps; peches
speed deeps
speeder speered
speedo epodes; depose
speedos deposes
speel peels; sleep

speeler   peelers; sleeper
speelers   peerless; sleepers
speeling   peelings; sleeping
speels   sleeps
speer   peers; perse; prees; prese;
  spree
speered   speeder
speers   preses; sperse; sprees
speir   épris; peris; piers; pries; prise;
  ripes; spire
speired   Perseid; predies; preside
speirs   prises; spires
speiss   pisses; sepsis
Speke   keeps; peeks; pekes
speldin   spindle
speldins   spindles
spell   pells
speller   respell
spellers   respells
spelt   pelts; slept
spelter   pelters; petrels
spend   pends
speos   pesos; poses; posse
sperling   springle
sperm   perms
spermaceti   imprecates
sperm-oil   implores; pelorism
sperse   preses; speers; sprees
spersed   depress; pressed
spersing   pressing; springes
spew   pews
Spey   espy; sype
sphaer   phares; phrase; raphes;
  seraph; shaper; Sherpa
sphaere   reshape
sphaeres   reshapes
sphaers   phrases; seraphs; shapers;
  Sherpas
sphenic   pinches
sphere   herpes; Hesper; pheers
spheric   ceriphs; ciphers
spial   lapis; pails
spica   aspic; Capis; picas
spicae   apices
spice   epics
spicer   cripes; Persic; precis; prices
spices   pisces
spick   picks
spider   prides; prised; redips;
  risped; spired
spider-crab   crispbread
spied   siped
spiel   piles; plies; slipe; spile

spieler   replies
spiels   plissé; slipes; spiles
spies   sipes
spignel   pingles, pin-legs
spike   kepis; kipes; pikes; Pisek
spikelet   pikelets
spiking   pigskin
spile   piles; plies; slipe; spiel
spiled   dispel; lisped
spiles   plissé; slipes; spiels
spiling   lisping
spill   pills
spillage   pillages
spilt   slipt; split
spin   nips; pins; snip
spina   pains; piñas; Spain
spinal   plains
spinate   panties; patines; sapient
spindle   speldin
spindled   splendid
spindles   speldins
spine   pcnis; pines; snipe
spined   piends; sniped
spinel   pensil; Pilsen; spline
spinels   pensils; splines
spines   snipes
spinet   instep; step-in
spinets   insteps; step-ins
spinier   inspire; pirnies
spink   pinks; Pinsk
spinner   pinners
spinnet   tenpins
spinode   dispone
spinodes   dispones
spins   snips
spinule   line-ups; lupines; up-lines
spiracle   calipers; replicas
spiral   prials
spirant   spraint
spire   épris; peris; piers; pries; prise;
  ripes; speir
spired   prides; prised; redips;
  risped; spider
spireme   empires; emprise;
  epimers; imprese; premise
spiremes   emprises; impreses;
  premises
spires   prises; speirs
spiring   prising; risping
spirited   tide-rips
spirits   tripsis
spirt   sprit; stirp; strip; trips
spirted   striped

spirting striping
spirts sprits; stirps; strips
spit pits; tips
spital plaits
spitcher pitchers
spite piets; piste; stipe
spites pistes; stipes
spitter pitters; tipster
spitters tipsters
splat plats; spalt
splats spalts
splatter partlets; platters; prattles;
  sprattle
splatters sprattles
splay palsy; plays
splaying palsying
splendid spindled
splenic pencils
splice clipes
spline pensil; Pilsen; spinel
splines pensils; spinels
splinters printless
split slipt; spilt
split ring stripling; triplings
splitter triplets
splore polers; proles
sploshing longships
Spock pocks
spode dopes; posed
spoiled despoil; diploes; dipoles;
  peloids; soliped
spoilers oil-press
spoilt pilots; pistol; postil
spoke pokes
spoliation positional
spoliator troopials
spondee depones
spongier reposing
spontoon pontoons
spoof poofs
spool loops; pools; sloop
spooled poodles
spooler loopers
spools sloops
spoon snoop
spooned snooped
Spooner snooper
spooning snooping
spoons snoops
spoor roops; sopor
sporadic picadors
spore pores; poser; prose; ropes;
  Soper

spores posers; proses
sport ports; strop
sported deports
sporter porters; pretors; reports
sporters portress
sports strops
sporule leprous
sposh shops; sophs
spot opts; post; pots; stop;
  tops
spots posts; stops
spotter potters; protest
spotters protests
spotty typtos
spout pouts; stoup
spouter petrous; posture; pouters;
  Proteus; septuor; troupes
spouters postures
spouts toss-up
sprag grasp
sprags grasps
spraid rapids
spraint spirant
sprang prangs
sprangle spangler
sprangles spanglers
sprat parts; prats; spart; strap; traps
sprats straps
sprattle partlets; platters; prattles;
  splatter
sprattles splatters
spray prays; raspy
sprayer prayers; respray
sprayers resprays
spread drapes; padres; parsed;
  rasped; repads; spared
spreads adpress
spreathing strap-hinge
spree peers; perse; prees; prese;
  speer
sprees preses; speers; sperse
sprig grips; prigs
springe pingers
springes pressing; spersing
springier reprising; respiring
springiest persisting
springle sperling
sprint prints
sprinter printers; reprints
sprit spirt; stirp; strip; trips
sprite esprit; priest; Pteris; ripest;
  stripe; tripes
spritely priestly

sprites   persist; priests; stirpes; stripes
sprits   spirts; stirps; strips
sprod   dorps; drops; prods
sprout   Proust; stroup; stupor
sprouted   postured; proudest
sprouting   outspring; posturing
sprouts   stroups; stupors
spruces   percuss
sprue   puers; pures; purse; super
sprues   purses; supers
spruit   purist; stir up; uprist
spruits   purists; stirs up
spud   puds
spued   dupes; pseud
spule   pules; pulse
spules   pulses
spuming   impugns
spun   puns
spunk   punks
spur   purs
spuriae   Piraeus; upraise
spurner   pruners
spurt   turps
sputa   sat up
sputter   putters
spying   pigsny
squad   quads
squail   quails
squatter   quartets
squeak   quakes
squeal   equals
squid   quids
squill   quills
squire   quires; Quseir; risqué
squireen   enquires
squit   quits
Sri   sir
stab   bast; bats; tabs
stabbed   tebbads
stabber   barbets; rabbets
stabile   astilbe; bestial
stable   ablest; ablets; bleats; tables
stabled   blasted
stabler   alberts; blaster; labrets; tablers
stablers   blasters
stabling   blasting
staccato   toccatas
stack   tacks
stacker   rackets; tackers
stacket   tackets
stade   dates; sated; stead

stades   steads
Stael   least; leats; slate; stale; steal; stela; taels; tales; teals; tesla
stag   gats; tags
stage   gates; geats
stager   grates; greats; targes
stages   sagest
stagey   gayest
stagged   gadgets
stagger   taggers
stagier   agister; gaiters; sea-girt; strigae; triages
stagnation   antagonist
Stahl   halts; laths; shalt
staid   adits; ditas
stain   saint; satin; Tanis
stained   Danites; detains; instead; sainted
stainer   nastier; ratines; resiant; retains; retinas; retsina; starnie; stearin
stainers   starnies; stearins
Staines   entasis; Saintes; sestina; tansies; tisanes
stainless   saltiness; slatiness
stains   saints; Säntis; satins; Sistan
stair   airts; astir; raits; sitar; Sitra; stria; tarsi; Trias
staired   asterid; astride; diaster; disrate; tirades
stairs   sistra; sitars
staithe   atheist
staithes   atheists
stake   Keats; skate; Skeat; steak; takes; teaks
staked   skated; tasked
stakes   skates; steaks
staking   skating; takings; tasking
stale   least; leats; slate; Stael; steal; stela; taels; tales; teals; tesla
staled   deltas; desalt; lasted; salted; slated
staler   alerts; alters; artels; laster; ratels; salter; slater; stelar; tarsal
stales   slates; steals; tassel; teslas
Stalin   instal; Latins
staling   anglist; lasting; salting; slating
stalk   talks
stalker   talkers
stamen   aments; mantes
staminal   talisman
stamp   tamps

195

stampede stepdame
stampedes stepdames
stamper tampers
Stan ants; tans
stance ascent; enacts; secant
stances ascents; secants
stanch chants; snatch
stanched snatched
stancher chanters; snatcher;
 tranches
stanchers snatchers
stanches snatches
stanching snatching
stander endarts; red ants
stane antes; etnas; nates; Nesta;
 Senta; stean; Teans
stanes assent; sanest; snaste; steans
stang angst; gants; gnats; tangs
Stanger garnets; Sargent; strange
Stanhope phaetons; Stephano
staniel eastlin; elastin; entails;
 salient; slàinte
staniels eastlins; salients
stank kants; tanks
stannate tannates
stannic tin cans
stap past; pats; spat; taps
stapes pastes; spates; speats
staple palest; palets; pastel; petals;
 plates; pleats; septal
stapler palters; per-salt; plaster;
 platers; psalter; spartel
staplers per-salts; plasters; psalters
staples pastels
staps pasts; spats
star arts; rats; tars; tsar
starch charts; scarth
starcher charters; Chartres
stardom tsardom
stare arets; aster; astre; earst; rates;
 reast; resat; strae; tares; tears; teras
stared adrets; daters; trades; treads
starer arrest; arrêts; raster; raters;
 Sartre; terras
starers arrests; rasters
stares assert; asters; astres; reasts;
 Stresa
staring ratings
stark karst; karts; skart; strak
starlet rattles; slatter; startle;
 tatlers; Telstar
starlets slatters; startles
starling ratlings

starn rants; tarns
starnie nastier; ratines; resiant;
 retains; retinas; retsina; stainer;
 stearin
starnies stainers; stearins
star-nose assentor; senators;
 treasons
star-noses assentors
starred darters; retards; traders
stars tsars; trass
starshine tarnishes
start tarts
started tetrads
starter ratters; restart
starters restarts
startle rattles; slatter; starlet;
 tatlers; Telstar
startler rattlers
startles slatters; starlets
startling rattlings
starve averts; tavers; traves; vaster
starved adverts
stashing Hastings
stasis assist
state taste; tates; teats; testa
stated tasted
stateless tasteless
statement testament
statements testaments
stater aretts; taster; taters; tetras;
 treats
staters tasters
states tastes
stateside steadiest
static attics
statical cat's-tail
stating Sittang; tasting
stational saltation
stator tarots
statue astute
stature Steuart
staunch canthus; chaunts
stauncher chaunters
stave vesta
staves vestas
staw swat; taws; twas; wast
stawed wadset; wasted
stawing wasting
staws swats
stayed steady
stayer estray; reasty; yarest
stayers estrays
staying Stygian

St. Clair Carlist
St. Dié deist; diets; dites; edits; id
  est; sited; stied; tides
stead dates; sated; stade
steaded dead-set; sedated
steadier readiest
steadiest stateside
steadily diastyle
steading d'Estaing; sedating
steads stades
steady stayed
steak Keats; skate; Skeat; stake;
  takes; teaks
steaks skates; stakes
steal least; leats; slate; Stael; stale;
  stela; taels; tales; teals; tesla
steale elates; stelae; teasel
stealer elaters; Laertes; relates
stealers tearless; tesseral
steales teasels
stealing eastling; Galenist; genitals
steals slates; stales; tassel; teslas
stealt latest
steam mates; meats; Mesta; tames;
  teams
steamer sea-term
steamers sea-terms
steamier emirates
steaming mintages
steamship shipmates
steamy mayest
stean antes; etnas; nates; Nesta;
  Senta; stane; Teans
steane ensate; sateen; senate
steanes senates
steans assent; sanest; snaste; stanes
stearin nastier; ratines; resiant;
  retains; retinas; retsina; stainer;
  starnie
stearine arsenite
stearins stainers; starnies
steel leets; sleet; stele
Steele eel-set
steeled deletes; sleeted
steelier leeriest
steeling gentiles; sleeting
steels sleets; steles
steely sleety
steen etens; teens; tense
steens tenses
steeped deepest
steeper estrepe
steepled depletes

steer ester; reest; reset; retes; stere;
  teers; terse; trees
steered reested
steering integers; reesting; streigne
steers esters; reets; resets; steres
Stefan fasten; nefast
steil islet; istle; stile; teils; tiles
steils islets; stiles
stein inset; neist; set in; tines
Steiner entires; entries; Teniers;
  trenise
steins insets; sets in; Tessin
stela least; leats; slate; Stael; stale;
  steal; taels; tales; teals; tesla
stelae elates; steale; teasel
stelar alerts; alters; artels; laster;
  ratels; salter; slater; staler; tarsel
stele leets; sleet; steel
steles sleets; steels
stell tells
Stella sallet
stellar tellars
St. Elmo molest; motels
stem tems
stempel pelmets; stemple; temples
stempels stemples
stemple pelmets; stempel; temples
stemples stempels
sten nest; nets; sent; tens
stencil clients
stend dents; tends
Stendhal Shetland
stens nests
Stenson sonnets; tensons
stent tents
stentor snotter
stentors snotters
step pest; pets; sept
stepdame stampede
stepdames stampedes
Stephano phaetons; Stanhope
step-in instep; spinet
step-ins insteps; spinets
steps pests; septs
stere ester; reest; reset; retes; steer;
  teers; terse; trees
steres esters; reests; resets; steers
steric trices
sterical articles; recitals
sterigma magister; migrates
sterile leister
sterlet letters; settler; trestle
sterlets settlers; trestles

sterling   ringlets; tinglers; tringles
stern   Ernst; rents; terns
sterna   antres; astern
sternal   antlers; rentals; saltern
Sterne   enters; Ernest; nester;
  rentes; resent; tenser; ternes
sterned   tenders
sternmost   sortments
sternum   Munster
steroid   editors; roisted; rosited;
  sortied; storied; tie-rods; triodes
sterol   ostier
sterols   ostlers
stet   sett; test
stetson   ostents; St. Neots
Steuart   stature
Steve   evets
Steven   events
stew   ewts; tews; west; wets
steward   strawed
Stewart   swatter; tewarts
stewed   tweeds; wested
stewer   sweert; tweers; wester
stewers   westers
stewing   twinges; westing
stews   wests
stey   stye; tyes
Steyr   resty; treys; tyres
St. Germain   emigrants; mastering;
  streaming
sthenic   ethnics
Stheno   honest; Sethon
stibbler   tribbles
stich   chits
stick   ticks
sticker   rickets; Sickert; tickers
stickle   tickles
stickler   strickle; ticklers; trickles
sticklers   strickles
stie   site; ties
stied   deist; diets; dites; edits; id est;
  St. Dié; sited; tides
sties   sites
stieve   evites
stiff   tiffs
stiffen   infefts
stiffer   restiff
stifle   filets; itself
stifler   filters; lifters; trifles
stile   islet; istle; steil; teils; tiles
stiles   islets; steils
stilet   titles
still   lilts; tills

stillage   legalist; tillages
stillages   legalists
stiller   rillets; tillers; trellis
stilt   tilts
stilter   litters; slitter; testril; tilters;
  titlers
stilting   slitting; Tlingits
stime   emits; items; metis; mites;
  smite; times
stimed   demits; misted
stimes   misset; smites; tmesis
stiming   misting; smiting; timings
Stimson   monists
stimulate   mutilates
stimulator   mutilators
sting   tings
stingaree   reseating
stinger   resting
stingo   ingots; tigons; tosing
stingray   straying
stink   knits; skint; tinks
stinker   Inkster; tinkers
stint   tints; 'tisn't
stinted   dentist
stinter   tinters
stipe   piets; piste; spite
stipes   pistes; spites
stipple   tipples
stippler   ripplets; tipplers; tripples
stir   rits
stirk   skirt
stirks   skirts
stirp   spirt; sprit; strip; trips
stirpes   persist; priests; sprites;
  stripes
stirps   spirts; sprits; strips
stirred   strider
stirs up   purists; spruits
stir up   purist; spruit; uprist
stitcher   chitters
stiver   rivets; strive; trevis
stivers   strives; treviss
St. Lô   lost; lots
St. Marie   Artemis; imarets;
  maestri; maister; misrate; semitar
St. Michael   alchemist
St. Neots   ostents; stetson
stoa   oast; oats; Sato; Taos
stoas   assot; oasts; Tasso
stoat   toast
stoats   toasts
stob   bots
stocked   dockets

stockier corkiest; rockiest
stockinger restocking
stodge godets
stoep estop; poets; potes; stope;
  topes
stoeps estops; posset; stopes
stoically callosity
stoker stroke
stokers strokes
stolen Solent; telson
Stolp plots; polts
stoma atoms; moats
stomacher chromates
stomatic masticot
stone Eston; notes; onset; seton;
  Tenos; tones
stone-coal consolate
stoned doesn't; Donets; Ostend
stone-mill millstone
stonen Neston; nonets; sonnet;
  tenons; tenson; tonnes
stone-pine Penistone
stone-pits pottiness
stoner noters; Reston; tenors;
  tensor; Terson; trones
stoners tensors
stones Nestos; onsets; setons; sets
  on
stonier in store; orients; triones
stonk knots
stook kotos
stool loots; lotos; tools
stoop Sopot
stoor roost; roots; torso
stoors roosts; torsos
stop opts; post; pots; spot; tops
stope estop; poets; potes; stoep;
  topes
stoped depots; despot; posted
stopes estops; posset; stoeps
stoping posting
stopings postings; signpost
stopper toppers
stopping toppings
stopple topples
stops posts; spots
storable bloaters; sortable
storax taxors
store estro; roset; rotes; tores; torse
stored Dorset; sorted; strode
storer resort; roster; sorter
storers resorts; rosters; sorters
stores rosets; sortes; torses; tosser

store-ship prothesis; sophister
store-ships sophisters
storey oyster; rosety; Troyes;
  tyroes; Yes Tor
storeys oysters
storied editors; roisted; rosited;
  sortied; steroid; tie-rods; triodes
stories rosiest; sorites; sorties
storing sorting; trigons
storm morts; Troms
story ryots; tyros
stot tost; tots
stotter stretto; totters
stound donuts
stoup pouts; spout
stoups spouts
stour roust; routs; sutor; torus;
  tours
stours rousts; sutors
stout touts
stove votes
stover strove; voters
stovies soviets
stow swot; tows; twos
stowed towsed
stower sowter; stowre; towers;
  towser; twoers
stowers sowters; stowres; towsers
stowing towsing; Wigston
stown towns; wonts
stowre sowter; stower; towers;
  towser; twoers
stowres sowters; stowers; towsers
stows swots
Strabo aborts; boarts; tabors
strack tracks
strad darts; drats
strae arets; aster; astre; earst; rates;
  reast; resat; stare; tares; tears; teras
strafe afters; faster
strafing ingrafts
straighten shattering
straik traiks
strain instar; santir; Sintra; trains
strained detrains; tan-rides
strainer restrain; terrains; trainers;
  transire
strainers restrains; transires
strains instars; santirs
strait artist; sittar; strati; traits
straiten intreats; nitrates; tartines
straitens resistant
straits artists; sittars; tsarist

strak   karst; karts; skart; stark
strakes   skaters; streaks; taskers
stramp   tramps
strange   garnets; Sargent; Stanger
stranger   granters; regrants
strangle   tanglers; trangles
strap   parts; prats; spart; sprat; traps
strap-hinge   spreathing
strapless   psaltress
strapper   trappers
strapping   trappings
straps   sprats
strata   Tatars
strati   artist; sittar; strait; traits
Straus   Rastus; sutras; Tarsus
straw   swart; warst; warts; wrast
strawed   steward
strawy   swarty
stray   satyr; trays
strayed   rest-day
straying   stingray
strays   satyrs
streak   skater; strake; takers; tasker
streaks   skaters; strakes; taskers
stream   armets; master; maters;
   tamers
streamed   mastered
streaming   emigrants; mastering;
   St. Germain
streamless   masterless
streams   masters
stream-tin   martinets
streamy   mastery
streel   Lester; relets
street   setter; tester
streets   setters; tersest; testers
streigne   integers; reesting; steering
strelitz   streltzi
streltzi   strelitz
Stresa   assert; asters; astres; reasts;
   stares
stressed   desserts
stretta   tatters
stretto   stotter; totters
strew   trews; wrest
strewed   wrested
strewer   wrester
strewers   wresters
strewing   wresting
strews   wrests
stria   airts; astir; raits; sitar; Sitra;
   stair; tarsi; Trias
striae   satire

striate   artiste; attires; tastier
striated   tardiest
strickle   stickler; ticklers; trickles
strickles   sticklers
stricter   critters; restrict
strid   dirts
striddle   tiddlers
stride   direst; driest
strident   tridents
strider   stirred
strife   refits; sifter
strig   girts; grist; grits; trigs
striga   gratis
strigae   agister; gaiters; sea-girt;
   stagier; triages
Striges   tigress
strigine   igniters; resiting
strike   trikes
striker   skirret
strikers   skirrets
striking   skirting
Strine   insert; inters; sinter; trines
string-bean   banterings
strinkle   tinklers
strip   spirt; sprit; stirp; trips
stripe   esprit; priest; Pteris; ripest;
   sprite; tripes
striped   spirted
stripes   persist; priests; sprites;
   stirpes
striping   spirting
stripling   split ring; triplings
stripper   trippers
strips   spirts; sprits; stirps
striptease   tapestries
strive   rivets; stiver; trevis
strived   diverts
striven   inverts; Ventris
strives   stivers; treviss
stroam   Martos; Mostar; stroma
stroaming   Montargis; sigmatron
stroams   matross
strobe   Osbert; sorbet
stroddle   strodled; toddlers
Stroheim   isotherm; moithers
stroke   stoker
strokes   stokers
stroma   Martos; Mostar; stroam
strongarm   Armstrong
strop   ports; sport
strophe   pothers; thorpes
strops   sports
Stroud   Tudors

stroup   Proust; sprout; stupor
stroups   sprouts; stupors
strout   trouts; tutors
strove   stover; voters
strow   trows; worst; worts
strowed   worsted
strowing   worsting
strows   worsts
struck   trucks
strudel   lustred; rustled
strum   turms
strumae   matures
strumpet   trumpets
strung   grunts
strut   sturt; trust
struts   sturts; trusts
St. Servan   servants
stub   bust; buts; tubs
stubs   busts
stuck   tucks
stud   dust
student   stunted
studs   dusts
study   dusty
stum   must; smut; tums
stumble   tumbles
stumbler   tumblers; tumbrels
stumbling   tumblings
stumer   estrum; muster
stumers   musters
stumper   sumpter
stumpers   sumpters
stums   smuts
stun   nuts; tuns; Unst
stunted   student
stupe   set-up; upset
stupes   upsets
stupor   Proust; sprout; stroup
stupors   sprouts; stroups
sturt   strut; trust
sturted   trusted
sturting   trusting
sturts   struts; trusts
stye   stey; tyes
Stygian   staying
style   yelts
styles   slyest
stylite   testily
styrene   yestern
Styx   xyst
suable   usable
sub   bus
subedar   daubers

suber   burse; rebus
sublet   bluest; bustle; subtle
subman   busman
suborn   bourns
suborned   bounders; rebounds
subpoena   bean soup
subs   buss
substation   bus station
substations   bus stations
substract   subtracts
substraction   subtractions
substractor   subtractors
subtle   bluest; bustle; sublet
subtler   bluster; bustler;
    butlers
subtractions   substraction
subtractors   subtractor
subtracts   substract
succade   accused
succor   crocus
such   Cush
suck   cusk
suckler   ruckles
sucks   cusks
sucrase   causers; cesuras; saucers
sucre   cruse; cures; curse
sucrose   courses; Croesus; sources
sudd   duds
sudder   udders
sue   use
sued   deus; dues; Duse; used
sues   uses
suet   Utes
Suez   Zeus
suffer   ruffes
sugar   Argus; gaurs
sugars   Sargus
Suhl   lush; shul
suing   using
suint   inust; Tunis; units
Suisse   issues
suit   Uist
suitcase   sauciest
suite   etuis
suites   tissue
suits   situs
sulcal   callus
sullied   illudes; ill-used
sullies   ill-uses
sulphured   desulphur
sultanic   lunatics
sum   Mus
sumac   Camus; caums; Musca

Sumer   mures; muser; Remus; serum
sumless   mussels
summae   Emmaus
summist   summits
summits   summist
sumph   humps
sumpter   stumper
sumpters   stumpers
sums   muss
Sunay   unsay
sunburned   unburdens
sun-cured   uncursed
sunder   nursed
sundering   undersign
sunders   undress
sun-dog   sungod; ungods
sun-dogs   sungods
sung   gnus; guns; snug
sungod   sun-dog; ungods
sungods   sun-dogs
sunhat   haunts; unhats; Ushant
sunlight   hustling
sunlit   insult
sunn   nuns
sunrise   insures
sunset   unsets
sunspot   unstops
sup   pus; ups
super   puers; pures; purse; sprue
supernal   purslane
supers   purses; sprues
supersonic   percussion
supine   puisne
supper   uppers
supple   peplus
supplier   periplus
supposer   purposes
supreme   presume
sups   puss
sura   rusa; Ursa
sural   Larus; Urals
suras   sarus
surat   sutra
surbase   abusers
sure   Reus; rues; ruse; ures; user
sureness   Suresnes
Suresnes   sureness
surf   furs
surfeits   surfiest
surfier   friseur; frisure
surfiest   surfeits
surge   urges

Surinam   uranism
surmise   misuser; mussier
surmises   misusers
surname   manures
surnamed   maunders
surreined   reinsured
Surya   saury
Susie   issue
suspire   uprises
suspiring   uprisings
sustain   issuant
sutler   luster; lustre; luters; result; rustle; ulster
sutlers   lusters; lustres; results; rustles; ulsters
sutor   roust; routs; stour; torus; tours
sutors   rousts; stours
sutra   surat
sutras   Rastus; Straus; Tarsus
suture   uterus
Svengali   leavings
swad   daws; wads
swaddle   dawdles; waddles
swaddler   dawdlers; waddlers
swag   wags
swage   wages
swain   wains
swale   Lawes; sweal; wales; weals
swaled   dwales
swales   sweals
swallow   wallows
swaly   swayl; yawls
swam   maws
swami   aswim
swan   awns; sawn
swang   gnaws; wangs
swank   wanks
swanker   wankers
swap   paws; spaw; waps; wasp
swaps   spaws; wasps
sward   draws; wards
sware   sawer; swear; wares; wears
swarm   mawrs; warms
swarmer   warmers
swart   straw; warst; warts; wrast
swarty   strawy
swarve   wavers
swash   shaws
swasher   hawsers; washers
swat   staw; taws; twas; wast
swath   thaws
swathe   wheats

swats   staws
swatter   Stewart; tewarts
sway   ways; yaws
swayer   sawyer
swayers   sawyers
swayl   swaly; yawls
sweal   Lawes; swale; wales; weals
sweals   swales
swear   sawer; sware; wares; wears
swearer   wearers
swears   sawers; wrasse
sweat   tawse; waste
sweatier   weariest
sweats   sawset; tawses; wastes
swede   sewed; sweed; weeds
Sweden   endews
Swedish   swished; whissed
swee   ewes; wees
sweed   sewed; swede; weeds
sweel   Lewes; sewel; weels; Wesel
sweels   sewels
sweep   weeps
sweeper   weepers
sweer   ewers; sewer; Weser
sweered   weeders
sweers   sewers
sweert   stewer; tweers; wester
sweet   ewest
sweir   swire; weirs; wires; wiser
sweirt   twiers; twires; writes
swell   wells
swelt   welts
swelter   welters; wrestle
swelters   wrestles
swig   wigs
swill   wills
swindles   wildness; windless
swine   sewin; sinew; wines
swines   sinews
swing   wings
swinge   sewing; winges

swinger   wingers
swingle   slewing
swingles   wingless
swingtree   westering
swink   winks
swinker   winkers
swipe   wipes
swiper   wipers
swire   sweir; weirs; wires; wiser
swished   Swedish; whissed
swisher   wishers
swishes   whisses
swishing   whissing
swith   whist; whits
swither   withers; writhes
swive   views; wives
swob   bows
swop   pows; sowp; wops
swops   sowps
sword   drows; words
sworder   rewords
swore   owers; serow; sower; worse
swot   stow; tows; twos
swots   stows
swound   wounds
sybarite   bestiary
sybo   boys; yobs
syboe   obeys
syce   scye
syces   scyes
sye   sey; yes
syed   deys; dyes
syke   keys; Skye; yesk
Sykes   yesks
syndicate   asyndetic
syne   yens
synod   Dyson
sype   espy; Spey
Syra   rays
syrtes   tressy
syrup   pursy; Pyrus

T

ta   at
tab   bat
tabards   bastard
tabbed   tebbad
tabes   abets; baste; bates; beast;
   beats; besat; Sebat
Tabitha   habitat
table   ablet; blate; bleat .

tableau   tabulae
tabler   albert; labret
tablers   alberts; blaster; labrets;
   stabler
tables   ablest; ablets; bleats; stable
tablet   battle
tablets   battels; battles
tabor   abort; boart; Rabot

tabored aborted; borated	**taigling** ligating
taboring aborting; borating	**tail** alit; Atli; Lita; tali
tabors aborts; boarts; Strabo	**tailed** detail; dilate
tabour rubato	**tailles** Liestal; tallies
taboured obdurate	**tailor** Rialto
tabouret obturate	**tailored** idolater
tabourets obturates	**Tain** ain't; Tina
tabret batter	**Taine** entia; tinea
tabrets batters	**taint** tanti; titan
tabs bast; bats; stab	**taints** tanist; titans
tabu abut; buat; tuba	**taish** saith; Thais
tabula ablaut	**taj** Jat
tabulae tableau	**tak** kat
tabus abuts; buats; tubas	**take** Kate; keta; teak
tach Cath; chat	**take-in** intake
tache cheat; teach; theca	**take-ins** intakes
taches chaste; cheats; sachet; scathe	**takers** skater; strake; streak; tasker
tachisme misteach	**takes** Keats; skate; Skeat; stake;
tacit attic	steak; teaks
tacker racket	**takings** skating; staking; tasking
tackers rackets; stacker	**taks** kats; skat; task
tackets stacket	**talar** altar; ratal
tackled talcked	**talars** altars; astral; tarsal
tackling talcking	**talc** clat
tacks stack	**talcked** tackled
tactic tic-tac	**talcking** tackling
tactics tic-tacs	**talcose** alecost; lactose; locates;
tactile lattice	scatole
Tadcaster castrated	**tale** et al.; late; leat; tael; teal; tela
tae ate; eat; eta; tea	**talent** Lanett; latent; latten
tael et al.; late; leat; tale; teal; tela	**taler** alert; alter; artel; later; ratel
taels least; leats; slate; Stael; stale;	**tales** least; leats; slate; Stael; stale;
steal; stela; tales; teals; tesla	steal; stela; taels; teals; tesla
taenioid ideation	**tali** alit; Atli; Lita; tail
taes east; eats; sate; seat; seta; teas	**talisman** staminal
tag gat	**talkers** stalker
tagged gadget	**talks** stalk
tagger garget	**taller** tellar
taggers stagger	**tallies** Liestal; tailles
taglioni intaglio; ligation	**tally-ho** loathly
taglionis ligations	**tallymen** mentally
Tagore orgeat	**talon** notal; tolan; tonal
tag-rag rag-tag	**Talos** altos; Salto; tolas
tags gats; stag	**talus** sault; Tulsa
Tagus Tsuga	**tam** mat
tahr hart; rath; thar	**tamal** Malta
tahrs harts; raths; thars; trash	**tamale** malate
tahsil latish	**tamales** malates
tai ait; ita	**Tamar** Marat
Taiden Danite; detain	**tamarin** martian
taigle aiglet; ligate	**tamarins** martians
taigled ligated	**tame** mate; meat; Meta; team; Tema
taigles aiglets; ligates	**tamed** mated

tameless   mateless; meatless
tameness   Massenet
tamer   armet; mater; trema
tamers   armets; master; maters;
  stream
tames   mates; meats; Mesta; steam;
  teams
tamin   matin
tamine   inmate
taming   mating
tamise   samite
tamises   asteism; Matisse; samites
tammies   mismate
Tampere   tempera
tampers   stamper
Tampico   potamic
tampion   ptomain
tampon   potman
tampons   postman
tamps   stamp
tams   mast; mats
tan   ant; Nat
Tancred   tranced
tang   gant; gnat
tanged   ganted
tangerine   Argentine
tangi   giant
tangible   belating; bleating
tangie   eating; ingate
Tangier   Geraint; granite; ingrate;
  tearing
tangies   easting; Gastein; genista;
  ingates; ingesta; seating; teasing;
  tsigane
tangiest   estating
tanging   ganting
tangle   Anglet
tangler   trangle
tanglers   strangle; trangles
tango   tonga
tangos   Gaston; Sontag; tongas
tangs   angst; gants; gnats; stang
tanh   than
Tanis   saint; satin; stain
tanist   taints; titans
tank   kant
tanks   kants; stank
tannates   stannate
tannic   tin can
tanrec   canter; carnet; creant;
  Cretan; nectar; recant; trance
tanrecs   canters; carnets; Cretans;
  recants; trances

tan-ride   detrain; trade-in; trained
tan-rides   detrains; strained
tans   ants; Stan
tansies   entasis; Saintes, sestina;
  Staines; Usanes
tansy   nasty
tanti   taint; titan
Tantra   rattan; tartan
Tantras   rattans; tartans
Tao   oat
Taoism   Maoist
Taos   oast; oats; Sato; stoa
tap   apt; pat
tape   pate; peat
taped   adept; pated
tapeline   petaline
tapen   paten
taper   apert; pater; peart; Petra;
  prate; trape
tapered   predate; red tape
tapers   paster; paters; Praest; prates;
  repast; trapes
tapes   paste; pates; septa; spate;
  speat
tapestries   striptease
tapir   atrip; parti
tapirs   rapist
taplash   asphalt
taps   past; pats; spat; stap
tapster   patters; spatter
tapsters   spatters
tar   art; rat
tara   rata
Tarbes   barest; baster; bestar; breast
tarcel   cartel; claret; rectal
tarcels   cartels; clarets; scarlet
tardier   tarried
tardiest   striated
tare   aret; rate; tear
tared   adret; dater; rated; trade;
  tread
Taree   arête; eater; reate
tares   arets; aster; astre; earst; rates;
  reast; resat; stare; strae; tears; teras
targe   grate; great; Greta; terga
targed   der Tag; grated
targes   grates; Greats; stager
targing   grating
tar-heel   leather
tar-heels   leathers
taring   rating
tarn   rant
tarnishes   starshine

205

tarns   rants; starn
taro   Orta; rota; Tora
taroc   actor; Crato; Croat
tarocs   actors; castor; Castro; Croats;
    scrota
taros   Astor; roast; rotas; Sarto;
    Troas
tarot   ottar
tarots   stator
tarpan   trapan
tarpans   Spartan; trapans
Tarpeian   Patarine
tarpon   patron
tarred   darter; dartre; retard; trader
tarried   tardier
tarries   tarsier
tars   arts; rats; star; tsar
tarsal   altars; astral; talars
tarsel   alerts; alters; artels; laster;
    ratels; salter; slater; staler; stelar
tarsels   artless; lasters; salters;
    slaters
tarsi   airts; astir; raits; sitar; Sitra;
    stair; stria; Trias
tarsia   arista; tiaras
tarsier   tarries
Tarsipes   pastries; piastres;
    raspiest; traipses
Tarsus   Rastus; Straus; sutras
tartan   rattan; Tantra
tartans   rattans; Tantras
tarted   ratted; tetrad
tartine   intreat; iterant; nattier;
    nitrate; tertian
tartines   intreats; nitrates; straiten
tartish   athirst
tartlet   tattler
tartlets   tattlers
tarts   start
tarty   ratty
tarweed   watered
tasar   ratas
tash   hast; hats
tashed   deaths; hasted; 'sdeath
tashes   ashets; hastes
tashing   hasting
task   kats; skat; taks
tasked   skated; staked
tasker   skater; strake; streak; takers
taskers   skaters; strakes; streaks
tasking   skating; staking; takings
Tasman   mantas
tasse   asset; sates; seats; Tessa

tassel   slates; stales; steals; teslas
tasses   assets
tassie   siesta
tassies   siestas
Tasso   assot; oasts; stoas
taste   state; tates; teats; testa
tasted   stated
tasteless   stateless
taster   aretts; stater; taters; tetras;
    treats
tasters   staters
tastes   states
tastier   artiste; attires; striate
tasting   Sittang; stating
Tatar   attar
Tatars   strata
tate   Etta; teat
tater   arett; tetra; treat
taters   aretts; stater; taster; tetras;
    treats
tates   state; taste; teats; testa
tath   that
tatler   latter; rattle
tatlers   rattles; slatter; starlet;
    startle; Telstar
tatters   stretta
tattier   attrite; titrate
tattler   tartlet
tattlers   tartlets
tatu   taut
tatus   tauts
taube   beaut; Butea; tubae
Tauber   arbute
taubes   beauts
taunted   attuned
taunting   attuning
taunts   tutsan
taurine   ruinate; uranite; urinate
taut   tatu
tauts   tatus
taver   avert; trave
tavered   averted
tavering   averting; vintager
taverns   servant; versant
tavers   averts; starve; traves; vaster
taw   twa; wat
tawer   water; wrate
tawers   waster; waters
tawery   watery
tawnier   tinware
tawny   wanty
taws   staw; swat; twas; wast
tawse   sweat; waste

tawses   sawset; sweats; wastes
taxer   extra
taxers   astrex; extras
taxes   Texas
taxors   storax
tayras   astray; satyra
tea   ate; eat; eta; tae
tea-bag   atabeg
tea-bags   atabegs
teach   cheat; tache; theca
teacher   cheater; hectare
teachers   cheaters; hectares
teaches   escheat
teaching   cheating
teacups   cuspate
teagle   eaglet; Galtee; gelate; legate;
    telega
teagles   eaglets; legates; telegas
teak   Kate; keta; take
teaks   Keats; skate; Skeat; stake;
    steak; takes
teal   et al.; late; leat; tael; tale;
    tela
teals   least; leats; slate; Stael; stale;
    steal; stela; taels; tales; tesla
team   mate; meat; Meta; tame; Tema
teaming   mintage; tegmina
teams   mates; meats; Mesta; steam;
    tames
teamwork   workmate
Tean   ante; Aten; etna; neat
Teans   antes; etnas; nates; Nesta;
    Senta; stane; stean
teapot   aptote
teapots   aptotes
tear   aret; rate; tare
tear-drop   parroted; predator;
    prorated
tear-drops   predators
tearer   re-rate
tearers   re-rates; serrate
tearing   Geraint; granite; ingrate;
    Tangier
tearless   stealers; tesseral
tea-rose   roseate
tear-pit   partite
tears   arets; aster; astre; earst; rates;
    reast; resat; stare; strae; tares; teras
teas   east; eats; sate; seat; seta; taes
tease   setae
teased   easted; seated; sedate
teasel   elates; steale; stelae
teasels   steales

teaser   arêtes; easter; eaters; reates;
    reseat; saeter; Teresa
teasers   easters; reseats; saeters;
    tessera
tea-set   estate; testae
tea-sets   estates
teasing   easting; Gastein; genista;
    ingates; ingesta; seating; tangies;
    tsigane
teat   Etta; tate
teats   state; taste; tates; testa
tea-urn   aunter; nature; Neutra
tea-urns   aunters; natures; saunter
tebbad   tabbed
tebbads   stabbed
Tebet   Bette
tec   etc.
tech   echt; etch
techs   chest
tectonic   concetti
tedious   outside
teem   meet; mete; Teme
teeming   meeting
teems   meets; metes; Temes; temse
teen   eten; nete; tene
teenager   generate; green tea;
    renegate
teenagers   generates; renegates
teens   etens; steen; tense
teer   rete; tree
teering   integer; treeing
teers   ester; reest; reset; retes; steer;
    stere; terse; trees
tees   Este; Sète
teeter   terete
teeth   thete
teg   get
tegmina   mintage; teaming
tegs   gest; gets
Teheran   earthen; hearten
Tehran   anther; thenar
tehrs   Herts.; Resht
teil   tile
teils   islet; istle; steil; stile; tiles
teind   tined
tel   elt; let
tela   et al.; late; leat; tael; tale; teal
telae   elate
telega   eaglet; Galtee; gelate; legate;
    teagle
telegas   eaglets; legates; teagles
telephony   polythene
teleran   eternal

telesis tieless
tellar taller
tellars stellar
teller retell
tellers retells
tells stell
tellurian ill-nature
tels elts; lest; lets
telson Solent; stolen
Telstar rattles; slatter; starlet;
  startle; tatlers
Tema mate; meat; Meta; tame; team
Teme meet; mete; teem
Temes meets; metes; teems;
  temse
tempera Tampere
temperated attempered
temperating attempering
Templar trample
Templars tramples
template palmette
templates palmettes
temple pelmet
temples pelmets; stempel; stemple
temporise peristome
temporises peristomes
tems stem
temse meets; metes; teems; Temes
ten net
tenable Beltane
tenace cetane
tend dent
tended dented
tender rented; terned
tenderising ingredients
tenders sterned
tending denting
tendon Denton
tends dents; stend
tene eten; nete; teen
Tenebrae bean tree
Tenedos denotes
tenesmus muteness
Teniers entires; entries; Steiner;
  trenise
tenioid edition
tenner rennet
tenners rennets
tennis sennit; sinnet
tenon nonet; tonne
tenoned Edenton
tenons Neston; nonets; sonnet;
  stonen; tenson; tonnes

tenor noter; trone
tenors noters; Reston; stoner;
  tensor; Terson; trones
Tenos Eston; notes; onset; seton;
  stone; tones
tenpins spinnet
tenrec center; centre; recent
tenrecs centers; centres
tens nest; nets; sent; sten
tense etens; steen; teens
tensed nested; sedent
tenser enters; Ernest; nester;
  rentes; resent; Sterne; ternes
tenses steens
tensing nesting
tension intones; Sonnite
tenson Neston; nonets; sonnet;
  stonen; tenons; tonnes
tensons sonnets; Stenson
tensor noters; Reston; stoner;
  tenors; Terson; trones
tensors stoners
tent nett
tentative attentive
tented detent; netted
tenters testern
tenting netting
tents stent
tenty netty
tenuis unites; unties
tenure neuter; retune; tureen
tenures neuters; retunes; tureens
Teos toes; tose
tequila liquate
terai irate
teraph threap
teras arets; aster; astre; earst; rates;
  reast; resat; stare; strae; tares; tears
terbia baiter; barite
terce Crete; erect
terefah feather
Teresa arêtes; easter; eaters; reates;
  reseat; saeter; teaser
Teresina trainees
terete teeter
terga grate; great; Greta; targe
tergiversation interrogatives
Termes merest; Mestre; meters;
  metres
terminal tramline
terminals tramlines
terminates martensite
termini interim; mintier

termless smelters
termly myrtle
termor tremor
termors tremors
tern rent
ternal altern; antler; learnt; rental
ternaries Eritreans; rain-trees;
  retainers
ternate entreat; ratteen
terne enter; rente; treen
terned rented; tender
ternes enters; Ernest; nester;
  rentes; resent; Sterne; tenser
Terni inert; inter; nitre; trine
terning renting; ringent
ternion intoner
ternions intoners
terns Ernst; rents; stern
terpenes pretense
terpsichorean cheiropterans
terra arrêt; rater
terrace caterer; retrace
terraced retraced
terraces caterers; retraces
terracing retracing
terrain trainer
terrains restrain; strainer; trainers;
  transire
terrapins transpire
terras arrest; arrêts; raster; raters;
  Sartre; starer
terrene enterer; re-enter
terrenes enterers; re-enters;
  resenter
terries étriers; reiters; retires;
  retries
terrine reinter; rentier
terrines reinsert; reinters;
  rentiers
territ ritter; triter
territs ritters
terrorise roisterer
terrorises roisterers
terry retry; tryer
terse ester; reest; reset; retes; steer;
  stere; teers; trees
tersely restyle
terser rester
tersest setters; streets; testers
Terson noters; Reston; stoner;
  tenors; tensor; trones
tertian intreat; iterant; nattier;
  nitrate; tartine

tesla least; leats; slate; Stael; stale;
  steal; stela; taels; tales; teals
teslas slates; stales; steals; tassel
Tess sets
Tessa asset; sates; seats; tasse
tessera easters; reseats; saeters;
  teasers
tesseral stealers; tearless
Tessin insets; sets in; steins
test sett; stet
testa state; taste; tates; teats
testae estate; tea-set
testament statement
testaments statements
test-ban battens
test-case cassette
test-cases cassettes
tested detest
tester setter; street
testern tenters
testers setters; streets; tersest
testes sestet; tsetse
testicular trisulcate
testier Trieste
testily stylite
testing setting
testril litters; slitter; stilter; tilters;
  titlers
test run entrust; nutters
test runs entrusts
tests setts
tetanic nictate
tetanus attunes
tetra arett; tater; treat
tetrad ratted; tarted
tetrads started
tetras aretts; stater; taster; taters;
  treats
Tetuán attune
tew ewt; wet
tewarts Stewart; swatter
tewing twinge
tewit twite
tewits twites
tews ewts; stew; west; wets
Texans sextan
Texas taxes
thae eath; hate; heat; Thea
Thais saith; taish
thaler halter; lather
Thales haslet; lathes; Shelta
Thame Meath
Thames smeath

than   tanh
thane   neath
thanes   Athens; hasten; snathe;
  sneath
thar   hart; rath; tahr
thars   harts; raths; tahrs; trash
Thasos   hoasts; hostas; shoats
that   tath
thaw   Wath; what
thawer   wreath
thawers   wreaths
thaws   swath
the   eth; het
Thea   eath; hate; heat; thae
theater   theatre; thereat
theaters   theatres
theatre   theater; thereat
theatres   theaters
Thebaid   habited
Thebes   behest
theca   cheat; tache; teach
thecal   chalet; Thecla
Thecla   chalet; thecal
thee   ethe
thees   sheet; these
theics   itches
thein   thine
their   Erith
theirs   Thiers
theism   Themis
Theiss   heists; shiest; shites; sithes;
  thesis
theist   Thetis; tithes
theistic   ethicist; itchiest
the Lamb   Lambeth
Thelma   Eltham; hamlet
themes   smeeth
Themis   theism
then   hent
thenar   anther; Tehran
thenars   anthers
theologic   ethologic
theological   ethological
theologist   ethologist
theologists   ethologists
theology   ethology
Thera   earth; Harte; hater; heart;
  Herat; rathe; thrae
there   ether; three
thereat   theater; theatre
therein   neither
Theresa   heaters; reheats
thermos   mothers; smother

these   sheet; thees
theses   sheets
thesis   heists; shiest; shites; sithes;
  Theiss
thete   teeth
Thetis   theist; tithes
thew   whet
thews   whets
thible   blithe
thicken   kitchen
thickened   kitchened
thickener   kitchener
thickeners   kitcheners
thickening   kitchening
thickens   kitchens
thickest   thickets; thickset
thickets   thickest; thickset
thicks   kitsch
thickset   thickest; thickets
Thiers   theirs
Thiès   heist; shite; sithe
thigh   hight
thighs   hights
thigs   sight
thin   hint; Nith
thine   thein
thing   night
things   nights
thinker   rethink
thinkers   rethinks
thins   hints
third   thrid
thirds   thrids
this   hist; hits; shit; sith; Tshi
thistle   Lettish; lithest
tho'   hot
thole   helot; hotel
tholes   helots; hostel; hotels
tholi   litho
Thor   thro'
Thora   Horta; Torah
thoracic   trochaic
thorn   north
thorned   northed; throned
thorning   northing; throning
thorns   norths
thorny   rhyton
thorpe   pother
thorpes   pothers; strophe
those   ethos; shote
thous   shout; south
thousand   hand-outs
thowel   howlet

thowels howlets
thrae earth; Harte; hater; heart; Herat; rathe; Thera
thrashes harshest
thraves harvest
thraw wrath
thread dearth; hatred; red-hat
threads dearths; hardest; hatreds; red-hats; trashed
thready hydrate
threap teraph
threat hatter
threats hatters; rathest; shatter
three ether; there
threes Esther; ethers; Hester
threne nether
thrice cither
thrid third
thrids thirds
thripses hipsters
thro' Thor
throb broth
throbs broths
throe other
throes others; Rothes; tosher
throne hornet; Horten
throned northed; thorned
thrones hornets; shorten
throning northing; thorning
throw worth; wroth
throwing ingrowth; Worthing
thru hurt; ruth; Thur
thrust truths
Thun hunt
Thur hurt; ruth; thru
Thurles hurtles; hustler
thus huts; shut; tush
thyrsi Irtysh; shirty
ti it
tiaraed radiate
tiaras arista; tarsia
Tiaret attire; ratite
Tib bit
Tiber biter; rebit; tribe
Tibet Betti
Tibur bruit
tic cit
tice Ceti; cite
tices cites
tickers rickets; Sickert; sticker
tickle Keltic
tickler trickle
ticklers stickler; strickle; trickles

tickles stickle
ticks stick
tics cist; cits
tic-tac tactic
tic-tacs tactics
tiddlers striddle
tide diet; dite; edit; tied
tided dited
tide-rips spirited
tides deist; diets; dites; edits; id est; sited; St. Dié; stied
tidiness insisted
tidying dignity
tied diet; dite; edit; tide
tieless telesis
tier Riet; rite; tire
tierce cerite; recite
tiercels sclerite
tierces recites
tiering igniter; tigrine
tie-rod editor; rioted; triode
tie-rods editors; roisted; rosited; sortied; steroid; storied; triodes
tiers reist; resit; rites; Siret; tires; tries
ties site; stie
tiffs stiff
tige gite
tiger Tigre
tiger-nut uttering
tiges gites
tigon ingot
tigons ingots; stingo; tosing
Tigre tiger
tigress Striges
tigrine igniter; tiering
tigs gist
Tijuana Juanita
tike kite
tikes kites; skite
til lit
tilde tiled
tildes idlest; listed; silted
tile teil
tiled tilde
tiler litre; relit
tilers lister; litres
tiles islet; istle; steil; stile; teils
till lilt
tillages legalist; stillage
tilled lilted
tiller rillet
tillered tredille

tillers   rillets; stiller; trellis
tilling   lilting
tills   lilts; still
tilted   titled
tilter   litter; titler
tilters   litters; slitter; stilter; testril;
   titlers
tilting   titling
tilts   stilt
timbale   limbate
timbales   balmiest
timber   betrim; timbre
timbers   betrims; timbres
timbre   betrim; timber
timbres   betrims; timbers
time   emit; item; mite
timed   demit
timer   merit; mitre; remit
timers   merits; mister; mitres;
   remits; smiter
times   emits; items; metis; mites;
   smite; stime
time-saving   negativism
timings   misting; smiting; stiming
Timon   Minot
Timor Sea   amortise; atomiser
tin   nit
Tina   ain't; Tain
tin can   tannic
tin cans   stannic
tind   dint
tinded   dinted
tinder   rident; trined
tinding   dinting
tinds   dints
tinea   entia; Taine
tinean   innate
tineas   tisane
tined   teind
tineid   indite
tines   inset; neist; set in; stein
tinged   nidget
tinges   ingest; signet
tingled   glinted
tingler   ringlet; tringle
tinglers   ringlets; sterling; tringles
tingles   glisten; singlet
tingling   glinting
tin god   doting
tings   sting
tink   knit
tinkers   Inkster; stinker
tinklers   strinkle

tinkles   lentisk
tinks   knits; skint; stink
tinned   indent; intend
tinner   intern
tinners   interns
tins   nits
tinsel   enlist; inlets; listen; silent
tinsels   enlists; listens
tinters   stinter
tints   stint; 'tisn't
tinware   tawnier
tip   pit
tipper   Pripet
tippler   ripplet; tripple
tipplers   ripplets; stippler; tripples
tipples   stipple
tips   pits; spit
tipster   pitters; spitter
tipsters   spitters
tiptoes   potties
tirade   airted; raited
tirades   asterid; astride; diaster;
   disrate; staired
Tiranë   Nerita; ratine; retain; retina
tirasse   satires
tire   Riet; rite; tier
tired   tried
tiredness   dissenter; residents
tireless   leisters
tires   reist; resit; rites; Siret; tiers;
   tries
Tir na n-Og   ignorant
tiro   riot; tori; trio
tiroes   sortie; tories
tiros   riots; roist; rosit; trios
tis   its; sit
tisane   tineas
tisanes   entasis; Saintes; sestina;
   Staines; tansies
'tisn't   stint; tints
tissue   suites
titan   taint; tanti
titans   taints; tanist
titfer   fitter
titfers   fitters
tither   hitter
tithers   hitters
tithes   theist; Thetis
titled   tilted
titler   litter; tilter
titlers   litters; slitter; stilter; testril;
   tilters
titles   stilet

titling tilting
titrate attrite; tattier
titration attrition
titre trite
titres sitter; trites
titters tritest
titup putti
Tiw Twi; wit
Tlemcen clement
Tlingits slitting; stilting
tmesis misset; smites; stimes
toad dato
toads datos
toady today
toast stoat
toaster Rosetta; rotates; to-tears
toasting Tsingtao
toasts stoats
Tobago Bogota
toccatas staccato
tocher hector; rochet; troche
tochered hectored
tochering hectoring
tochers hectors; rochets; torches;
  troches
toco coot
tocsin tonics
tocsins consist
tod dot
today toady
toddlers stroddle; strodled
tods dost; dots
toecap Capote
toenail elation
toes Teos; tose
tofore foetor; footer; refoot
tog got
toga goat; Göta
togaed dogate; dotage
togas goats; SOGAT
toggle goglet
toggles goglets
toho hoot; Otho
to-hunga hang-out
toil Loti
toile Eliot
toiler Loiret; loiter
toilers Estoril; estriol; loiters
toilet Lottie
toilets litotes; T. S. Eliot
toils Isolt; Solti
toko koto; took
Tokyo Kyoto

tola alto; lota
tolan notal; talon; tonal
tolas altos; Salto; Talos
told dolt
tole lote
Toledo looted; tooled
tolerance coeternal
toles lotes
tolu lout; Toul
tom mot
tombac combat
tome mote
tomes mesto; motes; smote
toms most; mots
tomtom motmot
tomtoms motmots
ton not
tonal notal; talon; tolan
Tonbridge Bridgeton
tone Eton; note
toned Donet; noted
toneless noteless
tones Eston; notes; onset; seton;
  stone; Tenos
tonga tango
tongas Gaston; Sontag; tangos
tonic Cinto
tonics tocsin
tonight hotting
toning noting
tonne nonet; tenon
tonnes Neston; nonets; sonnet;
  stonen; tenons; tenson
tons onst; snot
tonsorial torsional
tonsured roundest; unsorted
took koto; toko
tool loot
tooled looted; Toledo
tooler looter; Loreto; rootle
toolers looters; rootles
tooling looting
tools loots; lotos; stool
toom moot
toomed mooted
tooming mooting
tooms moots; smoot
toon Noto; onto; oont
toot Otto
tootsies sootiest
top opt; pot
tope poet; pote
toped depot; opted; poted

toper   Porte; repot; trope
topers   poster; presto; repost;
   repots; tropes
topes   estop; poets; stoep; stope;
top hat   hot tap
top hats   hot taps
topic   optic; picot
topical   Capitol; coal-pit; optical;
   pit-coal
topically   optically
topics   optics; picots
toping   opting; poting
topis   posit
top-line   pointel; pontile
topology   optology
toppers   stopper
toppings   stopping
topples   stopple
tops   opts; post; pots; spot; stop
topside   deposit; dopiest; posited
topsides   deposits; side-post
tor   ort; rot
Tora   rota; Orta; taro
Torah   Horta; Thora
toran   orant; trona
torches   hectors; rochets; tochers;
   troches
tore   rote
torero   rooter
toreros   rooster; rooters
tores   estro; roset; rotes; store;
   torse
tori   riot; tiro; trio
tories   sortie; tiroes
torments   sortment
torn   tron
tornado   donator; odorant
torpedo   trooped
torpid   tripod
torque   quoter; roquet
torques   questor; quoters; roquets
torret   retort; rotter
torrets   retorts; rotters
tors   orts; rots; sort
torsade   roasted
torse   estro; roset; rotes; store; tores
torses   rosets; sortes; stores; tosser
torsional   tonsorial
torso   roost; roots; stoor
torsos   roosts; stoors
tort   trot
tortile   triolet
tortilla   littoral

tortillas   littorals
tortoise   rootiest
torts   trots
torus   roust; routs; stour; sutor;
   tours
tory   ryot; troy; tyro
Tosca   Ascot; coast; coats; costa
tose   Teos; toes
tosed   dotes
tosh   host; hots; shot
toshed   hosted
tosher   others; Rothes; throes
toshing   hosting
tosing   ingots; stingo; tigons
toss   sots
tosser   rosets; sortes; stores; torses
tosses   Sestos
toss-up   spouts
tost   stot; tots
to-tear   rotate
to-tears   Rosetta; rotates; toaster
totem   motet; motte
totems   motets; mottes
totes   set-to
tother   hotter
Totnes   ostent
tots   stot; tost
totters   stotter; stretto
touch   chout; couth
toucher   retouch
tough   ought
toughs   sought
Toul   lout; tolu
toupets   outstep
tour   rout
Touré   outer; outré; route
toured   detour; douter; outred; red
   out; routed
tourer   retour; router
tourers   retours; routers; trouser
touring   ring out; routing
tours   roust; routs; stour; sutor;
   torus
toused   ousted
touser   ouster; outers; routes;
   souter; trouse
tousers   estrous; oestrus; ousters;
   sourest; souters; trouses; tussore
tousing   ousting; outings
tousled   loudest
touted   duetto
touts   stout
tow   two; wot

towel   owlet
towels   Elstow; lowest; owlets
tower   twoer; wrote
towers   sowter; stower; stowre;
   towser; twoers
towing   Wigton
towline   two-line
town   nowt; wont
towns   stown; wonts
tows   stow; swot; twos
towsed   stowed
towser   sowter; stower; stowre;
   towers; twoers
towsers   sowters; stowers; stowres
towsing   stowing; Wigston
trace   caret; carte; cater; crate; react;
   recta
traceable   creatable
traced   carted; crated; Dectra; redact
tracer   arrect; carter; crater
tracers   carters; craters
traces   carets; cartes; caster; caters;
   crates; Cresta; reacts; recast
tracing   carting
tracks   strack
trad   dart; drat
trade   adret; dater; rated; tared;
   tread
trade counters   unstercorated
traded   darted
trade-in   detrain; tan-ride; trained
trader   darter; dartre; retard; tarred
traders   darters; retards; starred
trades   adrets; daters; stared; treads
tradesmen   smartened
trading   darting
traduce   Decatur
tragedy   gyrated
tragion   orating
traiks   straik
trail   liart; trial
trailer   retiral; retrial
trailers   retrials
trailing   ringtail
trails   trials
train   intra; Nitra; riant; Trani
trained   detrain; tan-ride; trade-in
trainee   Aintree; retinae
trainees   Teresina
trainer   terrain
trainers   restrain; strainer; terrains;
   transire
trains   instar; santir; Sintra; strain

traipse   parties; piastre; pirates;
   praties
traipses   pastries; piastres; raspiest,
   Tarsipes
traits   artist; sittar; strait; strati
Tralee   relate
tram   mart
tramline   terminal
tramlines   terminals
trample   Templar
tramples   Templars
tramps   stramp
trams   marts; smart
trance   canter; carnet; creant;
   Cretan; nectar; recant; tanrec
tranced   Tancred
trances   canters; carnets; Cretans;
   recants; tanrecs
tranche   chanter
tranches   chanters; snatcher;
   stancher
trangle   tangler
trangles   strangle; tanglers
Trani   intra; Nitra; riant; train
transept   patterns
tranships   transship
transience   nectarines
transient   instanter
transire   restrain; strainer; terrains;
   trainers
transires   restrains; strainers
transom   Marston; matrons
transpire   terrapins
transpose   patroness
transship   tranships
trap   part; prat; rapt
trapan   tarpan
trapans   Spartan; tarpans
trape   apert; pater; peart; Petra;
   prate; taper
traped   depart; parted; petard;
   prated
trapes   paster; paters; Praest; prates;
   repast; tapers
trapesed   pederast; predates
traping   gin trap; parting; prating
trappean   apparent
trappers   strapper
trappings   strapping
traps   parts; prats; spart; sprat; strap
trash   harts; raths; tahrs; thars
trashed   dearths; hardest; hatreds;
   red-hats; threads

trass stars; tsars
trave avert; taver
travel varlet
traveled Arteveld
travels varlets; vestral
traves averts; starve; tavers; vaster
tray arty
trays satyr; stray
treacle Electra
treacles clearest
tread adret; dater; rated; tared;
  trade
treader retread
treaders retreads; serrated
treading derating; gradient; red
  giant
treadle alerted; altered; related
treads adrets; daters; stared; trades
treason senator
treasons assentor; senators;
  star-nose
treasurer serrature
treat arett; tater; tetra
treated aretted
treater retreat
treaters retreats
treaties ariettes; iterates; treatise
treating aretting
treatise ariettes; iterates; treaties
treats aretts; stater; taster; taters;
  tetras
treaty yatter
Tredegar garreted; gartered;
  regrated
tredille tillered
tree rete; teer
treed deter
treeing integer; teering
treen enter; rente; terne
treenail elaterin; entailer
treenails entailers
trees ester; reest; reset; retes; steer;
  stere; teers; terse
trefoil loftier
trellis rillets; stiller; tillers
trema armet; mater; tamer
tremor termor
tremors termors
trenail entrail; Latiner; latrine;
  ratline; reliant; retinal
trenails entrails; Latiners; latrines;
  ratlines
trencher retrench

trenise entires; entries; Steiner;
  Teniers
trenises sentries
trentals slattern
Trento rotten
trepan arpent; enrapt; entrap;
  panter; parent
trepans arpents; entraps; panters;
  parents; pastern
trephine nephrite
trepidation partitioned
Tresco corset; Cortes; coster;
  escort; scoter; sector
trespass sparsest
tress rests
tressed deserts; dessert
tressels restless
tressing trigness
tressy syrtes
trestle letters; settler; sterlet
trestles settlers; sterlets
trevis rivets; stiver; strive
treviss stivers; strives
trews strew; wrest
trey tyre
treys resty; Steyr; tyres
triable Alberti; librate
triacid triadic
triadic triacid
triads Astrid
triage gaiter
triages agister; gaiters; sea-girt;
  stagier; strigae
trial liart; trail
trials trails
triangle alerting; altering; integral;
  relating
triangles integrals
Trias airts; astir; raits; sitar; Sitra;
  stair; stria; tarsi
tribbles stibbler
tribe biter; rebit; Tiber
tribes bestir; bister; bistre; biters
tribunal turbinal
tribunate turbinate
tribune turbine
tribunes turbines
trice recti
triced credit; direct
Tricel relict
trices steric
Tricia iatric
trickle tickler

trickles   stickler; strickle; ticklers
tridents   strident
tried   tired
tries   reist; resit; rites; Siret; tiers;
   tires
Trieste   testier
trifle   filter; lifter
trifled   flirted
trifles   filters; lifters; stifler
trifling   flirting
trig   girt; grit
trigness   tressing
trigon   Girton; roting
trigons   sorting; storing
trigs   girts; grist; grits; strig
trikes   strike
trimester   remitters; trimeters
trimeter   remitter
trimeters   remitters; trimester
trimmed   midterm
trimness   minsters
trinal   ratlin
trine   inert; inter; nitre; Terni
trined   rident; tinder
trines   insert; inters; sinter; Strine
tringle   ringlet; tingler
tringles   ringlets; sterling; tinglers
trinket   knitter
trinkets   knitters
trio   riot; tiro; tori
triode   editor; rioted; tie-rod
triodes   editors; roisted; rosited;
   sortied; steroid; storied; tie-rods
triolet   tortile
triones   in store; orients; stonier
trios   riots; roist; rosit; tiros
trip   ript
tripe   petri; piert
tripes   esprit; priest; Pteris; ripest;
   sprite; stripe
triple   let rip
triplets   splitter
triplings   split ring; stripling
tripod   torpid
tripodic   dioptric
tripods   disport
tripos   prosit
triposes   ripostes
trippers   stripper
tripple   ripplet; tippler
tripples   ripplets; stippler; tipplers
trips   sprit; stirp; strip
tripsis   spirits

triremes   merriest; rimester
trismus   sistrum; truisms
trisulcate   testicular
trite   titre
tritones   interests; resistent
triter   ritter; territ
trites   sitter; titres
tritest   titters
triune   uniter
triunes   uniters
Troas   Astor; roast; rotas; Sarto; taros
trocar   carrot
trocars   carrots
trochaic   thoracic
troche   hector; rochet; tocher
troches   hectors; rochets; tochers;
   torches
trod   dort
trolls   stroll
Troms   morts; storm
Tromsö   motors
tron   torn
trona   orant; toran
trone   noter; tenor
trones   noters; Reston; stoner;
   tenors; tensor; Terson
Troon   Orton
troop   poort; Porto
trooped   torpedo
troopials   spoliator
troops   poorts
trope   Porte; repot; toper
tropes   poster; presto; repost;
   repots; topers
tropine   pointer; protein; pterion
tropism   imports
tropist   protist
tropists   protists
Troste   otters
trot   tort
trots   torts
trouble   blue-rot; boulter
troubles   boulters
trounce   cornute; counter; recount
trounced   cornuted
trounces   construe; cornutes;
   counters; recounts
trouncing   cornuting
troupe   pouter
troupes   petrous; posture; pouters;
   Proteus; septuor; spouter
trouse   ouster; outers; routes;
   souter; touser

trouser retours; routers; tourers
trouses estrous; oestrus; ousters; sourest; souters; tousers; tussore
trout tutor
trouts strout; tutors
trouvère overture
trouvères overtures
trove overt; voter
trow wort
trowed rowted
trowel wortle
trowels wortles
trows strow; worst; worts
troy ryot; tory; tyro
Troyes oyster; rosety; storey; tyroes; Yes Tor
truce cruet; cuter; eruct
truces cruets; cruset; Custer; eructs; rectus
trucial curtail
trucks struck
trudgen grunted
true Rute
true-love revolute
truest utters
truffle fretful
truisms sistrum; trismus
Truman antrum
trumpets strumpet
trundle rundlet
trundles rundlets
truss rusts
trussed dusters
trusses russets
trust strut; sturt
trusted sturted
trusting sturting
trusts struts; sturts
truths thrust
try Tyr
tryer retry; terry
try on Ryton
Tsabian abstain
Tsabians abstains
Tsana Santa; Satan
tsar arts; rats; star; tars
tsardom stardom
tsarina artisan
tsarinas artisans
tsarism Marists; Ramists
tsarist artists; sittars; straits
tsars stars; trass
T. S. Eliot litotes; toilets

tsetse sestet; testes
tsetses sestets
Tshi hist; hits; shit; sith; this
tsigane easting; Gastein; genista; ingates; ingesta; seating; tangies; teasing
Tsingtao toasting
Tsuga Tagus
tuan aunt; tuna
tub but
tuba abut; buat; tabu
tubae beaut; Butea; taube
tubas abuts; buats; tabus
tube Bute
tubed debut
tuber brute; rebut
tubers brutes; buster; rebuts
tubs bust; buts; stub
tucks stuck
Tucson counts
Tudors Stroud
tug gut
tugs gust; guts
tule lute
tules lutes
Tulsa sault; talus
tumbler tumbrel
tumblers stumbler; tumbrels
tumbles stumble
tumblings stumbling
tumbrel tumbler
tumbrels stumbler; tumblers
tums must; smut; stum
tun nut
tuna aunt; tuan
tunas aunts
tuner urent
tuners unrest
tunes unset; usen't
tungstic cuttings
tunic cut in; incut
tunics cuts in
Tunis inust; suint; units
Tunja jaunt; junta
tuns nuts; stun; Unst
tup put
tups puts
turacin curtain
Turanians Saturnian
turbaned breadnut
turbinal tribunal
turbinate tribunate
turbine tribune

turbines   tribunes
Turco   court
Turcos   courts; scruto
turdine   intrude; untired; untried
turds   durst
tureen   neuter; retune; tenure
tureens   neuters; retunes; tenures
Turin   rutin
Turk   kurt
Turkess   tuskers
turms   strum
turn   runt
turned   retund
turner   return
turners   returns
turnings   unstring
turnips   unstrip
turnover   overturn
turnovers   overturns
turns   runts
turps   spurt
turret   rutter
turrets   rutters
Tuscan   cantus
Tuscans   Sanctus
tush   huts; shut; thus
tuskers   Turkess
tussal   saltus; saults
tusser   estrus; russet
tussore   estrous; oestrus; ousters;
    sourest; souters; tousers; trouses
tutor   trout
tutors   strout; trouts
tutsan   taunts
Tver   vert
twa   taw; wat
twain   witan
twas   staw; swat; taws; wast
twat   watt
twats   watts

tweed   De Wet
tweeds   stewed; wested
tweers   stewer; sweert; wester
Twi   Tiw; wit
twice   twire; write
twiers   sweirt; twires; writes
twiner   winter
twiners   winters
twinge   tewing
twinges   stewing; westing
twire   twier; write
twires   sweirt; twiers; writes
twist   twits
twite   tewit
twites   tewits
twits   twist
two   tow; wot
twoer   tower; wrote
twoers   sowter; stower; stowre;
    towers; towser
two-line   towline
twos   stow; swot; tows
tye   yet
tyes   stey; stye
tyke   kyte
tykes   kytes; skyte
typical   clay-pit
typographer   petrography
typto   potty
typtos   spotty
Tyr   try
tyre   trey
tyres   resty; Steyr; treys
Tyrian   in-tray
Tyrians   in-trays
tyro   ryot; tory; troy
tyroes   oyster; rosety; storey;
    Troyes; Yes Tor
tyros   ryots; story

U

U-boat   about
U-boats   Basuto
U-bolt   boult
U-bolts   boults
udal   auld; dual; laud
udaller   allured
udals   Aldus; lauds
udder   dured
udders   sudder

udo   duo; Oud
ugh   hug
ugly   guly
Uhlans   unlash
Uist   suit
ulan   Luna; ulna
ulcer   cruel; lucre
ulcerous   urceolus
ulcers   cruels

219

ullages seagull
ulna Luna; ulan
ulnar lunar; urnal
ulnare neural; unreal
ulnares Laurens
ulster luster; lustre; luters; result;
  rustle; sutler
ulstered resulted
ulsters lusters; lustres; results;
  rustles; sutlers
ultimate mutilate
Ultonian Lutonian
Ultonians Lutonians
ultraism altruism
ultraist altruist
ultraistic altruistic
ultraists altruists
umbels umbles
umber brume; umbre
umbers umbres
umbles umbels
umbo ombú
umbos ombús
umbra Burma; rumba
umbral brumal; labrum; lumbar
umbrated drumbeat
umbre brume; umber
umbres umbers
Umbria barium
umlaut mutual
umph hump
umpire impure
umpired dumpier
unable Nabeul; nebula
unaired uranide
unaltered unrelated
unarm Namur
unarmed duramen; manured;
  maunder
unbar buran; urban
unbare unbear; urbane
unbares unbears
unbars burans
unbear unbare; urbane
unbears unbares
unboding bounding
unboiled unilobed
unbred burden; burned
unburden unburned
unburdens sunburned
uncage cangue
uncages cangues
uncarted underact; untraced

uncase usance
uncate Canute
uncertain encurtain; runcinate
unchal launch; nuchal
unchosen nonesuch
uncial Alcuin; Lucian; Lucina
unclaimed undecimal
unclear lucarne; nuclear
uncles Clunes
unclips insculp; sculpin
unclose counsel
unclosed enclouds
uncloses counsels
uncoil Culion
uncope pounce
uncoped pounced
uncopes pounces
uncoping pouncing
uncursed sun-cured
undam maund; Munda
undams maunds; Mundas
undated daunted
unde dune; nude
undecimal unclaimed
undelight unlighted
under Düren; runed; urned
underact uncarted; untraced
underacts undercast
underage dungaree; ungeared
underarm unmarred
underbrush undershrub
undercast underacts
underdo redound; rounded
underdog grounded
underdoing redounding
underfed refunded
underfur unfurred
undergo guerdon; ungored
underleased undersealed
underleasing undersealing
underlying enduringly
undernote undertone
undernotes undertones
undersealed underleased
undersealing underleasing
underset dentures; sederunt;
  undesert
undersets sederunts
undershrub underbrush
underside undesired
undersign sundering
undersigns undressing
undertone undernote

undertones   undernotes
undesert   dentures; sederunt;
   underset
undeserve   unsevered
undesired   underside
undies   indues
undoers   Oresund; resound;
   sounder
undrape   unpared
undrapes   unspared
undreamed   maundered
undreaming   maundering
undress   sunders
undressing   undersigns
unearth   haunter
unearths   haunters
unfelt   fluent
unfolder   flounder
unfolders   flounders
unfolding   foundling
unforced   frounced
unforested   unfostered
unfostered   unforested
unfurred   underfur
ungainly   unlaying
ungeared   dungaree; underage
ungilded   deluding; indulged
ungird   during
ungirth   hurting; unright
ungirths   unrights
ungods   sun-dog; sungod
ungored   guerdon; undergo
ungual   ungula
ungula   ungual
unhalsed   unlashed
unhasting   hauntings
unhat   haunt
unhats   haunts; sunhat; Ushant
unhorsed   enshroud
uniate   auntie
unilobed   unboiled
unions   unison
unison   unions
unite   untie
united   untied
uniter   triune
uniters   triunes
unites   tenuis; unties
units   inust; suint; Tunis
unlace   cuneal; launce; Lucena
unlaces   censual; launces; unscale
unlaid   Lindau
unlash   Uhlans

unlashed   unhalsed
unlay   yulan
unlaying   ungainly
unleased   unsealed
unleash   unshale
unlighted   undelight
unlisted   insulted
unlit   until
unloaded   duodenal
unmarred   underarm
unmastered   unstreamed
unmated   untamed
unmined   minuend
unnamed   mundane
unnoticed   continued
unorder   rondure; rounder
unorders   rondures; rounders
unpaired   unrepaid
unpared   undrape
unpent   punnet
unperch   puncher
unpoetical   peculation
unqueen   Neuquen
unraised   denarius; Eridanus
unreal   neural; ulnare
unrelated   unaltered
unrent   runnet
unrepaid   unpaired
unreserved   unreversed
unrest   tuners
unresting   insurgent
unreversed   unreserved
unright   hurting; ungirth
unrights   ungirths
unripe   punier; purine
unrobe   bourne
unrobed   bounder; rebound
unrobes   bournes
unsainted   inundates; unstained
unsay   Sunay
unscale   censual; launces; unlaces
unscored   crunodes
unsealed   unleased
unseals   sensual
unseat   nasute
unseats   nasutes
unseeing   ingénues
unseens   unsense
unsense   unseens
unset   tunes; usen't
unsets   sunset
unsettle   lunettes
unsevered   undeserve

unshale   unleash
unship   punish
unshod   hounds; Hudson
unsliced   includes; nuclides
unsocial   Alcinoüs
unsoiled   delusion; insouled
unsorted   roundest; tonsured
unspared   undrapes
unspent   punnets
unspoilt   Plotinus
Unst   nuts; stun; tuns
unstained   inundates; unsainted
unstated   Neustadt; untasted
unstayed   unsteady
unsteady   unstayed
unstercorated   trade counters
unstirred   intruders
unstop   puntos
unstops   sunspot
unstreamed   unmastered
unstring   turnings
unstrip   turnips
untame   unteam
untamed   unmated
untames   unteams
untasted   Neustadt; unstated
unteach   Chanute
unteam   untame
unteams   untames
untidy   nudity
untie   unite
untied   united
unties   tenuis; unites
until   unlit
untiled   diluent
untimely   minutely
untired   intrude; turdine; untried
untrace   centaur
untraced   uncarted; underact
untraces   centaurs; Etruscan;
   recusant
untried   intrude; turdine; untired
untrod   rotund
upbreak   break-up
upcast   catsup
upcasts   catsups
upclose   close-up; couples; opuscle
upcloses   close-ups; Scopelus
up-ends   send-up; upsend
uphold   hold-up
upholds   hold-ups
uplander   pendular
upled   duple; puled

up-line   line-up; lupine
up-lines   line-ups; lupines; spinule
upon   noup; Puno
uppers   supper
upraise   Piraeus; spuriae
uprear   parure
uprears   parures
uprise   Epirus
uprises   suspire
uprisings   suspiring
uprist   purist; spruit; stir up
ups   pus; sup
upsend   send-up; up-ends
upsends   send-ups
upset   set-up; stupe
upsets   stupes
uptrain   puritan
uptrains   puritans; Rasputin
uptrend   prudent
uracil   curial; Uralic
Uralic   curial; uracil
Urals   Larus; sural
uranide   unaired
uranism   Surinam
uranite   ruinate; taurine; urinate
urban   buran; unbar
urbane   unbare; unbear
urceolus   ulcerous
urdé   dure; rude; rued
ure   rue
urent   tuner
ures   Reus; rues; ruse; sure; user
uresis   issuer
urgent   gunter; gurnet
urges   surge
urinals   insular
urinate   ruinate; taurine; uranite
urinated   daturine; indurate;
   ruinated
urinates   Neustria
urine   inure
urn   nur; run
urnal   lunar; ulnar
urned   Düren; runed; under
urns   nurs; runs
Urodela   roulade
Ursa   rusa; sura
ursine   insure; inures; rusine
urticates   rusticate
usable   suable
usager   argues; augers; sauger;
   Segura
usance   uncase

use   sue
used   deus; dues; Duse; sued
used cars   crusades
Usedom   moused; soumed
usen't   tunes; unset
user   Reus; rues; ruse; sure, ures
users   Reuss; ruses
uses   sues
Ushant   haunts; sunhat; unhats
usher   huers
ushers   rhesus; rushes
using   suing
usurped   pursued
usurper   pursuer
usurpers   pursuers

usurping   pursuing
Utah   haut
utas   saut
utensil   luniest
uterine   retinue; reunite
uterus   suture
Utes   suet
Utopian   Opuntia
utterer   reutter
utterers   reutters
uttering   tiger-nut
utters   truest
uva   vau
uveal   Le Vau; value

V

Vaal   Alva; aval; lava
vacate   caveat
vacates   caveats
vade   Dave; deva; Veda
vaded   Vedda
vades   devas; saved; Vedas
vae   ave; Eva
vaes   Aves; save; vase
vaginate   navigate
vaguest   Gustave
vail   vali; vial
vails   Alvis; Salvi; silva; valis; vials
vain   Ivan; vina
vainer   Erivan; ravine; Vanier
vains   savin
vair   Ravi; riva
Valais   avails; saliva; salvia
vale   lave; leva; veal; vela
valence   enclave
valences   enclaves
valentine   Levantine
vales   Elvas; laves; salve; selva;
    slave; valse
valets   vestal
vali   vail; vial
valiant   Latvian
valis   Alvis; Salvi; silva; vails; vials
valise   Aviles; Leavis
vallar   larval
Valona   Avalon; Avlona
valse   Elvas; laves; salve; selva;
    slave; vales
valsed   salved; slaved
valses   salves; selvas; slaves

valsing   salving; slaving
value   Le Vau; uveal
vamose   amoves
vamper   revamp
vampers   revamps
vane   Evan; nave; Neva; vena
vanes   avens; Evans; naves; Sevan
vaneless   enslaves
Vanier   Erivan; ravine; vainer
vanishers   varnishes
vapid   pavid
Varde   drave; raved; Revda
vare   Arve; aver; rave; Vera
varec   carve; caver; crave
vares   avers; raves; saver
Varese   averse; reaves
varices   viscera
varier   arrive; Rivera
variers   arrives
varies   Servia
various   saviour
variously   savourily
varlet   travel
varlets   travels; vestral
varnishes   vanishers
vasa   Sava
vasal   lavas
vase   Aves; save; vaes
vases   saves
vast   vats
vaster   averts; starve; tavers; traves
vaticide   cavitied
vats   vast
vau   uva

vaulters vestural
veal lave; leva; vale; vela
Vectis civets; evicts
vector corvet; covert
vectors corvets; coverts
Veda Dave; deva; vade
Vedantic ci-devant
Vedas devas; saved; vades
Vedda vaded
Vedic viced
vee eve
veer ever
veered reeved
veering reeving
veers serve; sever; verse
vees eves
Vega gave
veil evil; Levi; live; vile; vlei
veils Elvis; evils; levis; lives; slive
vein vine
veined endive; envied
veinous envious; niveous
veins Nevis; vines; visne
vela lave; leva; vale; veal
velar laver; ravel; Reval
Veles elves
velour louver; louvre
velours louvers; louvres
vena Evan; nave; Neva; vane
venal elvan; levan; navel
venality natively
venation innovate
vender Denver; nerved; Verden
veneer enerve
veneers enerves
Vener erven; nerve; never; Verne
venerate enervate
venerated enervated
venerates enervates
venerating enervating
veneration enervation
venge Negev
venial alevin; alvine
Venice evince
Venlo novel; Vlonë
Ventris inverts; striven
Vera Arve; aver; rave; vare
verbose observe; obverse
Verden Denver; nerved; vender
Verdi diver; drive; rived
veriest restive
verifiers versifier
verily livery

veritable avertible
vermian Minerva
vernal nerval
vernation nervation
Verne erven; nerve; never; Vener
Verona Averno
Veronica Corvinae
versal lavers; ravels; salver; serval; slaver
versals salvers; servals; slavers
versant servant; taverns
versatile relatives
verse serve; sever; veers
versed served
verser revers; server
versers servers
verses serves; severs; Sèvres
versifier verifiers
versine enviers; inverse; Viersen
versines inverses
versing serving
version renvois
verso overs; roves; Serov; servo
verst verts
vert Tver
verticals cat-silver
verts verst
very ryve
Vespa paves
vespertine presentive
vest vets
vesta stave
vestal valets
vestas staves
vested devest
vestral travels; varlets
vestural vaulters
veto vote
vetoed devote
vets vest
vial vail; vali
vials Alvis; Salvi; silva; vails; valis
viand divan; Dvina
viands divans
vibes Bevis
vice cive
viced Vedic
vicegerent viceregent
vicegerents viceregents
vice-presidents predictiveness
viceregent vicegerent
viceregents vicegerents
vices cives

Vichy chivy
Vida avid; diva
vied Devi; dive
Viersen enviers; inverse; versine
vies Ives; vise
Viet-Cong coveting
view wive
viewer review
viewers reviews
views swive; wives
vigilante genitival
vikings skiving
vilde devil; lived
vile evil; Levi; live; veil; vlei
vilely evilly; lively
vileness evilness
Vilna Alvin; anvil; nival
vina Ivan; vain
vinas Sivan
vine vein
vinegar reaving
viner riven
vines Nevis; veins; visne
vintager averting; tavering
viola Oliva
violaceous olivaceous
violated dovetail
violet olivet
violets olivets
viperous pérvious; previous
viral rival
virent invert
virgin Irving; riving
visa Avis; siva
visaed advise; Davies
visas Sivas
viscera varices
visceral calivers; claviers

vise Ives; vies
vised dives
viséed devise; sieved
visitant nativist
vigilants nativists
visne Nevis; veins; vines
visored devisor; devoirs; voiders
vitrine inviter
vitrines inviters
vivers vivres
vivres vivers
vlei evil; Levi; live; veil; vile
vleis Elvis; evils; levis; lives; slive;
   veils
Vlonë novel; Venlo
void Ovid
voided devoid
voider devoir
voiders devisor; devoirs; visored
voile olive
vola Olav; oval
vole love
voled loved
voles loves; slove; solve
voling Gonvil; loving
volley lovely
Volsci Clovis
volt VTOL
vomer mover
vomers movers
vote veto
voter overt; trove
voters stover; strove
votes stove
vowels wolves
Vratca cravat
VTOL volt

W

wabble bawble
wabbles bawbles
wad daw
wadd dawd
wadded dawded
waddle dawdle
waddled dawdled
waddler dawdler; drawled
waddlers dawdlers; swaddler
waddles dawdles; swaddle
waddling dawdling

wade awed
wade in dewani; wained
wader Dewar; wared
waders sawder; Seward
wades sawed
wads daws; swad
wadset stawed; wasted
wae awe
waesome awesome
wafters fretsaw
wagered Edgware; ragweed

wages   swage
wags   swag
wail   wali
wailed   Dewali
wained   dewani; wade in
wains   swain
waist   waits
waisted   dawties
waister   waiters; wariest
waisters   waitress
waited   dawtie
waiters   waister; wariest
waitress   waisters
waits   waist
wake   weak; weka
waker   wreak
wakers   wreaks
wakes   askew; wekas
Walden   lawned
wale   weal
waled   dwale; lawed; weald
wales   Lawes; swale; sweal; weals
wali   wail
waling   lawing
walk   lawk
walks   lawks
wallets   setwall
wallows   swallow
waly   yawl
wan   awn
wand   dawn
wander   Andrew; Darwen; dawner;
   warden; warned
wandered   dawnered
wandering   dawnering
wanders   dawners; wardens
wands   dawns
wane   anew; Ewan; wean
waned   awned; dewan
wanes   sewan; weans
wang   gnaw
wangler   Wrangel; wrangle
wanglers   wrangles
wangs   gnaws; swang
waning   awning
wanker   Newark
wankers   swanker
wankle   knawel
wanks   swank
wanty   tawny
wap   paw
waps   paws; spaw; swap; wasp
war   raw

warble   bawler
warbled   brawled
warbler   brawler
warblers   brawlers
warbles   bawlers
warbling   brawling
ward   draw
warded   Edward
warden   Andrew; Darwen; dawner;
   wander; warned
wardens   dawners; wanders
warder   drawer; redraw; reward;
   warred
warders   drawers; redraws;
   rewards
warding   drawing
wards   draws; sward
ware   Rewa; wear
wared   Dewar; wader
warely   lawyer
wares   sawer; sware; swear; wears
warier   Rewari
wariest   waister; waiters
waring   rawing
warm   mawr
warmers   swarmer
warms   mawrs; swarm
warn   rawn
warned   Andrew; Darwen; dawner;
   wander; warden
warner   warren
warners   warrens
warns   rawns
warp   wrap
warper   prewar
warps   wraps
warred   drawer; redraw; reward;
   warder
warren   warner
warrens   warners
warst   straw; swart; warts; wrast
warts   straw; swart; warst; wrast
wary   awry
was   saw
wase   awes
wash   haws; shaw
washer   hawser; whares
washers   hawsers; swasher
wasp   paws; spaw; swap; waps
wasps   swaps
wast   staw; swat; taws; twas
waste   sweat; tawse
wasted   stawed; wadset

226

waster   tawers; waters
wastes   sawset; sweats; tawses
wasting   stawing
wat   taw; twa
watch-dog   dog-watch
water   tawer; wrate
watered   tarweed
waterfalls   Fats Waller
water-hen   wreathen
wateriness   earwitness
waters   tawers; waster
watery   tawery
Wath   thaw; what
watt   twat
watts   twats
wavers   swarve
way   yaw
wayboard   broadway
wayboards   broadways
ways   sway
weak   wake; weka
weal   wale
weald   dwale; lawed; waled
weals   Lawes; swale; sweal; wales
wean   anew; Ewan; wane
weans   sewan; wanes
wear   Rewa; ware
Weardale   Delaware
wearers   swearer
weariest   sweatier
wears   sawer; sware; swear; wares
weasels   aweless
weather   whereat; wreathe
weathers   wreathes
webster   bestrew
websters   bestrews
wed   dew
weds   dews
wee   ewe
weeders   sweered
weeds   sewed; swede; sweed
weedy   Dewey
weels   Lewes; sewel; sweel; Wesel
ween   enew
weened   enewed
weening   enewing
weens   enews; sewen
weepers   sweeper
weeps   sweep
wees   ewes; swee
weid   wide
weil   wiel; wile
weils   lewis; wiels; wiles

weir   wire
weird   wider; wired
weirs   sweir; swire; wires; wiser
weka   wake; weak
woltus   askew; wakes
weld   lewd
welder   lewder
welkin   winkle
well-doer   rowelled
well-doing   dowelling
wells   swell
Wels   slew
welters   swelter; wrestle
welting   winglet
welts   swelt
Wem   mew
wen   new
Wendic   winced
wens   news; sewn
went   newt
were   ewer
wersh   shrew
Werther   wherret
Wesel   Lewes; sewel; sweel; weels
Weser   ewers; sewer; sweer
Wesker   skewer
west   ewts; stew; tews; wets
wested   stewed; tweeds
wester   stewer; sweert; tweers
westering   swingtree
westers   stewers
westing   stewing; twinges
wests   stews
wet   ewt; tew
wets   ewts; stew; tews; west
wettish   whitest
wey   wye; yew
weys   wyes; yews
whale   wheal
whales   wheals
whalings   shawling
wham   hawm
whams   hawms; shawm
whares   hawser; washer
what   thaw; Wath
wheal   whale
wheals   whales
wheatear   a-weather
wheats   swathe
wheedle   wheeled
wheeled   wheedle
wheels   shewel
when   hewn

227

where hewer	**winced** Wendic
whereat weather; wreathe	**wincher** new rich
whereon Erewhon; nowhere	**winchers** Schwerin
wherret Werther	**winded** dwined
whet thew	**winder** rewind
whets thews	**winders** rewinds
whines newish	**winding** dwining
whinge hewing	**windless** swindles; wildness
whinges hewings; shewing	**windroses** rowdiness; wordiness
whirtles whistler	**wined** dwine; Edwin; widen
whissed Swedish; swished	**wines** sewin; sinew; swine
whisses swishes	**winge** Ewing
whissing swishing	**winger** Wigner
whist swith; whits	**wingers** swinger
whistler whirtles	**winges** sewing; swinge
whit with	**wingless** swingles
white withe	**winglet** welting
whiter wither; writhe	**wings** swing
white rose otherwise	**winker** Wrekin
whites withes	**winkers** swinker
whitest wettish	**winkle** welkin
whits swith; whist	**winks** swink
whity withy	**winsey** sinewy
who how	**winter** twiner
whoever however	**winters** twiners
whom Mhow	**winze** wizen
whores shower	**winzes** wizens
wide weid	**wipers** swiper
widely wieldy	**wipes** swipe
widen dwine; Edwin; wined	**wire** weir
wideness dewiness	**wired** weird; wider
widens dwines; Widnes	**wires** sweir; swire; weirs; wiser
wider weird; wired	**wiser** sweir; swire; weirs; wires
Widnes dwines; widens	**wishers** swisher
wiel weil; wile	**wist** wits
wield Wilde; wiled	**wit** Tiw; Twi
wieldy widely	**witan** twain
wiels lewis; weils; wiles	**with** whit
wigan awing	**withe** white
wiggler wriggle	**wither** whiter; writhe
wigglers wriggles	**withers** swither; writhes
Wigner winger	**withes** whites
wigs swig	**within** inwith
Wigston stowing; towsing	**without** outwith
Wigton towing	**withy** whity
Wilde wield; wiled	**witling** wilting
wildness swindles; windless	**wits** wist
wile weil; wiel	**wive** view
wiled wield; Wilde	**wives** swive; views
wiles lewis; weils; wiels	**wizen** winze
willer Irwell	**wizens** winzes
wills swill	**woalds** dowlas
wilting witling	**wobbly** by-blow

Woden endow; nowed; owned
woe owe
woes owes
wolf flow; fowl
wolfed flowed; fowled
wolfer flower; fowler; reflow
wolfers flowers; fowlers; reflows
wolfing flowing; fowling
wolves vowels
won now; own
wont nowt; town
wonts stown; towns
wop pow
wops pows; sowp; swop
wordier worried
wordily rowdily
wordiness rowdiness; windroses
words drows; sword
wordy dowry; rowdy
wore ower; owre
work-basket basketwork
worker rework
workers reworks
workhouse housework
work-master master-work
work-mate team-work
work-out outwork
workpiece piece-work
worried wordier
worse owers; serow; sower; swore
worsed dowers; dowser; drowse
worsen owners; rowens
worsens New Ross
worser rowers
worst strow; trows; worts
worsted strowed
worsting strowing
worsts strows
wort rowt; trow
worth rowth; throw; worth
Worthing ingrowth; throwing
wortle trowel
wortles trowels
worts strow; trows; worst

wot tow
wounder rewound
wounds swound
Wrangel wangler; wrangle
wrangle wangler; Wrangel
wrangles wanglers
wrap warp
wraps warps
wrasse sawers; swears
wrast straw; swart; warst; warts
wrate tawer; water
wrath thraw
wreak waker
wreaks wakers
wreath thawer
wreathe weather; whereat
wreathen water-hen
wreathes weathers
wreaths thawers
Wrekin winker
wrest strew; trews
wrested strewed
wrester strewer
wresters strewers
wresting strewing
wrestle swelter; welters
wrestles swelters
wrests strews
wriggle wiggler
wriggles wigglers
wringed redwing
wrist writs
write twier; twire
writes sweirt; twiers; twires
writhe whiter; wither
writhes swither; withers
writs wrist
wroken knower
wrong grown
wrote tower; twoer
wroth rowth; throw; worth
wye wey; yew
wyes weys; yews

X

xanthein xanthine
xanthine xanthein
Xema exam
xenial alexin

xerotic excitor
xylic cylix
xyst Styx
xysti sixty

Y

yacht Cathy
yager gayer
yah hay
Yahve heavy
yak Kay
yald lady
y'all ally
yam Amy; may; Mya
Yamal Malay
yamen Mayen; meany
yamens yes-man
yams mays
yanker Kearny
yap pay; pya
yaps pays; spay
yard adry; dray
yards drays
yare aery; Ayer; eyra; year
yarely yearly
yarest estray; reasty; stayer
yarn nary; Ryan
yarned denary
yarns snary
yarrow arrowy
yatter treaty
yaw way
yawl waly
yawled Dawley
yawls swaly; swayl
yaws sway; ways
ybet byte
ydred reddy
yea aye
yead Eday
year aery; Ayer; eyra; yare
yeard deary; deray; rayed; ready
yearded derayed
yearding deraying; readying
yeards derays
yearling layering; relaying
yearly yarely
yearn renay
yearned deanery; renayed
yearning renaying
yearns renays; senary
years eyras; sayer
yeas easy; eyas
yeast Yeats
yeasts sayest

Yeats yeast
Yecla lacey
yede eyed; yeed
yeed eyed; yede
yegg eggy
Yeisk skiey
yell Lely
yelts style
Yemen enemy
yen Ney
yens syne
yep Pye
yerd drey; dyer; Ryde
yerds dreys; dyers
yes sey; sye
yesk keys; Skye; syke
yesks Sykes
yes-man yamens
yestern styrene
Yes Tor oyster; rosety; storey;
   Troyes; tyroes
yet tye
yew wey; wye
yews weys; wyes
Yeysk skyey
Yezo oyez
Ygerne energy; greeny
yielder reedily
yill illy; lily
ylem elmy; Lyme
Ymir miry; rimy
yob boy
yobbo booby
yobs boys; sybo
yodel odyle; yodle
yodels yodles
yodle odyle; yodel
yodles yodels
yoga Goya
yogurt grouty
yon noy
yonder Rodney
Yonkers Orkneys
yore oyer
Ypres preys; pyres
Yssel lyses; sleys
yug guy
yulan unlay

Z

Zabian banzai
zabra bazar
zabras bazars
zaffer zaffre
zaffre zaffer
Zahle hazel
zeal laze
zebra braze

zebras brazes
zein Inez
Zelda lazed
zerda razed
zeriba braize
Zeus Suez
zo Oz
zoned dozen

Cognate Anagrams

A cognate anagram is a special variety of anagram in which the letters of a word or phrase are transposed to form another word or phrase which redefines, or is closely related in meaning to, the original. Listed here are some outstanding examples, both ancient and modern, of this most impressive aspect of the anagrammatic art.

ABANDON HOPE ALL YE WHO ENTER HERE
> Hear Dante! Oh, beware yon open hell

ABSENCE MAKES THE HEART GROW FONDER
> He wants back dearest gone from here

ACTIONS SPEAK LOUDER THAN WORDS
> Talk or airs can not show up deeds

ADELINA PATTI
> Italian adept

ADVERTISEMENTS
> i.e. tradesmen's TV

ADOLF HITLER
> Hated for ill

AFTERMATH
> At the farm

ALFRED TENNYSON, POET LAUREATE
> Neat sonnet or deep tearful lay

ALLEGORIES
Lies galore
ALPHABETICALLY
I play all the ABC
AMENITY
Any time
AMERICAN
Main race
AMERICAN INDIAN
I red man, I an Inca
ANAGRAMS
Ars Magna
AND WHEN DID YOU LAST SEE YOUR FATHER?
A roundhead: "Thy sire flew on Tuesday?"
ANGERED
Enraged
ANIMOSITY
Is no amity
ARABIAN DESERT
A date is barren
THE ARCTIC CIRCLE
Chart ice circlet
THE ARISTOCRACY
A rich Tory caste
ASININE
Is inane
ASPERITY
Yet I rasp
ASPERSION
No praises
ASSEVERATION
As one avers it
ASTRONAUT
Unto a star
ASTRONOMER
Moon-starer
ASTRONOMERS
On! More stars!
ATHLETICS
Lithe acts

AYE
   Yea
BALANCE SHEETS
   Cash table seen
BARGAIN SALE
   An aisle grab
BASTARD
   Sad brat
BATHING GIRLS
   In slight garb
BELLIGERENTS
   Rebelling set
BENEATH THE SOD
   Death—then be so
BENEDICTIONS
   Cited benison
BLANDISHMENT
   Blinds the man
THE BLARNEY STONE
   Blather sent on ye
THE BOARDING HOUSE
   This abode o' hunger
BRIGANDAGE
   A big danger
BROADCASTER
   Bred as actor
BURNISHING
   Shining rub
BUTTERFLY
   Flutter by
CARRIER PIGEONS
   Racing o'er spire
CHARITABLENESS
   I can bless earth
CHOIRMAN
   Harmonic
CHRISTIAN
   Rich saint
CHRISTIANITY
   Charity's in it

235

CIRCUMSTANTIAL EVIDENCE
Actual crime isn't evinced
CLEANLINESS
All niceness
COMBINE HARVESTERS
Betrim corn sheaves
COMPASSIONATENESS
Stamps one as so nice
COMPOUND INTEREST
Sum to do in per cent
CONIFER
Fir cone
CONSERVATIVE
Not vice versa
CONSIDERATE
Care is noted
CONSTRAINT
Can not stir
CONTEMPLATION
(i) On mental topic   (ii) Time to con plan
CONTRADICTION
Accord not in it
CONVERSATION
Voices rant on
THE COUNTRYSIDE
No city dust here
COUPLES
Up close
CROCODILE TEARS
Cries do act role
CURTAILMENT
Terminal cut
CUSTOMS AND EXCISE
Cussed 'incomes' tax
DANTE GABRIEL ROSSETTI
Greatest idealist born
THE DAWNING
Night waned
DEBENTURES
Ensure debt

DECIMAL POINT
   I'm dot in place
DECLARATION
   An oral edict
DELICATESSEN
   Ensliced eats
DESEGREGATION
   Negroes get aid
DESIGNATION
   Is a denoting
THE DETECTIVES
   Detect thieves
DEVOTIONAL SONGS
   God loves not a sin
DISCONSOLATE
   Is not solaced
DISCRETION
   Consider it
DISRAELI
   I lead, sir
DISTILLATION
   Do it in a still
DOLCE FAR NIENTE
   After indolence
DORMITORY
   Dirty room
DYNAMITE
   May end it
EARNESTNESS
   A stern sense
THE ECONOMIST
   He tots income
THE EIFFEL TOWER
   Few flit o'er thee
ELEVEN PLUS TWO
   Twelve plus one
ENDEARMENT
   Tender name
EPISCOPALIANISM
   Claim a pope is sin

ETERNAL DEVOTION
> I note ardent love

ETERNITY
> Entirety

THE EYES
> They see

FAINT-HEARTED
> Hinted at fear

FAITHLESSNESS
> This falseness

FAMILIES
> Life's aim

A FAREWELL TO ARMS
> Tale of war's realm

FLIRTING
> Trifling

FLOAT
> Aloft

FLORENCE NIGHTINGALE
> Flit on, cheering angel!

FOOL'S PARADISE
> So ideal for sap

FORESTER
> For trees

FOR MANY ARE CALLED BUT FEW ARE CHOSEN
> Half of a crowd? Nay, e'er a select number!

FRENCH REVOLUTION
> Violence run forth

A GENTLEMAN
> Elegant man

GOLDEN WEDDINGS
> Sign long wedded

GRAND FINALE
> A flaring end

THE GUARDIAN
> Naught I read

HAM SANDWICHES
> Dish a man chews

HAROLD WILSON
> (i) Who's 'n old liar?   (ii) All show or din

HENRY WADSWORTH LONGFELLOW
Won half the New World's glory
HMS PINAFORE
Name for ship
HORATIO NELSON
  (i) Lo! Nation's hero   (ii) Honor est a Nilo
HOUSES OF PARLIAMENT
A pile for us on Thames
IDENTIFIED
I defined it
IMPERSONATION
Apers in motion
INCOME TAXES
Exact monies
INCOMPREHENSIBLE
Problem in Chinese
INDIRA GANDHI
Had Indian rig
INDOMITABLENESS
Endless ambition
INNOMINATE
No name in it
INSURANCE POLICIES
Coin is in sure place
INSURGENT
Unresting
INTEGRAL CALCULUS
Calculating rules
IN THE GLOAMING
Main light gone
INTOXICATE
Excitation
INTRUSION
Is to run in
THE IRISH NATION
Oh, that is in Erin
IVANHOE BY SIR WALTER SCOTT
A novel by a Scottish writer
JAMES STUART
A just master

JEANNE D'ARC, MAID OF ORLEANS
As a man, rejoined old France
THE LAW OF SELF-PRESERVATION
What a preventer of life loss!
THE LEAGUE OF NATIONS
Ah, late foes get union
THE LEANING TOWER OF PISA
What a foreign stone pile!
THE LEGAL PROFESSION
Sole great help of sin
A LIBEL SUIT
I'll sue a bit
LIFE INSURANCE
I rule finances
LIKENESS
Ilk's seen
THE LORD'S PRAYER
Thy errors plead
THE LOST PARADISE
Earth's ideal spot
LOWSPIRITEDNESS
Depression wilts
LUBRICATION
Act, rub oil in
MADAM CURIE
Radium came
MANY A TRUE WORD IS SPOKEN IN JEST
Men joke and so win trusty praise
MARGARET THATCHER
(i) That great charmer
(ii) Great charm threat
(iii) Meg, the arch tartar
MARY WHITEHOUSE
I may rue the show
A MASTERPIECE
See me, I cap art
MATERNITY HOSPITAL
I pity natal mothers
MEADOWS
As mowed

MEASUREMENTS
  Man uses meter
MEAT BALLS
  Stale lamb
MEPHISTOPHELES
  The hopeless imp
METAPHYSICIANS
  Mystics in a heap
MICHAEL CURL
  I recall much
MIDWINTER WEATHER
  ´ Wind, rime, wet earth
MIGUEL CERVANTES DE SAAVEDRA
  Gave us a damned clever satire
MINCE PIES
  Spice in 'em
MISANTHROPE
  Spare him not
MISCHIEF-MAKER
  Mark if I scheme
MISFORTUNE
  Oft ruins me
MISREPRESENTATION
  Interpret one amiss
MODULATION
  I am not loud
THE MONA LISA
  Ah, not a smile?
MOONLIGHT
  Thin gloom
MOONLIGHT SERENADE
  An old-time song here
THE MORSE CODE
  Here come dots
MOUNTEBANK
  Meant bunko
MOUSTACHE
  Mouth case
MUTTERING
  Emit grunt

NESSITERAS RHOMBOPTERYX
(*Scientific name for the Loch Ness Monster, coined by Sir Peter Scott*)
> Monster hoax by Sir Peter S.

NOMINATE
> A mention

NUMERALS
> Mensural

NUMISMATIST
> Mint is a must

OLD ENGLAND
> Golden land

OLD-FASHIONED WINTER
> I folded earth in snow

OLD MASTERS
> Art's models

OLIVER WENDELL HOLMES
> He'll do in mellow verse

ONE-ARMED BANDIT
> A damned iron bet

ONE GOOD TURN DESERVES ANOTHER
> No, rogues never do endorse that!

ORATOR
> To roar

OUR FATHER WHO ART IN HEAVEN
> In woe, haven for a hurt heart

OUTSIDE BROADCAST
> Be sad, studio actors

PARISHIONER
> I hire parson

PATENIR
> Painter

PATERNAL
> Parental

PATRICK MOORE
> I'm a rocket pro

PAYMENT RECEIVED
> Every cent paid me

PETER OOSTERHUIS
> See pro hit so true

PIRATES
   Sea trip
PITTANCE
   A cent tip
POACHERS
   Cop hares
POCKET HANDKERCHIEF
   Oft reach'd pink cheek
POINT
   On tip
POLICEMAN
   Menial cop
POLICE PROTECTION
   Let cop cope in riot
POSTMAN
   No stamp?
THE POSTMASTER-GENERAL
   He's top letters manager.
PREDESTINATION
   I pertain to ends
PREMEDITATION
   I ponder it, mate
PRESBYTERIAN
   Best in prayer
PRODUCE
   Due crop
PROSECUTOR
   Court poser
PUNISHMENT
   Nine thumps
RALPH WALDO EMERSON
   Person whom all read
REALISTIC
   It is clear
REGINALD MAUDLING
   In a glaring muddle
REMUNERATION
   Our men earn it
REQUIESCAT
   (i) Quiet acres   (ii) 'e quits care

RESTRAINT
   Start rein
RETRACTIONS
   To recant, sir
REVOLUTION
   Love to ruin
RHAPSODY IN BLUE
   Rush led by piano
RIDICULOUS
   Ludicrous, I
ROALD AMUNDSEN
   Laud'd Norseman
ROBIN GOODFELLOW
   Wood elf or goblin
ROBINSON CRUSOE BY DANIEL DEFOE
   Friday—one boon on becursed isle
A ROLLING STONE GATHERS NO MOSS
   Stroller, on go, amasses nothing
SAINT ELMO'S FIRE
   Is lit for seamen
SAINT GEORGE AND THE DRAGON
   Aha! Strong giant ended ogre
SAINTLINESS
   Least in sins
SATISFACTION
   An act is so fit
SAUCINESS
   Causes sin
SAY IT WITH FLOWERS
   We flirt so this way
SCHOOLMASTER
   The classroom
SECLUSION
   Closes us in
SEMAPHORE
   See arm hop
A SENTENCE OF DEATH
   Faces one at the end
SEPARATION
   One is apart

A SHOPLIFTER
    Has to pilfer
THE SIGN OF THE CROSS
    He's right to confess
SILVER AND GOLD
    Grand old evils
A SILVER MINE
    I've minerals
A SIREN
    I snare
SKIN CARE
    Risk acne
SLANDEROUS
    Done as slur
SLITHERED
    Slid there
SLOT MACHINES
    Cash lost in 'em
SNOOZED
    Dozes on
SOFTHEARTEDNESS
    Often sheds tears
SOUTHERN CALIFORNIA
    Hot sun or life in a car
SPRING, SUMMER, AUTUMN, WINTER
    "Time's running past" we murmur
STAGHOUNDS
    A hunt's dogs
STANNIC
    Tin cans
STEALTHY
    At the sly
STEAMINESS
    Seen as mist
STIPEND
    Spend it
A STITCH IN TIME SAVES NINE
    This is meant as incentive
STONE DEAF
    Tones fade

STRAIT-LACED
  A deal strict
SUGGESTION
  It eggs us on
SURGEON
  Go, nurse
SUSPENDED ANIMATION
  Supine man is not dead
THE TAMING OF THE SHREW
  Her mate won the fights
TANTRUMS
  Must rant
TAX COLLECTION
  Exact coin toll
TED HEATH
  (i) Had teeth   (ii) The death
TEMPESTUOUS
  Seems put out
TEN COMMANDMENTS
  Can't mend most men
THEODORE ROOSEVELT
  Hero told to oversee
THIS EAR
  It hears
THUNDERSTORM
  Thor must rend
TORTOISE-SHELL BUTTERFLY
  O, it'll flutter by the roses
TOTAL ABSTAINER
  Is not late at bar
TRAGEDIAN
  Egad, I rant
TREACHEROUS
  Ruse or cheat
TREASURE ISLAND
  Sure is darn tale
TRIBULATIONS
  Is but on trial
A TRIP AROUND THE WORLD
  Hard to plan wider tour

TRUSTWORTHINESS
　　I now stress truth
T. S. ELIOT
　　Litotes
UNDIPLOMATIC
　　Mad, unpolitic
UNIFORMITY
　　I form unity
UNITED
　　In duet
UNRIGHTEOUSNESS
　　Guess then our sin
UPHOLSTERERS
　　Restore plush
VALETUDINARIAN
　　A nature invalid
VERSATILITY
　　Variety list
VICTORIA, ENGLAND'S QUEEN
　　Governs a nice quiet land
VIETNAMESE
　　Seem native
VILLAINOUSNESS
　　An evil soul's sin
VOCIFERATIONS
　　Strain of voice
A VOLCANIC MOUNTAIN
　　Lava in a conic mount
THE WAGES OF SIN IS DEATH
　　It's owed Satan high fees
WAITRESS
　　A stew, sir?
WESTERN UNION
　　No wire unsent
WHITHERSOEVER
　　Oh, wherever 'tis
WILDCAT
　　It claw'd
WILLIAM EWART GLADSTONE
　　(i) Wild agitator means well

    (ii) We want a mild legislator
    (iii) Wit so great will lead men
WILLIAM SHAKESPEARE
    We all make his praise

DISTRIBUTORS
for the Wordsworth Reference Series

**AUSTRALIA, BRUNEI,
MALAYSIA & SINGAPORE**

Reed Editions
22 Salmon Street
Port Melbourne
Vic 3207
Australia
Tel: (03) 646 6716
Fax: (03) 646 6925

**GERMANY, AUSTRIA
& SWITZERLAND**

Swan Buch-Marketing GmbH
Goldscheuerstraße 16
D-7640 Kehl am Rhein
Germany

GREAT BRITAIN & IRELAND

Wordsworth Editions Ltd
Cumberland House
Crib Street
Ware
Hertfordshire SG12 9ET

ITALY

Magis Books SRL
Via Raffaello 31/C
Zona Ind Mancasale
42100 Reggio Emilia
Tel: 0522-920999
Fax: 0522-920666

SPAIN

Ribera Libros S.L.
Poligono Martiartu, Calle 1-no 6
48480 Arrigorriaga, Vizcaya
Tel: 34-4-6713607 (Almacen)
     34-4-4418787 (Libreria)
Fax: 34-4-6713608 (Almacen)
     34-4-4418029 (Libreria)

PORTUGAL

International Publishing Services Ltd
Rua da Cruz da Carreira, 4B
1100 Lisboa
Tel: 01-570051
Fax: 01-3522066

SOUTHERN AFRICA

Struik Book Distributors (Pty) Ltd
Graph Avenue
Montague Gardens
7441
P O Box 193
Maitland
7405
South Africa
Tel: (021) 551-5900
Fax: (021) 551-1124

USA, CANADA & MEXICO

Universal Sales & Marketing
230 Fifth Avenue
Suite 1212
New York, NY 10001 USA
Tel: 212-481-3500
Fax: 212-481-3534